Working Scared
(Or Not at All)

Working Scared
(Or Not at All)

The Lost Decade, Great Recession, and Restoring the Shattered American Dream

Carl E. Van Horn

ROWMAN & LITTLEFIELD PUBLISHERS, INC.
Lanham • Boulder • New York • Toronto • Plymouth, UK

**331.1
V31W
2013**

Published by Rowman & Littlefield Publishers, Inc.
A wholly owned subsidiary of The Rowman & Littlefield Publishing Group, Inc.
4501 Forbes Boulevard, Suite 200, Lanham, Maryland 20706
www.rowman.com

10 Thornbury Road, Plymouth PL6 7PP, United Kingdom

British Library Cataloguing in Publication Information Available

Library of Congress Cataloging-in-Publication Data

Van Horn, Carl E.
  Working scared (or not at all) : the lost decade, great recession, and restoring the shattered American dream / Carl E. Van Horn.
     p.   cm.
  Includes index.
  ISBN 978-1-4422-1965-6 (cloth : alk. paper) — ISBN 978-1-4422-1966-3 (electronic)
  1. Unemployment—United States. 2. Labor market—United States. 3. Recessions—United States. 4. United States—Economic conditions—2009– 5. United States—Economic policy—2009– I. Title.
  HD5724.V358 2013
  331.10973—dc23

                                                                    2012043127

∞™ The paper used in this publication meets the minimum requirements of American National Standard for Information Sciences—Permanence of Paper for Printed Library Materials, ANSI/NISO Z39.48-1992.

Printed in the United States of America

This book is dedicated to
John and Regina Heldrich
and
American workers

Contents

Acknowledgments

This book is dedicated to John and Regina Heldrich, whose generous financial support brought about the John J. Heldrich Center for Workforce Development at Rutgers University and the creation of the ambitious research project *Work Trends: Americans' Attitudes about Work, Employers, and Government.* The endowment and operating funds provided by the Heldriches enabled the Center to survey nearly twenty-five thousand American workers from 1998 to 2012. The results of these surveys and in-depth follow-up interviews are the foundation for the findings presented in this book.

Although the analysis and conclusions presented here are mine alone, *Work Trends* was, from its inception, a collaborative undertaking, and I owe a great deal to my colleagues and collaborators. Professor Cliff Zukin, who has served as codirector of the project since 2008, contributed his excellent survey research skills and experience to strengthening the quality of the research and analysis. Over the past several years, he coauthored several groundbreaking reports with me on the experiences of unemployed workers and recent college and high school graduates during the Great Recession.

Professor Zukin and I were fortunate to work with several outstanding research assistants. Mark Szeltner contributed to several projects in 2012 and prepared the graphs and charts for the book. Other research assistants who worked closely with us on the *Work Trends* research include Charley Stone, Jessica Godofsky, Debbie Borie-Holtz, and Krista Jenkins.

From 1998 to 2005, the *Work Trends* surveys and reports were produced in partnership with the Center for Survey Research and Analysis (CSRA) at the University of Connecticut, which was directed by Professor Ken Dautrich. I am grateful to Professor Dautrich and CSRA for their significant contributions. Heldrich Center colleagues, past and present, including Duke Storen, K. A. Dixon, Aaron Fichtner, Scott Reynolds, Neil Ridley, Jeff Stoller,

Allison Kopicki, Bill Tracy, and Professor William Rodgers, chief economist at the Heldrich Center, also collaborated on *Work Trends* research projects and made important contributions.

Other colleagues at the Heldrich Center who contributed to this book by reviewing questionnaires and reviewing reports and draft chapters include Executive Director Kathy Krepcio and Maria Heidkamp. Another former Heldrich Center colleague, Nicole Corre, along with Ross Van Horn, effectively carried out numerous research tasks, including conducting detailed follow-up interviews of long-term unemployed workers. Robb C. Sewell helped prepare more than a dozen *Work Trends* research reports as senior writer/editor at the Heldrich Center. He also carefully reviewed the entire manuscript and prepared it for final publication along with the editors at Rowman & Littlefield. Nick Humez was responsible for indexing the book. Kathy Krepcio, Debbie Dobson, Janice Vasicek, and Dina Smiley were responsible for the Center's smooth functioning while I concentrated on writing this book.

Special thanks are due to Herb Schaffner, former director of communications at the Heldrich Center during the initial years of the *Work Trends* project. He has been a key collaborator in shaping the series and garnering attention for its findings. More recently, as the founder of the consulting firm Big Fish Media, he worked closely with me in all phases of preparing and revising the final manuscript. His keen insights, superb writing skills, and good counsel are gratefully acknowledged.

Christy Van Horn, my wife, also reviewed and commented on the entire manuscript and made numerous contributions to improving it. Her steadfast enthusiasm for the research and its value encouraged me to continue with the *Work Trends* project and write this book.

I also dedicate this book to the thousands of American workers who patiently and thoughtfully answered our surveys and provided detailed descriptions of their experiences and concerns. I hope that this book will contribute to ensuring a better future for them and the next generation of American workers.

Introduction

At the end of the twentieth century, with the economy booming and unemployment at historic lows, the American economy was a job-producing marvel. Opportunities for workers seemed endless; college students were getting bonuses from companies before they started working, and older workers were planning early retirement. The first decade of the twenty-first century was entirely different and a whole lot tougher. From the 9/11 terrorist attacks to surges in oil prices to bank failures and financial losses on Wall Street and in the housing market, millions either lost their jobs or feared they would. They watched helplessly as the value of their houses and retirement savings declined. At the end of the first decade of the twenty-first century, the United States endured the Great Recession, the worst economy in seventy years. In less than a decade, Americans experienced the best and the worst of times.

American workers are frustrated, angry, and scared. Already reeling from a decade of uncertainty and rapid labor market transformations, the Great Recession came along and crushed the lives of tens of millions of workers and their families. It forestalled careers, scrapped hopes for a college education, delayed retirements, and foreclosed family homes. As this book is published, the U.S. economy is still struggling to fully recover. Hopes for rapid economic growth and a return to full employment have evaporated. If robust labor market health does not return for five years, American workers will have endured an entire lost decade of high unemployment, stagnant or declining incomes, and anxiety.

The United States has undergone several significant economic transitions since World War II, but the decade ahead presents more troubling questions about the capacity of the economy to create and sustain broad-based growth and job opportunities. During this second decade of the twenty-first century, the nation confronts historic challenges in restoring economic growth and opportunity.

Working Scared (Or Not at All): The Lost Decade, Great Recession, and Restoring the Shattered American Dream presents findings based on over fifteen years of research that will help citizens, policymakers, educators, and business, union, and community leaders reach sounder decisions in the near future. *Working Scared* draws on nearly twenty-five thousand national random interviews with employed and unemployed Americans, conducted from 1998 to 2012, during one of the most volatile periods in U.S. economic history. Americans from all regions and in all occupations were interviewed, including unemployed and underemployed recent college and high school graduates, long-term unemployed workers with decades of work experience and no job prospects, out-of-work manufacturing union workers hoping to retrain for new careers, laid-off schoolteachers worried about budget cuts, anxious middle managers fearing new rounds of corporate layoffs, and real estate agents with no home buyers.

The entire set of over thirty research reports, including questionnaires and descriptions of survey methodology, from the project *Work Trends: Americans' Attitudes about Work, Employers, and Government*, is available on the John J. Heldrich Center for Workforce Development at Rutgers University's website (http://www.heldrich.rutgers.edu). Data from these surveys are also archived at the Roper Center for Public Opinion Research at the University of Connecticut (http://www.ropercenter.uconn.edu).The depth and range of survey data reported here are of substantial value to researchers, policymakers, journalists, and human resources executives. This is the first publication to make full use of the comprehensive data available from the *Work Trends* project, which was funded entirely by the Heldrich Center.

Collectively, the findings and observations from these surveys present a powerful witness to the anxieties and agony that swept the nation during this era. They provide one of the most comprehensive social science research portraits ever developed about the views of American workers about their jobs, the workplace, and government's role in the labor market. Also included in the *Work Trends* research is a special sample of workers who were laid off during the Great Recession. Their experiences and views were recorded during repeat interviews conducted in August 2009, March 2010, November 2010, and August 2011.

The Heldrich Center's *Work Trends* project was initiated and codirected by the author. Since 2008, the project's codirector has been Cliff Zukin, professor of political science and public policy, senior faculty fellow at the Center, and past president of the American Association for Public Opinion Research. From 1998 to 2005, Professor Ken Dautrich, a political scientist and former director of the Center for Survey Research and Analysis at the University of Connecticut, was the project's codirector. Significant contributions were also made by several graduate research assistants and professional staff affiliated with the Center, as noted in the acknowledgments.

Using the *Work Trends* findings as a foundation, this book presents a thematic narrative of the broad transformation of the American labor market in the first decade of the twenty-first century. In these pages, I describe and analyze what occurs in the friction between the changing nature of work and the experiences, beliefs, aspirations, and concerns of working men and women in a rapidly changing, globalized, knowledge-driven economy. By tracing the experiences of workers in times of economic prosperity and recession, I portray the shifting perceptions of America's workers as they are buffeted by new workplace realities.

The "voices" of American workers chronicled by the Heldrich Center tell a compelling story about a period of wrenching structural changes and two recessions. The book reports what workers think about government's role in training and education, the value of continuing education to success at work, the altered nature of retirement, the root causes of high unemployment, competition from foreign workers, the stress of unemployment, work–life balance concerns, workplace discrimination, health care, and job and career satisfaction.

In the first chapter, I describe the devastating consequences of the Great Recession. Not since the 1930s had the United States suffered as long or as deep an economic decline. More than twenty million Americans were laid off and plunged into months or even years of financial hardships. By the fall of 2012, more than three years after the recession was officially over, the U.S. economy had recovered only about half the jobs lost during the period.

Chapter 2 describes the powerful forces that reshaped the American labor market in the past twenty years, including globalization, offshoring, and corporate mergers as well as the rise of the knowledge- and technology-driven economy. The impacts of these profound and rapidly developing trends on the American workplace are discussed in chapter 3. It was a decade in which American workers grew increasingly dissatisfied with their working situations and more distrustful of their employers.

The unique difficulties experienced by older American workers in the recession era are examined in chapter 4. More than any other demographic group, unemployed workers in their fifties and sixties have struggled to navigate in the turbulent economy as their hopes for a secure job and dignified retirement slipped away. Chapter 5 explores the special challenges confronting recent high school and college graduates. Far too few of these young workers are employed in full-time jobs, and many doubt that they will be better off financially than the previous generation.

Chapter 6 assesses how the nation's policymakers responded to the Great Recession and outlines the "unfinished business" of public actions that could treat, if not heal, the damages to workers and the economy. The final chapter outlines the large-scale reforms necessary to restore the American dream of secure employment and intergenerational progress that benefits workers, employers, and the nation.

Chapter One

Working Scared in America and the Great Recession

The American Dream of working hard and being able to retire comfortably will not become a reality for many anymore. I think fear about the future will make the quality of our lives change, especially for our young people. They will never forget the economic downturn. . . . Their confidence in our country and in themselves has been forever broken.

—Unemployed worker interviewed in December 2010

The Great Recession that devastated the American economy and workforce officially began in late 2007 and ended in June 2009. Its lingering consequences raise fundamental questions: To what extent were the upheavals and sustained levels of high unemployment the product of short-term variations in the business cycle? Are these changes a harbinger of long-term structural changes and decline in the U.S. economy? How can American policymakers, employers, and workers successfully navigate these new realities? Will workers who get a good education and work hard succeed and be able to achieve the American dream of rising economic opportunity and financial security?

In the post–World War II era, the U.S. economy settled into the proverbial sweet spot of stable jobs and low levels of unemployment marred only by periodic recessions from which the economy quickly recovered. Completing high school used to guarantee millions of workers a good job with health and pension benefits. College graduates were quickly absorbed into good jobs and got a boarding pass to the middle class. It was not uncommon for American workers to remain with the same employer for their entire careers.

In the early twenty-first century, American workers alternate between two unwelcome worlds. Millions are unemployed, fighting for another job and suffering personal and financial agony. Among those who are still employed many desperately try to hang on to their jobs and live in a state of constant

1

anxiety. These Americans are "working scared" because, to them, it seems that virtually every job is temporary, threatened (directly or indirectly) by either technological change or global competition. With no certain routes to stable employment, American workers scramble for the education they need to remain employable and provide family sustaining wages. A college degree no longer brings automatic success in the labor market. American workers worry that the uncomfortable realities of a volatile labor market will plague them and their families for decades.

Well before the Great Recession ravaged the American economy, during the height of the 1990s boom, millions of job seekers were already anxious about their future and experiencing the harsh shocks of a rapidly churning labor market. Even before the collapse of the stock market and housing prices, the volatile twenty-first-century economy was transforming work as seismic changes in technology and finance swept aside small and giant corporations and up-ended entire industries. Before the Great Recession, workers at all educational and skill levels experienced job losses through downsizing, mergers, and acquisitions and were forced to search frantically for new opportunities.

These Americans are "working scared" because, to them, it seems that virtually every job is temporary, threatened (directly or indirectly) by either technological change or global competition.

In the early years of the twenty-first century, realities at work are radically different than they were in the mid- to late twentieth century (see table 1.1). Thirty years ago, most jobs were stable, or even permanent; now most jobs are temporary or contingent. Workers in the mid- to late twentieth century most likely could remain with a firm and ride the seniority escalator to better jobs and higher pay. Today's workers no longer have that expectation. Then, most employees felt loyal to the firms where they worked. Now, workers are more likely to distrust employers and look out for themselves.

In just a couple of decades, as a fairly stable economy rapidly evolved, it became much harder for specialists and average workers to predict what's going to happen next. Imagine, for a moment, college freshmen choosing among dozens of fields of study that will prepare them for a career that will take them deep into the first half of the twenty-first century. It's no wonder that many are dazed and confused about such choices. No matter which path these young people pursue, it is clear that ending one's education after attaining a high school diploma or college degree will not be sufficient to get and

Table 1.1. The Changing Realities of Work in America

Mid- to Late Twentieth Century	*Early Twenty-First Century*
Permanent	Temporary/contingent
Stable	Volatile
Advancement	Stagnation
Loyalty	Disaffection
One-and-done education	Lifelong learning
Health care from employer	Shared health care responsibility
Defined benefit pension	Defined contribution
"Early" retirement	"Never" retire

keep a good job. The notion of a "one and done" education has been replaced by the imperative of lifelong learning.

Expectations about retirement are also fundamentally different than they were a few decades ago. In the latter part of the twentieth century, most workers assumed that they would retire by age sixty-five or sooner. Now many Americans believe that they will never be able to afford to quit working because they do not have adequate savings: most Americans have more in credit card debt than savings. The baby-boom generation is just not leaving the workforce and opening up opportunities for younger workers because the value of their homes and their retirement savings took a major hit during the Great Recession. Fewer retired workers can look forward to guaranteed pension benefits from their employer. Often these have been replaced with "defined contribution plans" that offer no guarantees and depend on contributions to and investment earnings from the employee's account.

During the past decade or so, the labor market lost its moorings as employment surged and plunged. Stock market fluctuations and the collapse of housing prices rocked the U.S. economy. Public policymakers were paralyzed or unsure about how to cushion the blows. The hypergrowth bubbles of the late 1990s and early 2000s were spurred on by technological change, easy credit, government spending and tax cuts, and speculative gaming in the financial markets. The resulting double-digit growth may have lulled U.S. policymakers and citizens into thinking that what goes up does not have to come down. The economic growth and revenue benefits from these bubbles made it all too convenient for public and private leaders to kick the can of economic policy down the road. When the country needed a plan that involved making tough choices and allocating resources to build a more competitive economy and stable labor markets, it got more free poker chips and a discounted bus ride to the casino.

Billions of dollars over the past decade were invested by people and institutions that could not afford it on financial products that were anything but transparent and on industries that lacked sustainable markets. These actions created jobs that vanished and reappeared with the next infusion of cheap capital. The result can be measured in what we *did not* achieve—a national strategy for steady and sustained growth focused on investment, education, and workforce training. American policymakers did not have the vision to plan for a tech decade, a green decade, or a smart decade dedicated to reforming education. Instead, American workers experienced a lost decade.

The Great Recession and the decade preceding it were disasters for millions of working Americans and their families. These wild swings in the American economy were succinctly summarized by economists Harry Holzer and Marek Hlavac:

> During the 1980s, we first endured a severe recession, engineered by the Federal Reserve Bank to fight high rates of inflation, and then recovered with a lengthy period of expansion and economic growth. Another and milder recession in the early 1990s was followed by an even more robust period of expansion, often called the "Great Boom" or the "Roaring Nineties," during which high productivity and income growth returned to the U.S. economy. But in the decade of the 2000s, which once again began with a mild recession, the economic picture was more mixed; a shorter period of recovery, during which productivity growth was high but income growth was much lower, was followed by the most severe economic downturn since the 1930s, which is commonly known as the "Great Recession."[1]

Nobel Prize–winning economist Paul Krugman labeled the first decade of the twenty-first century the "Big Zero . . . a decade in which nothing good happened and none of the optimistic things we were supposed to believe turned out to be true." There was "basically zero job creation . . . zero economic gains for the typical family . . . zero gains for home owners" and "zero gains for stocks."[2]

THE "HURRICANE KATRINA" OF RECESSIONS

After a decade when average Americans experienced no wage or salary increases and many saw their paychecks decline and benefits disappear, the Great Recession piled misery on top of anxiety. No matter how hard they worked, American workers could not outrun the economic forces that made landfall in 2008. When the recession hit, many had nowhere to go, and the

After a decade when average Americans experienced no wage or salary increases and many saw their paychecks decline and benefits disappear, the Great Recession piled misery on top of anxiety.

search for safer ground became more urgent. Like Hurricane Katrina in 2005 that wrecked New Orleans and the Gulf Coast, killed over a thousand people, and cost over $150 billion, the Great Recession devastated the economic landscape, and its effects will damage millions of American workers for decades.

In the United States, no economic calamity of this magnitude had been experienced since the Great Depression of the 1930s. Except for a major recession in the early 1980s, American jobs grew at consistent pace until the end of 2007. As depicted in figure 1.1, the Great Recession was entirely different in depth and duration.

Among the key markers of the unprecedented economic crisis are the following:

- The longest recession on record.
- The unemployment rate rose to over 10 percent, the highest in 30 years.
- Unemployment for blacks reached 16.7 percent, the highest level since 1984.
- Over 20 million workers in 2010 were unemployed or were working in part-time jobs but wanted full-time employment or dropped out of the workforce.
- Long-term unemployment for six or more months was at the highest level it had been in more than sixty years.
- More private sector jobs were lost—nearly 9 million—than in the previous four economic recessions combined.
- Median family income fell from $49,600 in 2007 to $45,800 in 2010.[3]
- Family net worth declined from $126,400 in 2007 to $77,300 in 2010 because of the collapse of the real estate market.[4]
- Medicaid health care spending on low-income and disabled Americans topped $50 billion for the first time in its fifty-five-year history.[5]
- Three million children and 18 million adults received government assistance to buy food under the Supplemental Nutritional Assistance Program, better known as Food Stamps.[6]
- Over 8.1 million children under the age of eighteen were living in families with an unemployed parent.[7]

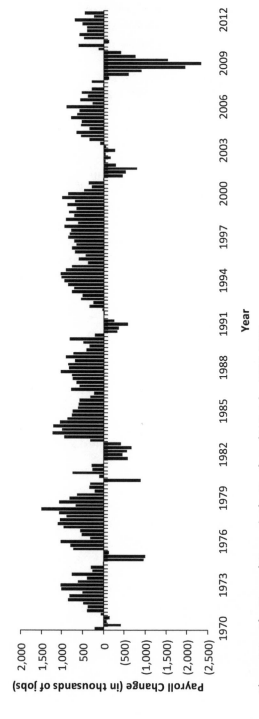

Figure 1.1. The Ups and Downs in the Number of U.S. Jobs, 1970–2012

Source: Employment Metrics—Monthly Change in Total Nonfarm Payroll (June 2012), St. Louis Federal Reserve, U.S. Department of Labor: Bureau of Labor Statistics, and data260.org.

Note: Quarterly change in nonfarm payrolls, 1970 to September 2012.

Americans' experiences during the Great Recession left lasting scars in psychological, social, economic, and policy terms. We know that job losses and displacements during natural disasters (such as Hurricane Katrina or Hurricane Sandy, the latter of which ruined dozens of northeastern shore communities) negatively affect the mental and emotional health of children. Over one-third of the affected children in displaced Katrina families have been clinically diagnosed with at least one mental health problem since the hurricane.[8] The impacts of lost homes and property, lost time in school, and damaged relationships for children and families when natural disasters strike is a phenomenon well understood by most Americans. The consequences of economic disasters are wider, more enduring, and perhaps less obvious.

Long-term unemployment is also associated with serious health problems.[9] The unemployed lose their health insurance coverage and cannot afford to renew it. They also often forgo health care treatment and visits to the doctor or dentist. Unemployed older workers in their fifties and early sixties are twice as likely to have heart attacks or strokes as people who are employed, according to research reported by William T. Gallo, professor of health policy at the City University of New York. Long-term unemployment also engenders adverse mental health symptoms, including stress and depression.[10] Job loss also affects child nutrition and health, according to the Children's Hospital of Philadelphia and First Focus, because families scrimp on food and lose health insurance.[11] Homelessness spiked for families and children during the first years of the recession; the number of homeless families with children who spent time in a shelter rose by 30 percent between 2007 and 2009.[12]

The Heldrich Center's *Work Trends* research documented the full scope of the personal, financial, and psychological impacts. The survey results and follow-up interviews revealed just how widespread and severe the problems were in society and put a human face on the official poverty, income, and health data reported by government agencies.[13] Here is what just a few of the hundreds of workers we interviewed in 2009 had to say:

After thirty-eight years . . . the company where I worked let six people go—three in billing where I worked. My seniority should have counted at that time. I wasn't mad—more shocked than anything. I gave 110 percent every day I worked there. I put my job before my husband—now "ex"—and before my kids.

I have tried to diversify, use my skills in other areas—and the longer the time passes, the more employers do not want to take the time to even look at my resume. . . . I fear for my family and my future. We are about to be evicted, and bills are piling. We have sold everything we possibly can to maintain, and are going under with little hope of anything.

When I went to a job fair, the [state] had canceled it because there were no companies hiring! This is a depression, not a recession.

THE SUDDEN COLLAPSE AND PAINFUL AFTERMATH

Fifteen million American workers were laid off from their jobs between 2007 and 2010. Most lost their jobs suddenly and without warning (see figure 1.2). Most had little or no time to prepare for the rocky road ahead. As one worker put it, "There was no warning at all. My boss said we'd work something out. Within a few hours I'm gone." With more than half of workers losing their jobs for the first time in at least five years, this upheaval struck like a powerful bolt of lightning. The vast majority got no assistance from their employers to cope with their plight. Over eight in ten received no severance pay. More than half of the jobless lost employer-provided health insurance. Only four in ten received partial temporary income support via the federal/state unemployment insurance system. Eight in ten of those who obtained unemployment benefits (which could last for up to ninety-nine weeks) feared that they would run out before getting their next job.

As noted above, between 2009 and 2011, the Heldrich Center surveyed nationally random samples of American workers who lost a job during the depths of the recession. Two years after our initial interviews with recession-era workers, we found the following:

- One in three was *still unemployed* and looking for work.
- Just over one in four had found a *full-time job*.
- Eight percent were *working part-time* and looking for full-time jobs.
- Seventeen percent were *out of the labor market entirely* because they had given up looking, had retired, or were enrolled in school.
- Part-time workers, not looking for full-time work or self-employed made up the remainder of those surveyed.

Among those who remained jobless, fully half had been seeking work for more than two years. Their continued unemployment was not due to a lack of effort. When they described their job search, it was clear that unemployed workers were actively seeking employment and using the strategies that usually succeed in better times. Nor were the jobless too picky about accepting job offers if they got one. Two of three unemployed workers said they were willing to take a pay cut or change careers in order to land a new job.

Even if a new job came, it did not happen quickly. About half were unable to find another job for six months; one in four searched for one or two years

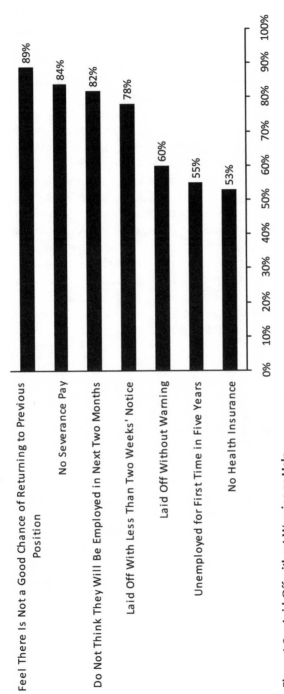

Figure 1.2.   Laid-Off without Warning or Help
Source: C. Van Horn and C. Zukin, "The Anguish of Unemployment," Heldrich Center for Workforce Development, Rutgers University, September 2009.

before getting another position. Just over half of the reemployed found what they regarded as a permanent job. Over half took a pay cut in their new jobs. Pay reductions were relatively minor for one in four reemployed workers, but nearly half of the rehired workers earned at least 20 percent less than in their prior job. Four in ten changed fields or careers, and, by a margin of two to one, they described their new jobs as a step down rather than a step up.

During this painful episode of economic turmoil, Heldrich Center surveys documented anguish and panic among the jobless. Most remained unemployed much longer than they expected, often exhausting both their personal savings and their unemployment insurance benefits. As the recession and their joblessness dragged on, six in ten of the Heldrich Center's panel of workers predicted there was just "no chance" they could return to their previous job. Seven percent feared that they would never work again. As one worker said, "There used to be pages of jobs every day and—in my industry—two columns in the paper. Now there are days where the entire list of available jobs in this city you can count on both hands!"

Job losses had a major impact on the families of over half of our respondents. Most described their finances as either flat-out poor or only fair. "I do receive food stamps, but that doesn't help me get back and forth to the grocery store, or buying laundry detergent to wash clothes, or even to buy new clothes for a possible job interview," commented one long-term unemployed worker. The unemployed suffered new harsh realities, including sharply reduced incomes and bleak prospects. Almost all immediately cut back on spending for entertainment and travel; seven in ten postponed plans for home improvement or canceled family vacations.

After making these difficult adjustments, the unemployed were forced into more painful choices. Fully one in three workers made do without something they considered *essential* for them and their families. Six in ten tapped into savings and retirement accounts. Even more startling, six in ten swallowed their pride and borrowed money from family and friends to make ends meet. Food and transportation expenses were curtailed by more than half of the unemployed workers. Significantly, 44 percent cut back on health care so much that it made a difference in the quality of day-to-day life. Nearly a third made different living arrangements, moving in with family or into a more affordable apartment or house. Older, unemployed workers faced more troublesome challenges, as detailed in chapter 4.

Millions of unemployed workers suffered financial devastation, losing income and assets. Credit cards were maxed out and mortgage payments skipped by more than half of our respondents. A staggering one in ten of the Heldrich Center's panel declared bankruptcy, and significant numbers also lost their homes. Nationally, home foreclosures more than doubled from

2006 to 2008, according to RealtyTrac, a real estate industry group. In all, 3.1 million homeowners filed foreclosure notices—one in every fifty-four households in the United States.[14]

Retirement plans were drastically altered by workers' prolonged unemployment. Some 70 percent said they changed their plans, with equal numbers saying they would retire earlier or later than they had originally planned. Just under half of those over the age of fifty expected to apply for Social Security as soon as they are eligible, even though this would lower their monthly benefit checks significantly. In most instances, those who expected to retire sooner said they simply could not find another job. Workers who now anticipate working longer were compelled to do so because their savings had been so depleted by their joblessness that they could not "afford to retire."

DID UNEMPLOYED WORKERS RECOVER?

After following a national sample of unemployed workers for two years, we wanted to estimate just how much progress they made in returning to where they were before the rug was pulled out from under them. In order to summarize the condition of the unemployed, the Heldrich Center created a typology of economic recovery in order to provide a summary of their experiences. The results of our analysis are displayed in figure 1.3.[15] Two years after our

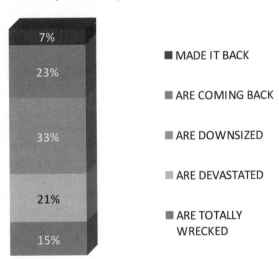

Figure 1.3. Most Unemployed Workers Did Not Fully Recover from the Great Recession
Source: C. Stone, C. Van Horn, and C. Zukin, "Out of Work and Losing Hope: The Misery and Bleak Expectations of American Workers," Heldrich Center for Workforce Development, Rutgers University, September 2011.

first interviews, only 7 percent could be considered to have "made it back." They are in good financial shape and have not suffered a decline in living standards. Another 23 percent believe they are on "their way back" because their standard of living changed only in a minor way or temporarily.

Other American workers have been much less fortunate. One in three was "downsized" by the recession. Their standard of living declined, but many believe the changes are minor and temporary. The remaining 36 percent experienced cataclysmic effects from the Great Recession. Based on their answers to our surveys, we classified 21 percent as "devastated" because they are in poor financial shape and have suffered major quality of life changes, even though some expect that these are temporary. Finally, there is the sizable 15 percent who seemed to have been "totally wrecked" by their experiences during and after the recession. Their finances are in poor condition, and they have suffered major, permanent lifestyle changes.

Bleak Outlooks

In light of these abysmal experiences, the bleak outlook of American workers during and after the Great Recession will come as no surprise. Shocked and dispirited, eight in ten of the unemployed were "very concerned" about the job market. (One in ten *employed* workers was very concerned about their own job security.) By the fall of 2011, their pessimism had deepened. Only one-third of the unemployed we surveyed in 2011 anticipate that the economy will improve within two years. And the share of the unemployed who think that the economy is undergoing fundamental negative changes grew from about 50 percent in August 2009 to over 70 percent in August 2011.[16]

Unemployed workers were further frustrated by the tattered safety net of government services that they hoped would be available in their time of need. Experienced workers who suddenly found themselves among the swelling ranks of the unemployed lamented the hardships and humiliation of taking public benefits. For some taking a lower-paying job meant receiving lower Unemployment Insurance benefits when they got laid off from that position than they would have received previously.[17] Others fell into the group of self-identified "99ers" who exhausted their unemployment benefits entirely. In response to a column in the *New York Times* by Bob Herbert, published in December 2010, a gentleman using the Internet "handle" PeppersDad commented,[18]

> You've already been updated with a list of the stigmas and barriers most 99ers face today. We are a cross-section of Americans which used to be middle class. Many of us—and the true unemployment statistics are grossly understated—were in the last decade or years of our careers. We're 50 and now 60 year olds.

We want to work. There's not one thing sexy, positive, or pleasant about accepting benefits.

Stephanie of Williamsville, New York, shared the heartache of losing unemployment benefits in a letter to Senator Bernie Sanders of Vermont:

> My benefits expired on September 5, 2010. I have gone through all my savings and sold everything that I can sell in order to survive and keep a roof over our heads. I have exactly $5 in my wallet and $46.77 in my checking account. My rent is due on December 15. I did apply for Food Stamps in September—never imagined that would happen to me—so I have been able to put food on the table, but I don't know what will happen next or where we will be even in the next month. I know that there are millions that have been without UI benefits since March of this year and I'm not sure how they are still able to survive. I don't know how I will, but I keep fighting—for my son. He deserves so much more than I can provide for him.[19]

A SILENT MENTAL HEALTH EPIDEMIC

For the jobless, especially for those out of work for extended periods, the psychological and emotional stress can be very difficult and sometimes devastating. One laid-off worker expressed her fears during an interview: "I am not married. My parents have passed away. So I am quite scared of what will happen if I do not land a job within the next couple months. . . . The thing I identified with the most—my work—has left me feeling lost." An overwhelming majority of the unemployed acknowledged feelings of depression or anxiety (see figure 1.4). One worker summarized his feelings: "Nobody has called me in seven months. I don't feel important. I'm not contributing to family finances." More than half of our respondents lost all hope that they would recover.

According to a national survey commissioned by Mental Health America, in 2009, 13 percent of unemployed workers reported problems with alcohol or drug abuse. Thirteen percent also said that "they have thought of harming themselves, making them four times as likely as full-time workers to report this symptom of mental illness."[20] Another study found that there is a very strong linkage between higher unemployment rates and increases in suicide rates in the United States.[21]

With more than 20 million Americans either unemployed or underemployed and millions more worried about what might happen next, the Great Recession created a silent and invisible mental health epidemic. The pathologies associated with long-term unemployment not only are limited to the jobless worker but also affect families and communities. Over half of the Heldrich

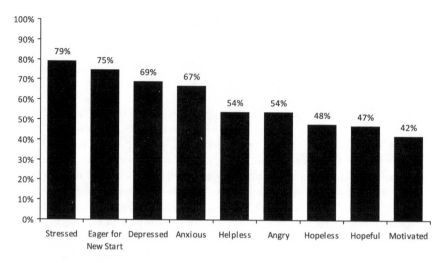

Figure 1.4. A World of Hurt for the Long-Term Unemployed
Source: C. Van Horn and C. Zukin, "The Anguish of Unemployment," Heldrich Center for Workforce Development, Rutgers University, September 2009.

Center's respondents reported that joblessness caused either a great deal or some stress in relationships with family and friends. More than four in ten unemployed workers said that they lost contact with close friends or avoided social situations with friends and acquaintances. While understandable, their behavior shut them off from one of the best techniques for finding another job. Activating your personal social network is a very effective method for learning about opportunities and getting recommendations to employers.[22]

While about four in ten jobless workers felt more motivated than ever to get back in the game, not everyone was capable of coping after enduring months or even years of rejection and corresponding financial catastrophes. With dim job prospects and plummeting self-esteem, nearly one in ten admitted to abusing drugs and alcohol. Nearly one in five of the jobless sought professional help from a therapist or counselor, but everyone cannot find or afford professional help. Many lost health care coverage or will not pay for counseling while they are trying to avoid hunger and homelessness. Even though many health care organizations and providers responded with lowered rates and online assistance, available counseling services could not handle the overwhelming demand for millions who would have benefited from it.[23]

A World of Hurt for the Long-Term Unemployed

Unemployed workers described a painful "world of hurt." One commented, "The lack of income and loss of health benefits hurts greatly, but losing the ability to provide for my wife and myself is killing me emotionally." Another reported, "I have been forced to sell personal property and am truly discouraged by the dim future I see ahead." Another said, "Being unemployed is frustrating, demeaning and, at this point, frightening."[24]

The jobless were not alone in suffering the consequences of an economic disaster. Facing mounting financial problems, millions of employed Americans took on more debt and made lifestyle changes to cope with the economic downturn. In September 2010, more than half of the employed and unemployed said they had financial debt other than their mortgage or rent. Americans working for large employers, those between thirty-five and fifty-four years of age, those paid hourly, women, blacks, and Hispanics all reported having more debt than their respective counterparts. Nearly 45 percent of Americans, interviewed for a 2010 MetLife survey, indicated that they would not be able to pay their bills for more than a month if they suddenly become jobless. Nearly two-thirds said they would be in deep financial trouble if an unemployment spell lasted for up to three months.[25]

Americans' dread about the economy was grounded in personal experiences. Three of every four U.S. workers were personally affected by the Great Recession, according to the Heldrich Center's September 2010 national survey, which found that Americans either lost a job themselves or knew a family member or close friend who lost a job during the 2007–2010 period. One in four Americans had no one among their family or friends lose a job in that period (see figure 1.5). Yet they too were surely well aware of the economic devastation as unemployment, bankruptcies, and home foreclosures soared in nearly every community in the United States.

Three of every four U.S. workers were personally affected by the Great Recession, according to the Heldrich Center's September 2010 national survey, which found that Americans either lost a job themselves or knew a family member or close friend who lost a job during the period.

Being unemployed or knowing someone who was unemployed meant that most employed workers sympathized with the struggles of jobless Americans. Few respondents blamed unemployed workers for their condition. Less than one in ten employed workers—and 3 percent of the unemployed—thought that the main cause of unemployment was that people just did not want to work, according to the September 2010 Heldrich Center survey. In fact, the views of employed and unemployed workers about the economy and labor market were strikingly similar.

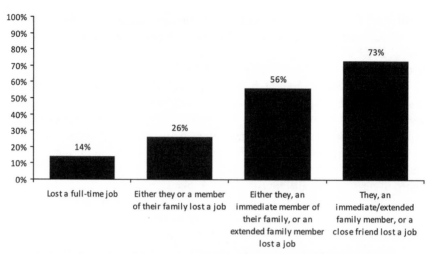

Figure 1.5. Most Americans Experienced Unemployment—Directly or Indirectly
Source: D. Borie-Holtz, C. Van Horn, and C. Zukin, "No End in Sight: The Agony of Prolonged Unemployment," Heldrich Center for Workforce Development, Rutgers University, May 2010.

There was, however, one significant difference between employed and unemployed Americans: half of the employed workers concluded that unemployed workers might be too selective about job offers, but only one in three jobless workers shared that view. In fact, the vast majority of unemployed workers said they were willing to take a cut in pay and benefits just to land a job and would accept a temporary job or one below their education and skill level in order to get back into the labor market.

BITTER LEGACIES

In response to the wide reporting about the Heldrich Center's *Work Trends* reports, unemployed workers wrote to me or commented on media websites about the bitter choices and trade-offs confronting them during the Great Recession. Audrey from Connecticut offered this incisive statement:

> This is the new world of corporate America we must face: my husband was "outsourced" by IBM (his job was sent to another country) in April 2009. Each of his team members faced this, like the ten little Indians, so we could see the writing on the wall. . . . Ironically, he was just rehired by IBM but at a lower salary, and with no guarantee of permanent status . . . THAT is the new reality in corporate America: Fire your employees, and then hire them back for less money and less secure situations.[26]

Both employed *and* unemployed workers held pessimistic outlooks about the U.S. economy between 2008 and 2012. That was not so surprising, but other twists in their story emerged, twists that will become important as we go deeper into this book. Over several different surveys conducted during this period, a majority of workers concluded that the recession ushered in a permanent, structural change in the economy rather than a temporary dip in the business cycle. In late 2009, less than half of employed Americans thought the economic downturn was "temporary," while the rest saw it as the beginning of fundamental and lasting changes.

During the recession era, Americans' confidence in their ability to find and keep jobs and in their belief that economic opportunities will be greater for the next generation declined sharply. In 1998, a Heldrich Center survey found that nearly three out of five Americans were extremely or very confident that they could find another job as good or better than the one they currently held. By 2010, less than half that percentage—one in five—felt confident they could find another job as good or better. In 1998, seven in ten believed it was a good time to find a job; by 2010, less than one in ten (7 percent) held that view. Between 1999 and 2009, the share of workers who agreed that job opportunities for the next generation would improve declined from 56 to 40 percent.[27]

After reading about the Heldrich Center's research in January 2011, Darren, an unemployed worker, wrote me,

> Two years ago I would have never thought it possible I would be in my current circumstance. Today, I have very little hope for my future. My biggest concern is what will the future hold for my seven-year-old daughter? It seems that the common view held by most elected officials is that our economy will shortly "bounce back" as it has in prior recessions. . . . I believe this is terribly wrong. What our country is currently experiencing is unlike the business cycle recessions of the past seventy years. We are in the midst of de-leveraging an enormous credit bubble combined while being woefully unprepared for the new era of global competition already in place. My job was not outsourced overseas, however, I have friends who have either lost high-salary jobs or are in constant fear of losing their jobs to outsourcing overseas. These factors have resulted in the make-up of our economy shifting permanently and will continue to do so while our government appears to be oblivious to all of this. I have never felt such a disconnect from the government as I do today.

A reader of a *New York Times* column by Bob Herbert that featured the Heldrich Center's research commented,

> Thanks for keeping us front and center. As one of the involuntarily retired, I regret that I wasted time on retraining (two years) and on applying for jobs. I wish I

had all of the money returned to me that I wasted on trying to create a new career. To my two children who are smart and capable, I recommend that you travel to a more prosperous country which I can see from here, but cannot get to.[28]

These workers' reversals of fortune reflect the perspectives of people living through a devastating recession. Millions of people were severely, perhaps permanently, harmed by the Hurricane Katrina of U.S. recessions. The next chapter examines the underlying forces transforming the American economy and the implications for American workers.

NOTES

1. "A Very Uneven Road: U.S. Labor Markets in the Past 30 Years," New York: Russell Sage Foundation, American Communities Project, March 2012, 1.

2. Paul Krugman, "The Big Zero," *New York Times*, December 27, 2009, A27.

3. Binyamin Applebaum, "Family Net Worth Drops to Level of Early '90s, Fed Says," *New York Times*, June 11, 2012, http://www.nytimes.com/2012/06/12/busi ness/economy/family-net-worth-drops-to-level-of-early-90s-fed-says.html.

4. Applebaum, "Family Net Worth Drops to Level of Early '90s, Fed Says."

5. "Kaiser Commission on Medicaid and the Uninsured, June 2010 Data Snapshot," December 20, 2011, http://www.kff.org/medicaid/upload/8050-04.pdf.

6. Julia B. Isaacs, "The Recession's Impact on Children," UpFront Blog, January 15, 2010, http://www.brookings.edu/opinions/2010/0115_recession_children_isaacs .aspx.

7. Julia B. Isaacs, "Families of the Recession: Unemployed Children and Their Families," June 2010, http://www.brookings.edu/research/papers/2010/01/14-fami lies-recession-isaacs.

8. "Legacy of Katrina Report Details Impact of Stalled Recovery on Mental Health Status of Children," *Science Daily*, August 26, 2010; National Center for Science Preparedness/Columbia University Mailman School of Public Health/Children's Health Fund, March 12, 2011, http://www.sciencedaily.com/ releases/2010/08/100823080629.htm.

9. Mitchell Hartman, "When Unemployment Runs Out—What's Next?," May 31, 2012, http://www.marketplace.org/topics/economy/when-unemployment-runs -out-whats-next.

10. William T. Gallo, Jennie E. Brand, Husn-Mei Teng, Linda Leo-Summers, and Amy L. Byers, "Differential Impact of Involuntary Job Loss on Physical Disability of Older Workers: Does Predisposition Matter?," *Research on Aging* 31, no. 3 (2009): 345–60; William T. Gallo, Elizabeth H. Bradley, Michelle Siegel, and Stanislav V. Kasl, "Health Effects of Involuntary Job Loss among Older Workers," *Journals of Gerontology. Series B, Psychological Sciences and Social Sciences* 56, no. 1 (2001): S3–S9.

11. Katherine Sell, Sarah Zlotnick, Kathleen Noonan, and David Rubin, "The Effect of the Recession on Child Well-Being," November 15, 2010, http://www.first focus.net/library/reports/the-effect-of-the-recession-on-child-well-being.

12. Sell et al., "The Effects of the Recession on Child Well-Being."

13. Carl E. Van Horn and Cliff Zukin, "Anguish of Unemployment," in *Work Trends* (New Brunswick, NJ: Heldrich Center at Rutgers, The State University of New Jersey, September 2009).

14. "Record 2.9 Million U.S. Properties Receive Foreclosure Filings in 2010 Despite 30-Month Low in December," http://www.realtytrac.com/content/press -releases/record-29-million-us-properties-receive-foreclosure-filings-in-2010-despite -30-month-low-in-december-6309.

15. Cliff Zukin, Carl E. Van Horn, and Charley Stone, "Categorizing the Unemployed by the Impact of the Recession," in *Work Trends* (December 2011).

16. Carl E. Van Horn, Cliff Zukin, and Charley Stone, "Out of Work and Losing Hope," in *Work Trends* (September 2011).

17. Bob Herbert, "The Data and the Reality," *New York Times*, December 27, 2010, http://www.nytimes.com/2010/12/28/opinion/28herbert.html.

18. Herbert, "The Data and the Reality."

19. Michael Thornton, "99rs Send Their Appeals for Help to Sen. Sanders," December 16, 2010, http://www.huffingtonpost.com/michael-thornton/99ers-send-their -appeals-_b_797444.html.

20. "Jobless Prone to Mental Woes," *Employment and Training Reporter*, October 19, 2009, 101.

21. Dean Baker and Kevin Hassett, "The Human Disaster of Unemployment," *New York Times*, May 29, 2012, 13.

22. Debbie Borie-Holtz, Carl E. Van Horn, and Cliff Zukin, "No End in Sight: The Agony of Prolonged Unemployment," in *Work Trends* (May 2010).

23. Christina Reardon, "Social Work Today," 2009, http://www.socialworktoday .com/archive/031109p12.shtml.

24. Gary Langer, "The Trauma of Unemployment," September 2009, http://abc news.go.com/blogs/politics/2009/09/the-trauma-of-unemployment.

25. Alison Linn, "Many Fear Job Loss, but Have No Savings for It," August 2010, http://www.msnbc.msn.com/id/38417262/ns/business-your_retirement/t/fear -job-loss-have-no-savings-it.

26. Herbert, "The Data and the Reality."

27. Carl E. Van Horn and Cliff Zukin, "What a Difference a Decade Makes," in *Work Trends* (December 2009).

28. Herbert, "The Data and the Reality."

Chapter Two

Is the American Worker Disposable?

There are just so many things that I feel should be done differently. I have a real problem with the number of jobs that are shipped overseas. It just slays me how we allow that and we continue to allow that. Companies are not in any way penalized, there's nothing really effective done to them, and yet that's not helping this country. That is really something that is almost painful for me to see, how we continue to do that.

—Sandra, Heldrich Center interview, March 2011

When I hear people talk about temp vs. permanent jobs, I laugh. The idea that any job is permanent has been well proven not to be true. We're all temps now.

—Barry Asin, Staffing Industry Analysts[1]

The United States is the wealthiest nation in the world, yet the overwhelming majority of American workers are worried about their job security, and millions are unemployed or underemployed. There are widespread fears about the availability and cost of health insurance and a college education. Pension and retirement benefits do not seem sufficient to most. The Heldrich Center's *Work Trends* surveys conducted over the course of a decade recorded their mounting concerns. What are the underlying causes of the new world of work?

During the period addressed in this book, some Americans prospered. The top income earners doubled their share of the nation's income in the past twenty-five years, as Paul Krugman and other leading economists have documented.[2] Millions of immigrants continued to seek jobs and opportunity in the United States, many risking their lives to do so. However, anxiety and fear remained stubborn realities for millions of low- and moderate-income families and individuals. Despite working hard and "playing by the rules," tens of millions of working adults were struggling or poor.[3]

Some observers predicted that the Great Recession was just another business cycle from which the nation would quickly recover.[4] They maintain that the United States will again experience widespread economic mobility, rising incomes, and wealth.[5] By late 2012, the *stock market* had nearly returned to its prerecession levels, but the *labor market* was still not healthy: only about half of the 8.7 million jobs lost during the Great Recession have returned to the economy. Corporate leaders present many success stories of American workplaces that invest in worker education, family benefits, and professional development as evidence that they still generate security and opportunity and are global models.[6] That is undoubtedly true, but American workers are increasingly skeptical that they too will benefit.

While there are still significant economic growth opportunities in some industries, the nature and scope of those opportunities were modified in significant but perhaps subtle ways. The turbulence of global competition and capital markets reshaped the American economy in the past two decades. A globalized economy cost the United States job losses in manufacturing and information technology. Free trade agreements, such as the North American Free Trade Agreement, had highly polarizing effects as major U.S. industries relocated all or part of their operations to other nations in search of lower taxes and less expensive labor. Federal policies intended to compensate the economic victims of new trade agreements reached only a small portion of laid-off workers in the manufacturing sector. Limited assistance was extended to service economy workers, according to reports by the Congressional Research Service and Heldrich Center research.[7]

During the past two decades, the practice of offshoring jobs from the United States spread from labor-intensive industries that produce low-value goods, such as toys; to complex products, such as automobiles; and services, such as interpreting radiology exams. Employees of all ranks, from the corporate suite to the mail room, learned that their industries and jobs are at risk. There are no safe havens; no corners of the economy are unaffected.

Employees of all ranks, from the corporate suite to the mail room, learned that their industries and jobs are at risk. There are no safe havens; no corners of the economy are unaffected.

It is fitting to begin with the godfather of U.S. corporate strategy, the late Peter Drucker, who described the symbiotic relationship between management and workers. In 2002, in a landmark article in the *Harvard Business Review*, Drucker asked, How should companies value and invest in people during the era of outsourcing?[8] He cited research by the consulting firm Mc-Kinsey & Company showing that large organizations could lower labor costs by one-quarter to one-third by outsourcing human resource functions. Noting the competitive implications of these choices, he described how outsourcing would transform the workplace. As large corporations move jobs to foreign corporations or specialty temporary service firms, he asked, how should organizations think of their human assets? Drucker wrote, "The attenuation of the relationship between people and the organizations they work for represents a grave danger to business." Businesses must think of their human assets not as just "employees" but as people who can bring a great deal of advantage to the organization. The last line of the article concludes, "Employees may be our greatest liability, but people are our greatest opportunity."

Less than a decade later, in an influential *Harvard Business Review* article, human resource expert Peter Cappelli of the Wharton School of Business critiqued corporate "talent management" strategies. He pointed out that it may no longer make sense for firms to recruit, develop, and retain workers on the assumption that they will spend most of their careers with a single firm.[9] In the same way that firms no longer stockpile components for products that will not be built for years or warehouse inventory that they may never sell, he concluded that firms often cannot afford to educate and retain workers that the company may never need. The Great Recession accelerated the trend to just-in-time labor forces, according to Cappelli: "Employers are trying to get rid of all fixed costs. First they did it with employment benefits. Now they are doing it with the jobs themselves . . . all risks are pushed on to employees."[10]

The choices made by employers about how they deploy their workforces represent one of the central economic policy issues of our era.

Are American workers a liability, a burden representing costs that must be slashed in order to achieve higher profits? Should employers make greater investments in human talent development and prepare employees for higher-order thinking and innovation? Can companies afford to value only a handful of highly educated professionals at the "core" of the firm and provide the minimum to everybody else? Are employees the firm's most valued asset or a disposable commodity? The choices made by employers about how they deploy their workforces represent one of the central economic policy issues of our era.

This chapter examines how global, competitive forces made once-secure jobs vulnerable. It examines these business and public policy decisions and their impacts on American workers who can rarely make their voices heard. I consider the degree to which the competitive pressures of the global economy have frayed the implicit mutually beneficial compact between worker and employer and examine the costs and the consequences.

WHAT HAPPENED TO
THE EMPLOYER/EMPLOYEE COMPACT?

In a complex society, citizens understand "normal" as rules and expectations that govern their behavior with others and with institutions. Norms shape our sense of obligation to family, community, and employer. These norms are shaped by institutions, personal experiences, customs, and cross-cultural and cross-regional exchanges via mobility, migration, and the media. Naturally, these influences lead to the evolution over time of what is understood as "normal" and desirable. Our adaptation of these norms (say, "getting a good job" after attending college) are reinforced by societal rewards (money and approval) and penalties as well as legal and regulatory boundaries. For example, if you refuse to work when you are able to do so, eventually you will receive no assistance from the government.

In the U.S. workforce, a shared set of beliefs defined a widely understood "compact" between employers and workers in the decades following World War II. All the elements of this workplace compact never existed for every worker, especially those with limited education, minorities, or women. Nevertheless, for many Americans, these norms were either the reality or the foundation of what they hoped to achieve in a job and career.

There has never been a formal agreement, outside of union contracts, about what employers owe to their employees in return for their hard work or loyalty. Yet most American workers want more than just a good day's pay for a good day's work. Rather, they expect their steadfast contributions to a company to be rewarded with a "permanent job" that enables them to retire with dignity. Naturally, employees hope for reciprocity from their employers. If they are loyal and work hard for the firm, they expect loyalty and honest dealings from their employer.

Data from the Heldrich Center's *Work Trends* surveys reveal that workers clearly perceive an asymmetry in their relationship with employers. More than eight in ten (85 percent) workers said that they were loyal to the organization where they work, but only 63 percent said that their employers were loyal to them.

Craig, a fifty-nine-year-old from Wisconsin, commented to Heldrich Center interviewers in 2011,

> My view today is that there is no career. There is no loyalty, no longevity, there is a just a role and a function . . . there is going to be more job hopping because there's constant change out there and as we advance technology wise. . . . It is all changing so fast, so hard to keep up with it. Unless the individual keeps changing with it, moving from organization to organization, they're not going to feel comfortable. How does that affect the community of the business? There's a loss of community in the corporation.

Even fewer workers (58 percent) trusted their employer to tell them the truth about the economic health of their company, and only 50 percent trusted employers to tell them about the security of their jobs. The extent to which workers trust and feel a sense of employer loyalty varies somewhat, but it is notably similar across gender, age, race, education, and income groups (see table 2.1).

American workers held consistent views throughout a decade of volatile swings in the U.S. economy. In 1998, at the peak of one of the nation's greatest episodes of economic growth, 65 percent said they felt a sense of loyalty from their employer, compared with 63 percent of workers in 2009 during one of the nation's worst recessions. In matters of trust, 58 percent of employees in 1998 said employers would tell the truth about the company's economic health, and 56 percent trusted them to tell the truth about their job security. In 2009, those numbers were 56 and 50 percent. Workers' attitudes about trust and loyalty, therefore, were not shaped by the Great Recession but rather were influenced by broader structural changes that led many workers to question whether they and their employer were working together for mutual benefit. In 2002, *New York Times* reporter Steven Greenhouse wrote,[11]

> In a strong departure from the 1990's when C.E.O.'s were often hailed as heroes, workers are voicing a sense of anger, even betrayal, toward top executives. Among experts in human resources, a sharp debate is underway about whether workers' commitment to their employers has waned in response to corporate downsizing and a sense that many top executives have betrayed workers and investors.

FOUR FORCES DOWNSIZING THE AMERICAN WORKER

It is a well-established principle of economics that market economies create and destroy jobs.[12] Repetitive, physically demanding, dangerous jobs have been reduced or eliminated by technological innovations in such industries as

Table 2.1. Workers Doubt That Their Loyalty to Employers Is Reciprocated (percent who agree)

	Total	Men	Women	White	Nonwhite	High School	Some College	BA or Higher	Under $35K	$35–$70K	$70K–$100K	$100K+
I feel a sense of loyalty to the company or organization that I work for.	85%	84%	85%	86%	81%	84%	86%	85%	86%	82%	85%	86%
The company or organization I work for feels a sense of loyalty toward me.	63%	63%	63%	65%	56%	70%	55%	63%	72%	64%	59%	56%
How much do you trust your employer to tell the truth about the economic health of your company, a lot?	56%	60%	52%	58%	49%	60%	47%	60%	55%	54%	54%	61%
How much do you trust your employer to tell the truth about the security of your job at your company, a lot?	50%	51%	51%	53%	44%	54%	44%	53%	57%	48%	44%	54%

Source: C. Van Horn and C. Zukin, "What a Difference a Decade Makes: The Declining Job Satisfaction of the American Workforce," Heldrich Center, Rutgers University, September 2009.

coal mining and steel production. Productivity gains are achieved by finding how to work not only faster but also smarter—and with fewer employees. As the knowledge economy evolved, many rightly celebrated the triumph of brain over brawn. Former Federal Reserve Board chairman Alan Greenspan promoted the views of economist Joseph Schumpeter, who stated, "Capitalism expands wealth primarily through creative destruction—the process by which the cash flow from obsolescent, low-return capital is invested in high-return, cutting-edge technologies."[13] Greenspan, who served as chairman from 1987 to 2006, maintained that rapid productivity gains driven by paradigmatic shifts in information technology would reward nimble workers and firms. Former Clinton administration treasury secretary Lawrence Summers, chief economic adviser during the first two years of President Obama's administration, called the new economy "Schumpeterian" because of the "avalanche" of creative destruction.[14]

It is important to understand the potential benefits and costs of how technology restructures work. Schumpeter argued that in large economies with massive corporations, the spark of entrepreneurial innovation is often co-opted within bureaucratic firms. According to Schumpeter, when industries become more established, workers become more educated, and government regulators gain power, then large companies will collaborate with government institutions to protect their monopoly or near-monopoly status. Creative destruction is slowed by democratic socialism. An implication of this trend is that information specialists, financiers, executives, lawyers, analysts, and consultants with advanced skills will prosper in a protected monopolistic cocoon because they have esoteric skills that are difficult to outsource. Workers in the service, technical, manufacturing, and related sectors compete in the raw, less regulated global markets churning with creative destruction. However, outsourcing and offshoring jobs have also reached the legal and medical professions because law firms and health insurance companies are also scrambling to reduce costs by hiring well-trained professionals in other countries.[15]

Unlike previous economic revolutions, the information technology revolution occurred so quickly that policymakers did not always understand or respond promptly. The industrial revolution spanned a century and a half, from early eighteenth-century textile spinning machines to the machine processes of the nineteenth century and the early twentieth century's internal combustion engine and assembly line production.[16] The enormous dislocations in the U.S. automotive industry unfolded over a period of more than forty years. The industry's golden age ended with the rise of imports in the 1970s and intensified in the 1980s as carmakers reengineered cars and organization charts with "total quality management," faster supply chains, and plant automation through robotics. The 1990s brought better times for U.S. automakers with the rise of new luxury vehicles and sport-utility vehicles, but non-U.S. auto brands became American fixtures. The Great Recession forced another key overhaul both in management structure and in competitive hybrids and fuel-efficient cars.[17]

The information technology revolution swept quickly through the economy in the mid-1990s and brought about huge changes in the structure of American firms and employment on a society-wide scale. This upheaval in the U.S. labor market can be pinned to four major forces that revamped nearly every major industry. The rapid pace and broad scope of change destabilized the careers of millions of American workers.

Each of these broad forces was accelerated by the rise in global competition driven by networked, broadband information technology, low-cost labor and trade agreements that eliminated tariffs and eroded protections for U.S. workers, and, most notably, policy and legislative support for economic liberalization. Deregulation of financial institutions and the emergence of hedge funds and private equity and the free flow of capital gave rise to more powerful financial institutions that deployed their funds to leverage mergers and corporate restructuring and quicker profits.[18]

The four broad forces driving labor market transformations are the following:

• Globalization and offshoring
• Mergers, acquisitions, and restructuring
• A transition from industrialization to a knowledge/service economy
• Deunionization

By examining the impact of these trends on industries, skills, jobs, and wages, one can better understand the fault lines moving beneath the lives of American workers. Will the economic forces transforming the national and world economy be beneficial to workers and their children and grandchildren? (Of course, when you are living through an economic disaster, you may not care whether things will improve in the long run.)

Who benefits during the transformation? What groups might be left behind or lose privileged positions in the current order? We know that low-skilled manufacturing workers lost out to low-wage workers in foreign countries for decades. Will this trend also appear in engineering, medicine, and law? Let's begin with the practice of relocating jobs from the United States to other countries, what has come to be known as offshoring.

Globalization and Offshoring

In his influential book *The World Is Flat*, journalist Thomas Friedman pointed out that the flattening forces brought about by the free flow of capital, the Internet, and work flow software have doubled the potential global workforce and created a new global playing field for collaboration and competition.[19] Thousands of firms and millions of U.S. workers who were once sheltered from this global competition were suddenly thrust into an entirely different economic environment. Distributing work that had been conducted entirely in the United States to other locations around the globe—a business practice that was unimaginable in the late 1980s—was now not only possible but also perhaps desirable.

Researchers vary in their estimates of the impact of offshoring U.S. jobs (a number of analysts have raised concerns about how the U.S. Bureau of Labor Statistics measures the phenomenon), but there is no doubt that global competition and the resulting offshoring of jobs had substantial impacts on major industries and occupations.[20] Research reported by Ann Harrison and Margaret McMillan of the University of California and Tufts University found that offshoring directly replaced home-country low-wage jobs, but they were skeptical about its impact on professional, high-skill jobs.[21] Researchers at the National Bureau of Economic Research also concluded that offshoring's greatest impact was on low-wage jobs but argued that cost savings and efficiencies make up for jobs lost and push native workers into more communication-intensive and lucrative jobs.[22] A 2007 analysis by the Organisation for Economic Co-operation and Development confirmed that offshoring of low-wage jobs to lower-wage nations depressed U.S. job opportunities in key sectors, although the total impact is far lower than other structural factors, such as technological advances.

Other respected economists, including Alan Blinder of Princeton University, however, argue that the impact of offshoring could be far greater in the coming decades. In his view, the only jobs not vulnerable to offshoring are ones that depend on direct contact with the purchaser, such as a carpenter. In 2006, Blinder estimated that 40 million U.S. jobs, in a workforce of about 150 million, could be moved to other countries.[23] With the rapid evolution of technology, that number could increase.

Offshoring U.S.-based service sector jobs began in the early 1980s when economic slowdowns spurred employers to "invest in their core" and "contract out" peripheral activities to other U.S. and foreign businesses. The terrorist events of September 11, 2001, convinced many companies to shift more U.S. jobs overseas. With technology improvements and broadband Internet services that enable the transmission of complex images and documents, waves of higher-value occupations, including engineering, radiology, research science, and some legal services, joined the migration. IBM established a research-and-development lab in New Delhi, India, and hired thousands of "software inventors," such as software engineers, cloud computing analysts, researchers in optimization and analytics, and many other technical positions.[24] Following IBM's lead are Motorola, which operates sixteen research-and-development centers in China employing 1,800 engineers, and other companies. However, the telephone and technology giant learned many bitter lessons, including theft of technology and intellectual property by Chinese firms that were once its suppliers.[25]

The rise of a global information technology workforce helps explain why the 1998 U.S. Bureau of Labor Statistics forecast of 1 million new, U.S.-based computer support specialist and systems analyst jobs over ten years did not materialize.[26] The pace of this repositioning of work from one country to the next has quickened. For example, in 2002, Forrester Research analysts predicted that over the next fifteen years, over 3 million U.S. white-collar jobs, accounting for $136 billion in wages, would move overseas. Two years later, Forrester revised its estimate upward.[27]

Prominent executives were quick to embrace the new imperative of globalization. In 2004, Carly Fiorina, chief executive officer of Hewlett-Packard, testified before Congress that "there is no job that is an American's God-given right anymore." Years later, that frank assessment might have contributed to her losing a U.S. Senate election in California.[28] Nandan Nilekani, the chief executive of the India-based Infosys Technologies, said memorably at a 2004 World Economic Forum, "Everything you can send down a wire is up for grabs."

The rise in offshoring over the past two decades reflects how the global economy both encourages and forces companies to move their operations where they can dramatically cut labor costs. It also reflects the dispersion of viable consumer markets around the globe, with an expanding middle class in several nations, including China, Brazil, and India. In 2000, developing countries were home to 56 percent of the global middle class, but by 2030 that figure is expected to reach 93 percent. China and India alone will account for two-thirds of the expansion, with China contributing 52 percent of the increase and India 12 percent, according to the World Bank and the Wharton School.[29]

Asked by the Heldrich Center in 2010 to assess the causes of high levels of unemployment and personal economic strife during the Great Recession, three out of every four American workers blamed "global competition and cheap labor from other countries."

Even as economists and policymakers continue to debate the net results from offshoring, two things are already clear. These new global realities introduced greater uncertainty and anxiety into the American economy and workplace. Second, millions of American workers have already concluded that offshoring harms them and the U.S. economy. Asked by the Heldrich Center in 2010 to assess the causes of high levels of unemployment and personal economic strife during the Great Recession, three out of every four American workers blamed "global competition and cheap labor from other countries." In contrast, just over four in ten respondents attributed high unemployment to the actions of Wall Street bankers: a similar number said that illegal immigrants had taken jobs away from Americans and contributed to high unemployment.[30]

Dozens of respondents to Heldrich Center surveys in December 2010 commented on the negative effects of these trends. Here is a grim assessment from one of those workers:

> Higher unemployment will become the norm because of excessive outsourcing of jobs to foreign countries for cheaper wages and higher profits. The middle class will be smaller or squeezed out of existence. The gap between the "haves" and the "have nots" will continue to widen. The standard of living will continue to decline and bottom out.

Mergers, Acquisitions, and Restructuring

Although many companies were not moving production or service delivery from the United States to another country, frequent ownership turnovers and reorganizations brought about through mergers and acquisitions further dislocated millions of American workers. In an effort to improve operations, productivity, and profitability, thousands of firms merged with their competitors or acquired them entirely. Driven by relentless market demands for quarterly profits, publicly traded companies are under pressure to reduce their head count by realigning departments and offshoring jobs. Some employees benefit from restructuring and receive more responsibilities and higher wages; others are discarded when the companies consolidate. Managers also seek technology solutions that might increase productivity by reducing personnel. Through automated phone and Internet-enabled customer service systems, human resource functions, data analysis, and information dissemination, firms are finding technology solutions that shrink their workforces.

The potential value of using technology to redesign business practices and reduce layers of management to improve productivity were popularized in *Reengineering the Corporation* by management consultants Michael Hammer and James Champy.[31] They argued that successful corporate restructurings that improve long-term profitability require management and employees to receive extensive training and buy-in to the new order. However, in thousands of companies where reengineering occurred, the goal of eliminating jobs was achieved without improving the business. Employees feared for their jobs, and many managers received inadequate training. Too many companies took the path of least resistance and automated their information technology processes and "back-office" operations and administration. The short-term profits often did not last, while shortcomings in product, services, innovation, training, and customer engagement emerged.[32]

Mergers and acquisitions are far from a sure bet to increase a company's return on investment. After examining eighty acquisitions completed from 2002 through 2005, the consulting firm Accenture concluded that around six in ten acquirers were unable to generate increased revenue growth in the second year after the deal closed compared with what their growth had been before merging. Gains were not realized when managers put customer service and satisfaction on the back burner to single-mindedly pursue cost savings, leading existing customers to jump ship.[33]

While mergers may or may not be the path to higher earnings, they are a shortcut to smaller workforces. When companies combine, overlapping positions are cut, and layoffs follow. What are the employment impacts of the corporate restructuring era? Between 2001 and 2006, changes in business ownership on average led to a 6 percent workforce reduction, according to Dina Itkin at the *Monthly Labor Review*.[34] Occupations least likely to be retained after an ownership turnover were those that performed analytical, clerical, and production work, while workers performing direct services, such as health care and education, were more likely to remain with the new firm.

Deindustrialization to Knowledge Economy

For over thirty years, there has been a steady decline of manufacturing in the United States. Whether it was automobile plants closing with relentless frequency or solar panel manufacturers in 2012, it sometimes seems like America does not make much anymore. In fact, between 1996 and 2010, employers in the United States laid off over 28 million people in large plant and office closings.[35] In 1980, approximately a third of the U.S. workforce was in manufacturing; by 2009, that sector employed only one-tenth of the workforce.[36] Since 1997, approximately one-third of the jobs in the entire manufacturing sector disappeared.[37]

The loss of America's leadership position in manufacturing downsized pay and tenure for workers who remain in that sector. Manufacturing employment historically paid better wages and provided abundant opportunities for workers with no more than a high school education. These industries were often stable because economic cycles relating to goods design, transport, and production played out over longer periods of time.

While some advanced manufacturing sectors have remained relatively strong, even emerging industries, such as in the energy sector, face global challenges. A few years ago, U.S. policymakers and business leaders predicted that the manufacturing of so-called green products, like solar panels, would create significant job growth. That did not happen. Major solar panel manufacturers are moving to China in search of lower production costs. The chief executive officer of one company that is moving its operations to China commented, "While the United States and other Western industrial economies are beneficiaries of rapidly declining installation costs of solar energy, we expect the United States will continue to be at a disadvantage from a manufacturing standpoint."[38]

In many respects, the United States of America is now the "United States of Services." American workplaces are more likely to be offices, laboratories, schools, and clinics than factories or assembly plants. Some types of work, such as health and education, are anchored in a single location because workers must be close to one another and to the people they serve. For thousands of other firms, the information and ideas—and the jobs—that form the productive base of a knowledge economy can be moved anywhere in the country or the world quickly. The high costs associated with moving industrial raw materials and finished goods pose no barrier in an economy based on brainpower.

The mobility of service delivery and capital affords companies more flexibility to move their operations from one community to another or from one country to another. It is far easier for companies to transfer operations and shift functions from one site to another. *Capital is very mobile; American workers are not.* Most households cannot easily leave their communities without incurring significant financial and personal costs. The depressed real estate and property values that accompanied the Great Recession are major barriers standing in the path of workers who might be willing to relocate to another town or city. During the housing crisis and recession, millions saw their home values plummet; moving became less desirable, if not impossible.

The prototypical postindustrial firm is no longer a stand-alone plant dependent on roads, rails, and water transport but rather a node within a national and global network connected by fiber-optic and wireless technology. While these arrangements have important competitive advantages for employers, they blur the lines between work, family, and community. Thousands of reliable, sustainable employers with a proven set of products have been replaced by companies that can deliver services using the Internet and door-to-door package delivery.

Consider the transformation of the iconic global giant General Electric (GE). During its strategic reinvention over the past thirty years, GE "financialized" its manufacturing business model. GE pared back industrial

operations, basing its manufacturing business on government-based contracts. The firm drove growth and profits by expanding financial services to
envelop its core of government contract manufacturing. In the book *Financialization and Strategy: Narrative and Numbers*, Froud, Johal, Leaver, and
Williams write,

> The story of GE Capital is a story of upward mobility, as GE has found growth
> of sales revenue by moving beyond captive finance into many other lines of
> financial business. GE has sold financial services since the 1930s, starting with
> domestic credit for refrigerators, a classic form of captive finance. Up to the
> late 1970s, GE was arguably not so different from other U.S. corporates, such
> as GM or Westinghouse, with a financial-services division whose central activ-
> ity was captive finance. However, through the 1980s and 1990s, GE Capital
> greatly expanded and increased its offering in everything from LBO finance to
> store cards.[39]

Relationships between GE and its workers and host communities were up-
ended. For decades, GE was a rock of stability in upstate New York, with union
workers making refrigerators and lightbulbs. Today, GE is a "financial services"
firm that depends on information technology and personnel around the globe.
The devastating impact on those who worked for the "old GE" is a familiar story
for millions of workers who hoped that if they worked hard and remained with
the company, they could ride the seniority escalator to better jobs, higher pay,
and a secure retirement. Without these expectations, employees are less likely
to feel positive attachment to their companies. Workers are much more likely to
distrust the firms they work for and to look out for themselves.

Millions of workers now must collaborate with colleagues located in dis-
tant cities and time zones. This necessitates new working methods, including
the electronic tether of e-mails and "smart phones" that practically guarantee
that employees will be "always on" for their employers. These unpredictable
circumstances create pervasive dissatisfaction among workers (explored further in chapter 3).

Deunionization

Union members and their political clout were largely responsible for many
laws and social changes that benefited hundreds of millions of American
workers. The forty-hour workweek, paid vacations, employer-provided
health and retirement benefits, family and medical leave, workplace safety,
and equal opportunity laws were legislative victories achieved by the union
movement and spread throughout much of the rest of the U.S. workforce.
Organized labor's support was essential for the enactment of major social

programs, from Medicare in the 1960s to the Affordable Care Act in 2010. Unions were the main champions of organizing rights for workers and of the gradual evolution of Social Security into a strong foundation for dignified retirement.

A *New York Times*/CBS News poll from February 2011 confirms that a majority of Americans favor collective bargaining.[40] The value of unions to American workers was summarized in a compelling essay by Jacob Hacker and Paul Pierson in the *Washington Post* in March 2011:

> Unions also push for broad federal policies that reduce gaps in income and wealth. In the United States, they have resisted the rampant deregulation of financial markets and the soaring growth of executive pay. They have been one of the few organized voices that have consistently pressed back against the string of tax-cut bills for the rich that began in the late 1970s. All of this makes the decline of unions—which has been far steeper in the United States than in Europe and Canada—a huge political and economic challenge. Private-sector union membership in America has fallen from roughly a third of workers in the middle of the 20th century to less than 7 percent today. Even including the public sector, the share is just over 1 in 10. Despite these declines, labor continues to be the only large-scale membership organization consistently representing Americans of moderate means on pocketbook matters.[41]

The precedents set by union contracts affected wages, benefits, and workplace fairness, especially for low- and middle-income workers without a college education. As economist Larry Mishel has noted, "Unions have a positive impact on the wages of non-union workers in industries and markets in which unions have a strong presence."[42]

With the unionized workforce declining, especially in the private sector, their bargaining power and influence on the American workplace have weakened considerably in the twenty-first century. Unionization has declined faster and in more industries in the United States than in other advanced industrialized nations.[43] Union contracts also helped establish practices that evolved into cultural and social norms. Union wage setting frequently established standards of what nonunion workers could demand from their employers. Union grievance procedures, which provide "due process" in the workplace, were adopted in many nonunion workplaces.

As large employers restructured their firms, shed labor costs, established global sourcing operations, and offshored functions, they not only reduced union representation but also gained strong leverage when negotiating with union leaders. For example, the economic crisis of 2008–2009 led to another round of major "givebacks" by the United Auto Workers (UAW) as policymakers and auto industry managers negotiated the conditions for government loans. Union members gave up two lump-sum payments previously agreed to as substitutes for pay raises, cut back on the UAW job bank (which paid workers supplemental wages during layoffs), agreed to major cuts in auto company contributions to health and welfare, and accepted less generous wages and benefits for new employees.

Because of reductions in union membership stemming from layoffs in construction, manufacturing, and teaching and public service positions, union membership's share of the American workforce declined from 15 percent in 1995 to 12 percent in 2011.[44] Private sector union membership fell by 339,000 to 7.1 million in 2010 and made up only 7 percent of all workers—the lowest percentage in more than a century. In the same year, public sector union membership declined by 273,000 to 7.6 million.[45] Also of note is the following:

- Between 1983 and 2010, the union membership rate for men declined by almost half (12.1 percentage points), while the rate for women declined by 3.5 percentage points.
- In 2010, among major race and ethnicity groups, black workers were more likely to be union members (13.4 percent) than workers who were white (11.7 percent), Asian (10.9 percent), or Hispanic (10.0 percent).
- Union membership was highest among fifty-five- to sixty-four-year-old workers (15.7 percent) and lowest for those ages sixteen to twenty-four (4.3 percent).

Median weekly earnings for union members in 2012 were $917—$200 more than the median weekly earnings for nonunion workers, according to the U.S. Bureau of Labor Statistics.[46]

The highest concentrations of union members in the public sector are in education and public safety functions, including teachers, police officers, and firefighters. Private sector industries with high rates of union membership include transportation and utilities (22 percent), telecommunications (16 percent), and construction (13 percent). In 2010, the lowest unionization rates occurred in agriculture and related industries (1.6 percent) and financial services (2.0 percent).

The four factors downsizing the American worker—globalization and

The four factors downsizing the American worker—globalization and offshoring, mergers and acquisitions, deindustrialization, and deunionization—transformed the American workplace and are likely to intensify over the next decade.

offshoring, mergers and acquisitions, deindustrialization, and deunionization—transformed the American workplace and are likely to intensify over
the next decade. Companies, people, and national economies will encounter
greater competition, challenges, and uncertainty in this era of Darwinian globalization. The nations that adapt most quickly will prosper. In order to keep
up with a rapidly changing labor market, American workers will need education and training frequently during their careers. Will they get it?

EDUCATION AND TRAINING GAPS

A knowledge-based economy increases pressure on workers not only to be
better prepared when they enter the workforce but also to upgrade their skills
throughout their working lives. Heldrich Center surveys in the late 1990s and
early 2000s consistently found strong support for significant federal government assistance to help workers get additional education so they can adapt to
the changing economy. Government-supported training for incumbent workers and for college students were endorsed by approximately three of every
four American workers.

Whether through schools, colleges, local training programs, or on the Internet, workers must learn to perform a broader range of complex tasks. They
need to know more about data analysis and management, communication,
and software application skills. In addition, the motile factors in our labor
market mean that people with access and ability to learn more complex skills
are more likely to get highly paid jobs. Because fewer employers provide job
training for new or incumbent workers, the costs of acquiring education and
training have shifted to individuals.

Persistent and growing income disparities in America are a by-product of
an economy that rewards better-educated workers. Education and skills gap
between lower-income and better-off workers are widening. Women at all
educational levels also earn less than men (see figure 2.1). In 2012, adults
twenty-five years and older with high school diplomas had median weekly
earnings of $659, while for college graduates with a bachelor's degree, me-
dian weekly earnings were $1,070—a difference of just over $400.[47] In 1996,
median earnings for high school graduates were $520 versus $795 for adults
with a bachelor's degree, a difference of $275.[48]

In the contemporary economy, advanced education and skills are the sine
qua non of labor market and economic success. To what extent are public
policies and employers responding to this challenge? Are investments being
made to keep the U.S. economy growing and competitive (and its citizens
solvent)? Are those investments appropriately focused on those who need

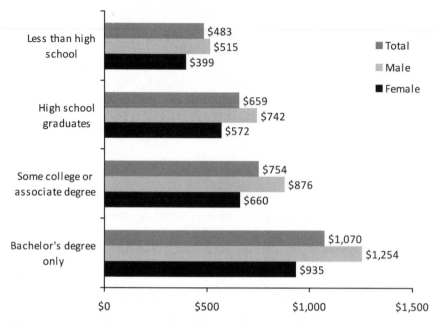

Figure 2.1. More Education Yields Higher Earnings at Work, but Men Do Better Than Women
Source: U.S. Bureau of Labor Statistics, "Usual Weekly Earnings of Wage and Salary Workers, Second Quarter, 2012," USDL 12-14-1419, July 2012.

it most? Are there gaps between our intentions and our needs and between investments in education before and after adulthood?

Education Spending P-20

State governments allocated over $332 billion to elementary and secondary education in fiscal year 2011, representing 20 percent of all spending. Education spending is greater than any other category, except Medicaid, which consumed 23.6 percent of state budgets. By comparison, only 7.6 percent of state funds go to transportation; public assistance programs consumed only 1.6 percent of state funds.[49]

The federal government, during the same years, spent about $55 billion on elementary and secondary education, representing about 9 percent of all education spending in K–12 programs.[50] The Department of Education and the Department of Health and Human Services channeled most of these funds through 150 programs, including Head Start for early childhood education, grants to improve reading and math through the No Child Left Behind program, and aid to bolster developmental educational programs for children with learning disabilities.

Colleges and universities receive substantial but, in comparison to K–12, less funding from state governments. Here, too, however, states spent four times more than the federal government. In 2011, state support for higher education was $164 billion, 10.1 percent of state budgets. Per capita aid to K–12 education has been rising for years, but state support for higher education has been either flat or declining since 1990 as more of the responsibility for paying tuition and fees shifted to students.[51]

Job Training Programs for the Unemployed

Far less government money is devoted to training or retraining workers who do not complete a high school or college education or for the long-term unemployed needing new skills. In fiscal year 2012, the principal federal job training and workforce development programs spent $3.2 billion after the sunset of the one-time increases in workforce spending contained in the Recovery Act. Of this amount, $770 million was allocated to adult training and education and $1.2 billion for dislocated workers. Other key federal programs target assistance to several groups with special needs, such as migrant and seasonal farmworkers, the reintegration of ex-offenders, and Indian and Native American programs.[52]

Given these modest amounts of funding, state and local agencies administering federal job training programs cannot possibly serve the millions of people who might be unemployed at any given point in time. Available funds are sufficient to train only about six hundred thousand people. Recall that as many as 20 million people were unemployed during the depths of the Great Recession. Political leaders in both parties have been loath to support significant investments in job training programs for decades, preferring instead to extend unemployment insurance benefits when the economy stalled. States are unlikely to fill the void given that they also faced huge deficits due to the Great Recession.

Training at Work

Does the private sector fill the void created by governments' limited investments in job training programs for employed and unemployed workers? The available evidence is not encouraging. According to a report issued in 2009 by the Society for Human Resource Management, the American Society for Training and Development, the Conference Board, and Corporate Voices for Working Families, corporate workforce readiness and remedial training programs do not meet the needs of employees or businesses. They often deliver unsatisfactory results for those who are enrolled in short-term training programs. Of particular note, more than 40 percent of employees identified the importance of programs to bolster critical thinking skills; more than 70 percent identified a high need for programs to enhance creative thinking. Employees saw these very skills as essential for competing globally but were not receiving or satisfied with training in these areas.[53]

Other research documents substantial reductions in private sector training budgets and programs. A 2009 study by Bersin & Associates, done in conjunction with *Workforce Management*, reported steep drops in private sector training and development spending:

> For the second straight year, companies sliced their spending on learning and development by 11 percent—to $714 per learner. Large companies, which are those with ten thousand or more employees, scaled back the most, by 12 percent. But smaller companies did not escape the budget knife. Small firms, which employ 100 to 999 employees, cut training budgets by 10 percent.[54]

Roughly six in ten companies routinely reported that they cannot find sufficient numbers of skilled, qualified workers, according to our *Work Trends* data.[55] However, most employers are unable or unwilling to invest in education and training because they do not know how long employees will remain with their firms or whether workers will take their new skills to a competitor. As global competition expands and during periods of slow economic growth, employers are not likely to alter these practices.

Management experts and millions of American workers believe that their best protection against the strong forces of economic change is to constantly enhance the skills of the workforce. According to management guru Peter Drucker, improving the talent of a firm's workforce is essential:

> It's one thing for a company to take advantage of long-term freelance talent or to outsource the more tedious aspects of its human resources management. It's quite another to forget, in the process, that developing talent is business' most important task—the sine qua non of competition in a knowledge economy.[56]

American workers agree. Between 1999 and 2009, Heldrich Center surveys found that seven in ten workers thought that opportunities to learn new skills at work were extremely or very important.[57] Enrollment in community colleges increased in eight of the ten years between 2001 and 2011 and grew by 15 percent between 2008 and 2010, according to the American Association of Community Colleges and National Center for Education Statistics data.[58] College graduates have also concluded that their BA or BS degree is not likely to be sufficient in the U.S. economy of the future. In national surveys of recent college graduates from the classes of 2006 to 2011 by the Heldrich Center, approximately two in three expected that they would need to obtain additional education in order to be financially successful.

Even though American workers know they need to learn more to be successful, they are finding it difficult to figure out what they need to know and how to pay for it. Workers complained that employers are unwilling to pay for educational and training programs or give them time off from work to attend schools. Over half said their employers did a poor job of providing them with training opportunities. From 1999 to 2009, workers who said they were "very satisfied" with educational and training opportunities from their employer never rose above 40 percent and dropped to 28 percent in 2009. Younger workers under age forty were particularly disappointed, with their satisfaction levels dropping from 56 percent in 1999 to 26 percent in 2009.

The situation is even more difficult for the working poor. Over eight in ten low-income workers said more education is essential for improving their job prospects, according to Heldrich Center *Work Trends* research. Yet fewer than one in five of the working poor received financial support from an employer to attend education or training outside of the workplace. (Fewer than one in three obtained government support for that purpose.[59]) Workers at the lower end of the income scale are especially eager to acquire the skills necessary to improve their opportunities and earnings in the workplace, but they are the least likely group to receive them.

Low-income American workers also found it hard to attend college after the Great Recession. For example, research commissioned by the Community Service Society of New York City in 2012 shows that fewer black and Latino high school graduates (groups that are disproportionately working poor) were enrolled in the City University of New York system after the recession. According to the report,

> By 2010, black students comprised 10 percent of entering freshmen at the top five CUNY colleges—Baruch, Hunter, Brooklyn, City, and Queens colleges—down from 17 percent in 2001 and 14 percent in 2008. Latino students made up 19 percent of entering freshmen at top schools in 2010, down from 22 percent in 2008. These changes coincided with a significant increase in the number of black and Latino high school students taking the SAT.[60]

Working poor adults also lag far behind better-off Americans in access to computers and technology. By the 2010s, more Americans in every income and racial group used the Internet at home than in 1999, but significant disparities remained in who had access to Internet and broadband technology. Senior citizens, Spanish speakers, adults with less than a high school education, and those living in households earning less than $30,000 were least likely to have Internet access, according to research by the Pew Internet and American Life Project. Among American adults in August 2011, 80 percent of white non-Hispanics, 71 percent of black non-Hispanics, and 68 percent of Hispanics were online. While 97 percent of adults living in households with incomes above $75,000 are online, only 62 percent of people earning less than $30,000 have Internet access. Similar gaps were found among levels of educational attainment. In February 2001 and at the time of our *Work Trends* report, about half of adults were online, and only a few percent had access to broadband. By 2011, more than six in ten Americans had obtained broadband access.[61]

The deficiencies of U.S. education and training policies have serious implications for America's workforce. For many workers, it is no longer feasible to learn enough by age eighteen or twenty-two to remain productive throughout one's entire career. Workers need periodic skills upgrading, but fewer are receiving it from employers. The federal government has not made significant and sustained investments in workforce development for incumbent or unemployed workers. The United States is falling behind several of its competitors and now spends less per capita on P-20 education than five other advanced economies, including Austria, Denmark, Norway, and Switzerland.[62]

Workers understand that in the knowledge economy, training should not be the emergency response to a job loss but rather a long-term career advancement strategy. Throughout the Heldrich Center's *Work Trends* research, Americans consistently emphasized the importance of technology, acquiring occupational and soft skills, and job training. They are willing to pay for education and training but also support tax incentives that would help them establish flexible lifelong-learning accounts. While they also strongly favor quality higher education and K–12 education, American workers no longer see a college degree as a safe conduct pass during hard times.

The global, knowledge-based economy requires a much greater emphasis on lifelong learning, flexibility, and core competencies so that workers and employers can transition from one job to the next or from one career to a new one. Workers understand that a good high school or postsecondary education is essential, but so is career and job-related training that meets current labor market needs. In our interviews with workers, they expressed concern over misplaced priorities in education. As Jeff, a fifty-four-year-old from Florida told us,

> My basic education wasn't that valuable. . . . I have a college degree in psychology. I think most people are not prepared for life by their education because they don't have enough information on what their choices are, what their opportunities are. It's a big problem with the education system in this country. People are

not adequately prepared for life or taught how to use their abilities, how to figure out what they want to do.

Or John, a forty-one-year-old from Wisconsin:

> If I realized I would be going into construction, I wouldn't have gone to college to earn a degree in ceramics, which is worthless. I read in the *New York Times* about how college students are realizing [some professions are less appealing] because there aren't a lot of jobs [with recent technology]. For example, legal research is being replaced by computers. I think they're realizing that spending all this money for education is not always worth it. In some fields it's worth the expense, but maybe we have to rethink things we have held traditionally that it's worth going into debt for because maybe you'll never catch up.

TRANSFORMING AMERICAN ATTITUDES

While moderate economic growth in 2011 and 2012 was welcomed, persistent high levels of unemployment remain a huge barrier to a sustained economic recovery. The anemic labor market, confusing and underfunded workforce programs, a shaky banking system, and political gridlock in Washington, D.C., badly eroded the trust between workers and employers and left scars that may affect economic behavior for years to come.

Working Americans are losing faith that their children and grandchildren will have better lives, losing hope that government and policymakers can fix the economy, losing trust in their employers, and becoming deeply frustrated about inadequate training and educational programs for unemployed workers.

Through nearly twenty-five thousand survey answers and hundreds of personal interviews with American workers, we identified four dramatic shifts in behavior and attitudes. Working Americans are losing faith that their children and grandchildren will have better lives, losing hope that government and policymakers can fix the economy, losing trust in their employers, and becoming deeply frustrated about inadequate training and educational programs for unemployed workers.

The Great Recession added to the numbers of the working poor and deepened their already severe financial stress, according to research released in

2010 by the Working Poor Families Project, and the Annie E. Casey, Ford, Joyce, and Mott Foundations. Forty-five million people, including 22 million children, lived in low-income working families in the depth of the recession in 2009, according to their analysis of census data. Over 30 percent of all American working families struggled to meet their basic needs during the recession, up from a figure of 27.4 percent in 2002.[63] For example, Joanne, a fifty-nine-year-old living in Detroit, lost her job in 2010, and while she eventually secured part-time work, her finances were destroyed:

> I no longer have a career, that's over with. What happened economically, it adjusted everybody's situation. I bought my first home in 2005, and it took me thirty years to save up for that, and one day everything just quit. I lost that home last year. It took all of my savings I put down in that home and the savings I had been living on. . . . I loved my job, when we were selling homes it was the best job I had ever had. I worked my way through that job up to a sales position. I thoroughly enjoyed it. There's nowhere else to go for that job.

Linda, a fifty-four-year-old North Carolina resident, found a new job in retail after a long bout of unemployment, but her income was less than half of what she earned before. She told us, "I ended up having to deplete resources that I never wanted to have to touch: 401ks, savings, retirement. . . . I have never been scraping the bottom of the barrel like this in my life."

In the early years of the twenty-first century, a majority of Americans do not believe that job, career, and employment opportunities will be better for the next generation. Half of workers believed it will be harder for young people to afford college and that they will never feel as secure in their jobs as they once did. Many workers we interviewed echoed the words of Joyce, who lives in rural Oregon. When asked about America's economic prospect, she said,

> I think we are going downhill fast. I keep trying to tell myself we will turn things around. It seems like things are getting worse and worse around here. [To help people get jobs we need to] lower the corporate tax rate and bring back people who have gone overseas. If the taxes were not so high then people wouldn't leave to go overseas. We should at least retax them for stuff they make overseas and bring back here. If we don't quit sending all of our jobs overseas we are going to be a ghost country.

Carrie, a highly educated professional in Baltimore, Maryland, said,

> I don't think we'll ever be in the same state we were before because of the financial institutions and their implications. . . . I don't feel like that industry is ever going to recover, and when you have a major industry like that, that will never recover, it's going to change the nature of our economy.

In the following chapter, I examine the new realities in the American work-place that emerged during an era of shocking transformations.

NOTES

1. Michelle Conlin, Moira Herbst, and Peter Coy, "The Disposable Worker," January 7, 2010, http://www.businessweek.com/magazine/content/10_03/b4163032935448.htm.
2. Paul Krugman, *End This Depression, Now* (New York: Norton, 2012).
3. U.S. Department of Labor, Bureau of Labor Statistics, "Working Poor Rate 7.2 Percent in 2010," April 5, 2012, http://www.bls.gov/opub/ted/2012/ted_20120405.htm.
4. Catherine Rampell, "Dissent on Recession's End," *New York Times Economix Blog*, April 12, 2010, http://economix.blogs.nytimes.com/2010/04/12/dissent -on-recessions-end; Chris Palmeri, "Worst Recession since the 1930s Will End in 2009," January 2, 2009, http://www.businessweek.com/the_thread/hotproperty/archives/2009/01/worst_recession.html; Julianne Pepitone, "Economists: Recession to End in 2009," CNNMoney, May 27, 2009, http://money.cnn.com/2009/05/27/news/economy/NABE_recovery_outlook.
5. Paul L. Winfree, "Analyzing Economic Mobility: Measuring Inequality and Income Mobility," May 31, 2007, http://www.heritage.org/research/reports/2007/05/analyzing-economic-mobility-measuring-inequality-and-economic-mobility; James Sherk, "Job to Job Transitions: More Mobility and Security in the Workforce," Heritage Foundation, September 2, 2008; Steve Forbes, *How Capitalism Will Save Us* (New York: Crown, 2009).
6. "Fortune 100 Best Companies to Work for 2012," May 2012, http://money.cnn.com/magazines/fortune/best-companies.
7. James R. Storey, "Trade Adjustment Assistance for Workers, Proposals for Renewal and Reform," Congressional Research Service, October 3, 2000; Meredith E. Staples, "Trade Adjustment Assistance Program," in *Work in America*, eds. Carl E. Van Horn and Herb Schaffner (Santa Barbara, CA: ABC-CLIO, 2002); Carl E. Van Horn, "A Rescue Plan for American Workers," October 17, 2008, http://www.industryweek.com/public-policy/viewpoint-rescue-plan-american-workers.
8. Peter F. Drucker, "They're Not Employees, They're People," *Harvard Business Review*, http://hbr.org/2002/02/theyre-not-employees-theyre-people/ar/1.
9. Peter Cappelli, "Talent Management for the Twenty-First Century," *Harvard Business Review*, March 2008.
10. Cappelli, "Talent Management for the Twenty-First Century."
11. Steven Greenhouse, "The Mood at Work: Anger and Anxiety," *New York Times*, Working Special Section, October 29, 2002, 9.
12. William J. Baume, *The Free-Market Innovation Machine* (Princeton, NJ: Princeton University Press, 2003).
13. Alan Greenspan, "Stock Options and Related Matters," keynote speech, Financial Markets Conference of the Federal Reserve Board, Sea Island, Georgia, October 2, 2002.

14. Lawrence Summers, "The New Wealth of Nations," keynote speech, Hambrecht & Quist Technology Conference, San Francisco, May 10, 2000.

15. Jayanth Krishnan, "Outsourcing and the Globalizing Legal Profession," *William & Mary Law Review* 48, no. 2189 (2007); Alan Garner, "Offshoring in the Service Sector," *Economic Review* (Kansas City: Federal Reserve Bank of Kansas City, 2004).

16. Raissa Muhutdinova-Foroughi, "Industrial Revolution and Assembly Line Work," in Van Horn and Schaffner, *Work in America*.

17. Michael Berger, *Automobile in American History and Culture* (Westport, CT: Greenwood, 2001).

18. Robert Atkinson, *The Past and Future of America's Economy: Long Waves of Innovation That Power Cycles of Growth* (London: Edward Elgar, 2005).

19. Thomas Friedman, *The World Is Flat* (New York: Farrar, Straus & Giroux, 2005).

20. Michael Mandel, "The Real Cost of Offshoring," *BusinessWeek*, June 2007.

21. Ann Harrison and Margaret McMillan, "Offshoring Jobs? Multinationals and U.S. Manufacturing Employment," *Review of Economics and Statistics* 93, no. 3 (August 2011): 857–75, August 2011.

22. Gianmarco I. P. Ottoaviano, Giovanni Peri, and Greg C. Wright, "Immigration, Offshoring, and American Jobs," National Bureau of Economic Research, NBER Working Paper No. 16439 (October 2010).

23. Alan S. Blinder, "Offshoring: The Next Industrial Revolution?," *Foreign Affairs*, March–April 2006, 113.

24. IBM Career Opportunities Page, http://www-07.ibm.com/in/research/careerops.html.

25. Vinay Couto, Mahadeva Mani, Arie Y. Lewin, and Carine Peeters, "The Globalization of White Collar Work," October 31, 2006, Booz Allen Hamilton, http://www.booz.com/media/uploads/The_Globalization_of_White-Collar_Work.pdf.

26. "More Than Two-Thirds of Projected Fastest Growing Occupations Are in High Wage Jobs," December 9, 1999, Bureau of Labor Statistics Employment Projections Program, 1998–2008, http://www.bls.gov/opub/ted/1999/Dec/wk1/art04.htm.

27. Amy Waldman, "More 'Can I Help You' Jobs Migrate," *New York Times*, May 11, 2003.

28. Daniel Drezner, "Outsourcing Bogeyman," *Foreign Affairs*, May–June 2004.

29. World Bank/Knowledge at Wharton, Wharton School, "The New Global Middle Class: Potentially Profitable—but Also Unpredictable," July 9, 2008, http://knowledge.wharton.upenn.edu/article.cfm?articleid=2011.

30. Carl E. Van Horn and Cliff Zukin, "Americans Assess an Economic Disaster," in *Work Trends* (New Brunswick, NJ: Heldrich Center at Rutgers, The State University of New Jersey, September 2010).

31. Michael Hammer and James Champy, *Reengineering the Corporation*, rev. and updated ed. (New York: HarperCollins, 2003).

32. Thomas Davenport, "The Fad That Forgot People," 1995, http://www.fastcompany.com/magazine/01/reengin.html; Steve Denning, "What HBR Won't Say: Why BPR Failed," The Leader's Guide to Radical Management, July 2010, http://ste

vedenning.typepad.com/steve_denning/2010/07/what-hbr-wont-say-why-bpr-failed .html.

33. Accenture, "Leveraging Sales & Marketing to Maximize the Value of Mergers & Acquisitions, 2008, http://www.accenture.com/SiteCollectionDocuments/PDF/ MAPOV22April08.pdf.

34. Dina Itkin, "The Effect of Business Ownership Change on Occupational Employment and Wages," U.S. Department of Labor, *Monthly Labor Review*, September 2008.

35. Bureau of Labor Statistics, "Mass Layoff Events and Initial Claimants for Unemployment Insurance, Private Nonfarm, 1996 to 2012, Not Seasonally Adjusted," 2012, http://www.bls.gov/mls/mlspnfmle.htm.

36. Richard Deitz and James Orr, "A Leaner, More Skilled U.S. Manufacturing Workforce," *Current Issues in Economics and Finance*, New York Federal Reserve Bank, February/March 2006, http://www.newyorkfed.org/research/current_issues/ ci12-2.pdf; U.S. Bureau of Labor Statistics, "Employment by Major Industry Sector," November 2009, http://www.bls.gov/emp/ep_table_201.htm.

37. Justin Lahart, "Even in Recovery, Some Jobs Won't Return," *Wall Street Journal*, January 12, 2010, http://online.wsj.com/article/SB126325594634725459.html.

38. Keith Bradsher, "Solar Panel Maker Moves," January 14, 2011, http://www .nytimes.com/2011/01/15/business/energy-environment/15solar.html.

39. Julie Froud, Sukhdev Johal, Adam Leaver, and Karel Williams, *Financialization and Strategy: Narrative and Numbers* (Oxford: Routledge, 2006). Thanks to Rortybomb.wordpress.com, Mike Konczak's blog.

40. http://www.nytimes.com/interactive/2011/02/28/us/28union-poll-results.html.

41. Jacob S. Hacker and Paul Pierson, "The Wisconsin Union Fight Isn't about Benefits. It's about Labor's Influence," *Washington Post*, March 6, 2011.

42. Lawrence Mishel and Matthew Walters, "How Unions Help All Workers— EPI Briefing Paper," Economic Policy Institute, August 2003, http://www.epi.org/ page/-/old/briefingpapers/143/bp143.pdf.

43. Ross Eisenbrey, "Strong Unions, Strong Productivity," June 20, 2007, http:// www.epi.org/publication/webfeatures_snapshots_20070620.

44. Union Membership and Coverage Database, Census Population Survey data, Barry Hirsh and David Macpherson, http://www.unionstats.com.

45. Union Membership and Coverage Database.

46. U.S. Department of Labor, Bureau of Labor Statistics, "Median Weekly Earnings of Full-Time Wage and Salary Workers by Union Affiliation and Selected Characteristics," January 27, 2012, http://www.bls.gov/news.release/union2.t02.htm.

47. U.S. Department of Labor, Bureau of Labor Statistics, "Usual Weekly Earnings of Wage and Salary Workers, Second Quarter, 2012," USDL 12-14-1419.

48. U.S. Department of Labor, Bureau of Labor Statistics, "Usual Weekly Earnings of Wage and Salary Workers, Second Quarter, 1996," USDL 96-291.

49. National Association of State Budget Officers, *NASBO State Expenditure Report*, December 13, 2011, 1.

50. "Overview of K–12 and Early Childhood Education Programs," GAO Federal Education Funding, GAO-10-51, January 27, 2010.

51. National Association of State Budget Officers, *NASBO State Expenditure Report*, 1.

52. FY 2013, Department of Labor Budget in Brief, 2012, http://www.dol.gov/dol/budget/2013/PDF/FY2013BIB.pdf.

53. American Society for Training and Development, Conference Board, Society for Human Resource Management, Corporate Voices for Working Families, "The Ill-Prepared US Workforce," July 2009.

54. "Downturn Prompts a Change in Learning Initiatives," October 2009, http://www.workforce.com/article/20091027/NEWS02/310279987.

55. Carl E. Van Horn and Cliff Zukin, "What a Difference a Decade Makes," in *Work Trends* (December 2009).

56. Drucker, "They're Not Employees, They're People."

57. Carl E. Van Horn and Cliff Zukin, "What a Difference a Decade Makes," in *Work Trends* (December 2009).

58. Sandy Baum, Kathleen Little, and Kathleen Payea, "Trends in Community College Education," Trends in Higher Education Series, College Board 2011, http://advocacy.collegeboard.org/sites/default/files/11b_3741_CC_Trends_Brief_WEB_110620.pdf.

59. Carl E. Van Horn and Duke Storen, "Working Hard but Staying Poor," in *Work Trends* (January 1999).

60. Lazar Treschan and Apurva Mehortra, "Unintended Impacts: Fewer Black and Latino Freshmen at CUNY Senior Colleges after the Recession," May 2012, http://www.cssny.org/publications/unintendedimpacts.php.

61. Kathryn Zickhur and Aaron Smith, "Digital Differences," Pew Internet and American Life Project, April 2012, http://pewinternet.org/Reports/2012/Digital-differences/.aspx.

62. "Economic, Environmental and Social Statistics," in *OECD Factbook 2011*, Organisation for Economic Co-operation and Development, 2011.

63. Brandon Roberts, Deborah Povich, and Mark Mather, "Working Poor Families Project Policy Brief," Winter 2010–2011, http://www.workingpoorfamilies.org/pdfs/policybrief-winter2011.pdf.

Chapter Three

New American Workplace Realities

I have no savings, no investments, no health insurance, no life insurance—all I got is me. I don't have family. I'm here, myself, just making a living.

—Lyn[1]

We used to think of people we hired as like adopting a member of the family. Now we look at them as someone who's just visiting for a day.

—Employer interview, Heldrich Center, December 2010

The economic upheavals of the past twenty years and the painful Great Recession and its aftermath spurred companies to redefine the relationships and responsibilities between employers and employees. American workers know that the rules have changed, and they don't like what happened. A "permanent job with good benefits" is beyond reach for most American workers. Perhaps only federal judges and tenured professors are insulated from the forces of workplace transformation, and even they face new challenges to their now rare, privileged status.

Few if any firms promise or even imply that new hires might be able to have a permanent job. Blue-chip companies that regularly appear on "best companies to work for" lists can be suddenly rocked by competition or mergers. For example, Quicken Loans, ranked by *Fortune* magazine as the twenty-ninth "best company to work for" in 2009, reduced its workforce by 41 percent that year. Firms offering what were once traditional benefits, such as pensions and health care insurance, are also declining in number.

Relationships between public employees and their government employers have been altered in ways that seemed unimaginable just a decade ago. A fiscal crisis caused by political leaders who allocated more funds than they collected in revenue worsened during the Great Recession, and the federal government plunged into even deeper financial trouble. In response, elected officials in both parties cut government jobs. In just three years—from mid-2009 to mid-2012—over 650,000 public sector jobs were eliminated. Put another way, if the government had not eliminated these jobs, the U.S. unemployment rate would be a full percentage point lower.[2]

Retirement and health care benefits for teachers, police officers, and government managers were also cut. In more than half the states, public sector employees were required to contribute more of their salary toward pensions and health care insurance premiums. These new "conditions of employment"—most of which were legislated rather than negotiated—came on top of worker givebacks, including unpaid furloughs and layoffs. In 2011, for example, Democratic governors in New York, Oregon, and Connecticut pressured public employee union workers to make greater contributions toward their pension benefits.

From the perspective of state elected officials trying to balance budgets, good arguments can be advanced for asking public employees to make sacrifices that help prevent budget catastrophes. From the standpoint of the public employees, however, workplace conditions have suddenly become grim. Many feel they were unfairly blamed for budget crises that had many causes, not just union worker pay and benefits, and for contracts that were willingly entered into by government officials during better economic times.

American workers in the public and private sectors still long for the "good old days" when their employers provided health benefits, workplace flexibility and fairness, a secure retirement, and access to education and training. Because employers may be even less able or inclined to reinstate those policies because of the Great Recession, we need to ask, How are workers adjusting to these new realities in the workplace? How does their dissatisfaction affect their loyalty to the firm or organization where they work?

DECLINING SATISFACTION AT WORK

Traditionally, Americans expected their jobs to produce not just a paycheck but also health benefits, retirement, and opportunities for promotion. Now, American workers have been forced to take greater responsibility for managing and paying for their health care, continuing education, and retirement benefits. As pillars of the work-based safety net weakened during the past decade, workers' job satisfaction, measured in the Heldrich Center's *Work Trends* surveys, followed a downward arc.

Between 1999 and 2009, the share of workers who said they were very satisfied with their job dropped from 59 to 49 percent. For Americans with a college degree, job satisfaction declined from 62 percent in 1999 to 49 percent in 2009. Workers were also less pleased with their health and medical coverage: satisfaction dropped from 43 percent in 1999 to 31 percent in 2009. Only one in

Now, American workers have been forced to take greater responsibility for managing and paying for their health care, continuing education, and retirement benefits.

three workers was very satisfied with health and medical coverage by 2009 (see figure 3.1).

Satisfaction with their opportunities for education and training at work declined from 40 percent in 1999 to 28 percent in 2009. Workers very satisfied with their ability to balance work and family fell from 51 to 40 percent during that decade. Even smaller shares of college-educated workers under age forty were very satisfied with work-based educational and job training opportunities.

Heldrich Center surveys during the past decade also revealed widening gaps between what Americans believe is important at work and what employers offer. Most Americans worry that the benefits and job security that once brought a higher standard of living for them and their families are disappear-

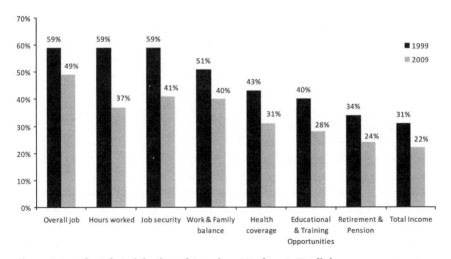

Figure 3.1.   The Job Satisfaction of American Workers Is Declining
Source: C. Van Horn and C. Zukin, "What a Difference a Decade Makes: The Declining Job Satisfaction of the American Workforce," Heldrich Center for Workforce Development, Rutgers University, September 2009.

ing and gone forever. American workers are losing confidence in the idea that economic opportunities will be greater for their children and grandchildren.

What workers want—and expect—from their employers remained quite stable throughout the *Work Trends* studies conducted by the Heldrich Center. Between 1999 and 2011, the vast majority of workers said that while their total annual income was very or extremely important, they also wanted more from their employers. Workers valued learning new job skills, balancing work and family, having health and retirement benefits, and job security. Ratings for these varied by just a few points over the course of twelve years:

- In 1999, 88 percent of Americans rated work and family balance as extremely or very important—in 2009, 86 percent said this.
- In 1999, 71 percent of Americans regarded learning new skills at work as extremely or very important—by 2010, 69 percent gave education and training at work a high rating.
- Similarly, 85 percent of workers rated employer-provided health insurance as extremely or very important in 1999, and in 2009, 79 percent of the sample still said it was essential.
- Retirement and pensions supported by employers were judged to be extremely or very important to 77 percent of American workers in 1999 and 64 percent of American workers in 2009.[3]

Heldrich Center surveys measured workers' opinions during the economic boom of the late 1990s, the brief recession of 2001–2002, and the Great Recession era from 2007 to 2012 and beyond. Americans described the changing landscape of health benefits, retirement, work and family policies, race and discrimination, career opportunities, and the emergence of the digital workplace dominated by information technology. They spoke out about policies governing time at work, compensation, and workplace benefits.

Although workers value these workplace practices and policies, few are aware that many of these benefits and protections are rooted in federal laws. For decades, federal policy and enforcement carried the load of ensuring basic standards in safety and hiring practices. Landmark legislation setting national standards for the workforce include New Deal–era laws, such as the Fair Labor Standards Act of 1938, the Equal Pay Act of 1962, the Civil Rights Act of 1964, the Americans with Disabilities Act of 1990, and the Family and Medical Leave Act of 1993. These and other laws improved working conditions, forbade discrimination, and broadened opportunity for hundreds of millions of people. For the most part, these policies were enforced not by an army of inspectors but rather through self-regulation by employers and by lawsuits brought by aggrieved parties.[4]

In the early twenty-first century, federal government and court pressure on employers eased somewhat. Only two new labor laws were enacted by Congress and the president during the past twenty years. The Family and Medical Leave Act was adopted in 1993. In 2009, Congress passed the so-called Lilly Ledbetter Law; this law expands opportunities for people filing class-action wage discrimination lawsuits in reaction to a Supreme Court decision striking down a wage discrimination case because of a disputed statute of limitations.

President George W. Bush's administration and Republicans in Congress from 2001 to 2006 did not place a high priority on advancing policies to improve workplace conditions. If anything, policymakers during that period weakened federal enforcement actions. Barton Gelman's award-winning book about the Bush administration, *Angler: The Cheney Vice Presidency*, documented the vice president's pursuit of a pro-business agenda that included a hands-off approach to regulating the American workplace. The Bush administration cut mine safety inspectors and the budget of the Occupational Safety and Health Administration (OSHA). Workplace regulations and inspections were replaced with "voluntary compliance" programs. Proposed ergonomics standards designed to protect workers from repetitive motion industries were shelved.[5]

Although the Obama administration supported stronger workplace regulations, including new National Labor Relations Board rules that lessened barriers to union elections, the demands of managing an economic recovery and Republican electoral gains in Congress hampered the administration's effectiveness. After Democrats lost control of the U.S. House of Representatives in the 2010 midterm elections, the Obama administration sought agreement from the business community before issuing new OSHA ergonomics standards and construction work noise standards.[6]

American workers recounted to us their displeasure with the new workplace realities that they must accept. Many sense that they now inhabit a harsher, less caring environment at work and fewer options when they contemplate retirement from work. According to Jon, a married fifty-two-year-old scientist living in Montana,

> With every company I've worked for, at every switch, I became less optimistic about retiring. Five years before the recession I was already working for a company starting to falter . . . so when it hit, the recession really accelerated feelings I had about retirement anyway. The company that I worked for in St. Louis had a 401K and pension plan . . . that's one of the reasons I came here, it was so good. It wasn't even two years before they flat out dropped the pension plan.

The workplace conditions that workers like Jon complain about are, from the perspective of many employers, inescapable consequences of global competition and the free flow of capital. These powerful trends swept aside the possibilities of permanent jobs and employer-based safety nets. Just as firms must fight for survival in the unforgiving marketplace, so too, many business leaders believe that most Americans must give up the notion of long-term job security. According to Cornell labor economist Kevin F. Hallock, employers' proposition to employees is, "You can absorb more risk, or you're going to lose your job. Which would you prefer?"[7]

THE WORK–FAMILY IMBALANCE

It was not just the harsh realities of the economy, however, that dramatically transformed the American workplace. Significant social and demographic changes also altered the composition of the workforce and workers' needs. As described in a March 2010 report by President Obama's Council of Economic Advisers titled *Work-Life Balance and the Economics of Workplace Flexibility*,

> American society has changed dramatically over the past half century. Women comprise nearly one-half of the labor force; in nearly one-half of all households all adults are working. And yet, children still need to be taken to the doctor and elderly parents still need care. Moreover, more adults are attending school. These and other changes have caused many workers to face conflicts between their work and personal lives. These changes also inspire the need and desire on the part of workers for more flexibility in the workplace.

Several major trends are coursing through the American workplace:

- In 1968, nearly half of children grew up in households where the father worked full-time, the mother was not in the labor force, and the parents were married. By 2008, only one in five children lived with these arrangements.
- In 1968, one in four children lived in households where the residing parent or parents were working full-time; forty years later, that figure had nearly doubled (see figure 3.2).
- In 1950, women constituted about less than a third of the labor force; in 2009, they made up nearly half.
- With people living longer, more adults have responsibilities for the care of older family members. According to the National Alliance for Caregiving, over 43 million Americans, the majority of them women, served in roles as unpaid caregivers to a family member over the age of fifty in 2008.
- Nearly one-fifth of employed people in 2008 provided care to a person over the age of fifty.[8]

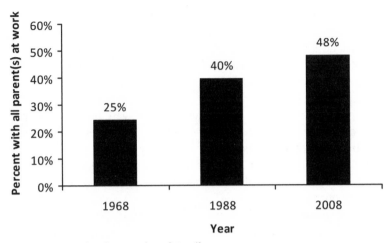

Figure 3.2. Balancing Work and Family
Source: Current Population Survey, Council of Economic Advisers, Executive Office of the President, "Work-Life Balance and the Economics of Workplace Flexibility," data from the Current Population Survey, http://www.whitehouse.gov/files/documents/100331-cea-econom ics-workplace-flexibility.pdf, March 2010.
Note: Full-time workers were employed for at least fourteen weeks in the previous year, working at least thirty-five hours per week. Sample is persons under age eighteen with at least one parent in the household.

Before the economic downturn in 2008, the Families and Work Institute reported that eight in ten employers offered workplace flexibility benefits to *some* employees; however, less than one in four employers provided workplace flexibility benefits to *all* employees.[9] When the Great Recession arrived, secular trends reshaping job security and working conditions accelerated. With huge increases in qualified applicants, employers with job openings were in a buyer's market for talent. They soon adjusted salaries and benefits.

According to the Families and Work Institute, the period between 2005 and 2012 was marked by two broad trends in the provision of workplace flexibility. On the one hand, greater numbers of employers offered policies that helped employees manage the times and places where they work. These include "flex time (from 66 to 77 percent); flex place (from 34 to 63 percent); and daily time off when important needs arise (from 77 to 87 percent)."[10] However, during this same time span, employers were less likely to permit workers to spend significant amounts of time away from full-time work, including reducing career breaks to take care of personal or family responsibilities (from 73 to 52 percent).[11] Management resistance, employee anxiety, and cultural issues contributed to the decline of flextime and family-friendly benefits.[12]

Employers and workers in firms with fewer than five hundred employees were also surveyed by the Families and Work Institute in order to compare their experiences with huge companies that are more likely to adopt work–family balance policies. In 2010, the Families and Work Institute reported the following comparisons:

- Firms with fewer than five hundred employees were less likely to provide their workforce with choices about which shifts they work than larger organizations: 36 versus 45 percent, respectively.
- Employees of firms with fewer than five hundred employees reported having more control over their schedules than those who work for slightly larger organizations.
- Seventy-seven percent of the firms with fewer than five hundred employees provide traditional flex time compared with 86 percent of larger companies.
- Thirty-six percent of small organizations provide compressed workweeks, compared with 48 percent of larger firms.
- Forty-seven percent of firms with fewer than five hundred workers offer occasional telecommuting compared with 64 percent of larger ones.
- Twenty percent of smaller organizations provide the option for regular telecommuting compared with 38 percent of larger ones.[13]

Annual surveys of human resource executives, conducted by the Society for Human Resource Management (SHRM), found that nonsalary and wage benefits declined substantially between 2006 and 2010. All but one of the twenty "family-friendly benefits" offered by employers were less widely available by 2010. Significant reductions occurred in the support of graduate and professional education, job sharing, flextime schedules, child care, and elder care referral services. Support for part-time telecommuting went up—the only benefit to do so. However, the opportunity for workers to telecommute on a full-time basis declined.

Research conducted by the Boston College Center for Work and Family in 2008 discovered that fewer employees took advantage of family-friendly benefits when they were available. Its report *Overcoming the Implementation Gap: How 20 Companies Are Making Flexibility Work*, confirmed the mismatch between employee needs and employer policies:

[Since the 1990s] numerous programs, policies, and initiatives for flexible work arrangements have been rolled out with much fanfare and optimism. Indeed, many benefits accrued for organizations at the forefront of this movement. . . . For a while, it looked as if the utilization rate of these policies was increasing year by year. Recently, however, the utilization of these policies has stabilized or even declined . . . we have learned that these flexible work arrangements are available but not widely used, some would say, not usable.[14]

Well before the Great Recession, the Heldrich Center's *Work Trends* reports reached similar conclusions about the gap between what workers want to help them achieve a good balance between work and family and what employers offer them. Roughly half of U.S. employers offered some form of flexibility around daily work hours, but far fewer provided more significant flexibility. A survey conducted by the Heldrich Center during the strong late 1990s economy found that most employers did not furnish the benefits American workers value the most. While nearly nine in ten workers said flexible work hours were at least somewhat important, only 61 percent of employers offered the benefit.[15] About half of workers felt that on-site child care was at least somewhat important but said that only 12 percent of employers provided for it. Telecommuting opportunities were favored by nine in ten employees, but only 17 percent of employers offered it.

LEARNING AT WORK

Opportunities for learning on the job have not improved in the past decade and may have declined. Employers are reluctant to support training in the basic technology and computer skills required for middle managers, technical, clerical, and support workers, a trend exacerbated by the recession. Jeff, a professional living in Washington, D.C., expressed his frustration with the situation during an interview in 2011 with the Heldrich Center:

> Training and keeping your skills current are valuable in my field. Employers see employees as a cost center, not a resource. They don't want to train employees; they expect you to come to a job and have the skill set already. If you're unemployed, you can't afford training. The trick is trying to acquire those skills to meet the demands of the labor market.

As noted above, in recent years, employers substantially reduced in-house education and training budgets as well as financial support for workers who want to acquire education and training outside of work hours. Examinations of corporate training and development budgets in 2009 and 2010 by a range of organizations found that the private sector made major budget cuts as the recession deepened. One report found the corporate training market shrank from $58.5 billion in 2007 to $56.2 billion in 2008, the greatest decline in more than ten years.[16]

These developments are occurring in a global labor market where a premium is placed on highly skilled workers, including those who manipulate and use computers, information technology, business software, and social media. In Heldrich Center surveys conducted over the past decade, workers recognized how critical these skills are for their own success. In 1999, over 70 percent of workers said that opportunities to learn new skills were "very" or "extremely important," and eight in ten workers said they would take advantage of tuition subsidies for continuing education, yet only one-third of employers offered them. In 2009, nearly two-thirds of workers surveyed said they would like more education and training to advance their careers, while half of workers said education and training were indispensible. Workers know they must master new technologies to advance their careers. One in two workers said they needed more advanced computer skills, and 44 percent complained that their employers did not provide sufficient computer training opportunities. Workers with the least know-how about new technologies expressed concern: nearly three-quarters of those with limited technology experience reported in Heldrich Center surveys that their employer was not helping them improve their computer skills.

Our research on employer-based education and training demonstrates that an elite group of megafirms that compete for the "best and brightest" workers will continue to provide gold-standard benefits. Their competitive market position and resources enable them to supply the benefits workers want. Corporate leaders, such as Jack Welch and the late Steve Jobs, were heralded for years in the management press for creating "learning organizations" where employees are expected to extend their work hours to master new areas of knowledge and participate in ongoing education. Corporations stage conferences and meetings to focus on new strategies, programs, systems, and ideas. Executives are sponsored to participate in high-profile speeches and meetings.

Leading companies, such as Johnson & Johnson and Motorola, allocate three times more than the national average on education and training. Most firms spend only modest amounts on educating their workers or nothing at all. In fact, 84 percent of employees in firms with fifty or more employees receive at least some formal training at work, according to the U.S. Department of Labor.[17] Yet more than 94 percent of the U.S. workforce are employed in firms with fewer than fifty employees where formal training is much less likely to occur.[18]

AN UNHEALTHY INSURANCE TREND

Another adverse trend for American workers has been the erosion of employer-based health care benefits during the past decade. Annual out-of-pocket costs for health care increased for Americans as insurers raised premiums and copays for health care services, limited coverage of preexisting conditions, and/or excluded basic medical procedures from coverage. For example, as the U.S. auto industry and other manufacturers declined in size and influence, their employee compensation and benefits packages no longer set high standards for the workforce as a whole. In 2009, with bankruptcy at American automakers looming, the United Auto Workers union agreed to further pay and benefit reductions, particularly for retirees who no longer received dental and vision benefits.

In 2010, an employee benefits survey reported that more than nine in ten large employers with over five hundred employees offered prescription drug benefits, dental insurance, or a mail-order prescription program. However, the percentage of employers offering other health care benefits declined in the past five years. Between 2006 and 2010, employers rolled back health benefits for contraceptive coverage, cancer insurance, long-term care insurance, retiree health care insurance, hospital indemnity insurance, and health coverage for spouses and foster children. On a positive note, more employers offered employee assistance programs, such as counseling for drugs, alcohol, and other addictions, and expanded eligibility for benefits to same-sex and opposite-sex domestic partners.[19] Undoubtedly, these surveys reflect a more positive employee benefit picture than for the entire economy because SHRM surveys only human resource executives from midsize and larger companies.

Surveys of workers show significant declines in the share of low- and moderate-income working families offered health insurance by their employers between 1998 and 2009, according to the Kaiser Family Foundation and the National Health Interview Survey.[20] For families with incomes at or above the median, insurance remained relatively stable during this period, but health insurance coverage declined for working families at or below the poverty line.[21] In short, lower-income workers took the brunt of health insurance cutbacks during the 2000s. Major health insurance firms and the Kaiser Foundation reported that new provisions in the Obama health care law were leading to tens of thousands of small businesses deciding to provide health insurance.[22]

Long-standing public policies and corporate consensus that workers' primary health care and pension coverage will be provided through work-based compensation are changing. The implementation of President Obama's health care expansion, known as the Affordable Care Act, will significantly change the health care insurance landscape. While the law was upheld by the U.S. Supreme Court in June 2012, the full implications of the new law for the health care coverage of American workers will not be known for several years. The law provides for access to health care insurance for most American workers through the private market, but some employers may continue to

either eliminate health insurance coverage or require their employees to contribute more toward it. What will employers do when the economy improves
or when the living standards of our global competitors improve?

A WORKPLACE DIVIDED

The composition of the U.S. workforce has undergone major transformations
in the past few decades. It is no longer mainly male and white but one where
more minorities and women are not only working but also leading organizations (see table 3.1).The share of the workforce that is white declined from 85
percent in 1990 to 80 percent in 2012.[23] In 2010, the U.S. population was 63.7
percent Caucasian, 12.4 percent African American, 16.3 percent Hispanic or
Latino, and 5.6 percent Asian.

By 2050, U.S. census demographers predict Hispanics may increase from
one-fifth to as much as one-third of the U.S. population. The African American population will expand more slowly, the census predicts, reaching a share
of 12.8 to 14.4 percent. Most likely, the non-Hispanic white population will
drop below 50 percent by 2050, making the United States a "majority minority" nation (see figure 3.3).[24]

While increasing diversity in the American workplace is positive, it also
brings new challenges for managers, workers, and policymakers. As diversity
increases, perceptions of bias and concerns about fairness may become more

Table 3.1.   The Growth of Women, Minorities, Immigrants, and Older Workers in the
Workplace

	1970	1990	2010
Rate of labor force growth down	1.7% (1960–1970)	1.6% (1980–1990)	1% (2000–2015)*
Women labor force participation rate	43%	57.50%	62%
Hispanics and Asians are expanding workforce share	8% (1980)	14.6% (2000)	19.40%
Whites and non-Hispanics are losing workforce share	82% (1980)	73% (2000)	69%
Median age of the workforce	39	37	41
Percent foreign born in the workforce	5.20%	9.30%	16%

Source: U.S. Bureau of Labor Statistics and U.S. Census (1970, 1990, 2010).
*Estimated rate.

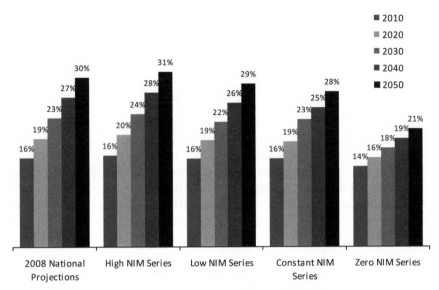

Figure 3.3. Hispanic Workers Projected to Increase in the Coming Decades (percent of total population)
Source: J. Ortman and C. Guarneri, United States Population Projections 2008 to 2009, U.S. Census Bureau, 2009, http://www.census.gov/population/www/projections/analytical-document09.pdf, 9.
Note: NIM = net international migration.

common. Managing racial and cultural diversity—and in multinational firms learning to work globally—requires better training and employer practices. Networked communications create opportunities for some, but it also erects barriers for those who are unable to afford computer hardware and to upgrade their skills. It will be a major challenge for workers, employers, and policymakers to ensure that technological advances are widely shared.

In 2002, the Heldrich Center conducted a survey that examined workers' views and experiences with race relations and discrimination at work.[25] The Heldrich survey found that white workers characterized their workplaces as places where equitable treatment was accorded to most and where few people personally experienced discrimination. Few white workers supported affirmative action to address current or past discrimination against African Americans and other minority workers.

Nonwhite workers described a very different workplace in which unfair treatment was more common and where hiring and promotion policies were often unfair to minorities. They also supported corrective government action and employer practices to promote more equitable workplaces. What are the implications of a workplace divided?

In principle, employers and workers concur that an equitable workplace is conducive to worker productivity and morale, providing all workers with equal opportunity for satisfaction and advancement. The Heldrich Center survey of American workers, conducted in 2002, drilled deeper to determine how workers perceived the incidence and scope of discrimination at their place of employment. Our research built on landmark research in 1997 by Diane Hughes and Mark Dodge that explored perceptions of bias among African American women and Philip Moss and Chris Tilley's remarkable book, *Stories Employers Tell: Race, Skill, and Hiring in America*, which revealed systemic discrimination against black men and other minorities in the hiring process.[26] Considering the demographic shifts that will occur in American workplaces, this racial divide may deepen and become more complex as individuals of various ethnic and racial identities perceive fairness and opportunity in ways others do not comprehend.

The Heldrich Center survey highlighted a glaring divide between the experiences of white and minority workers regarding discrimination at work. The determining factor in how workers perceived the treatment of minorities at work was not whether they worked for the public or private sector, their occupation, education, or income but rather whether the worker was black, Hispanic, or white. Half of African American workers believed that African Americans were the most likely group to be treated unfairly in the workplace, compared to just 10 percent of whites and 13 percent of workers of other races. The following was also found:

The Heldrich Center survey highlighted a glaring divide between the experiences of white and minority workers regarding discrimination at work.

- More than half of higher-income minority workers believed that African Americans were the most likely to experience discrimination, compared to only 33 percent of whites in the same income group.
- Far more African Americans (28 percent) and Hispanic Americans (22 percent) said they had personally experienced unfair treatment at work, compared to just 6 percent of white workers.
- Over half of African Americans said a coworker had suffered discrimination at work, compared to 13 percent of white workers.
- While 49 percent of whites agreed that firms should be required by law to maintain diversity in the workplace, 83 percent of African Americans agreed with the policy.

- African American workers were more likely than white workers or workers of other races to support the idea of preferential treatment to address past discrimination: half of African Americans agreed with this kind of affirmative action, and one-third strongly agreed, while only 15 percent of white workers agreed.

Heldrich Center research also found that most of America's small businesses do not have diverse workforces. Two-thirds of workers in firms with fewer than twenty-five workers reported that they had no African American colleagues and 57 percent had no Hispanic American coworkers. Larger firms are more proactive about recruiting and retaining diverse workforces, have developed antidiscrimination policies, and take instances of discrimination seriously.

Across the ethnic and income spectrum, respondents agreed that employers and workers should have greater responsibility for addressing employment discrimination than government policymakers. While most workers believe their employers aspire to create bias-free workplaces, there were significant differences between the races about how effectively employers actually responded when employees complained about discrimination:

- Large majorities of white workers (86 percent) and about three-quarters of workers of other races agreed that their employer took incidents of discrimination seriously, but only 61 percent of African Americans did so.
- Almost two-thirds of the minority workers who believed they were treated unfairly said that their employer ignored their complaint and took no action in response to the incident.
- Fifty-seven percent of minorities complained that their employer did not respond in a prompt or satisfactory manner to a complaint of discriminatory treatment or harassment.

Few rigorous surveys of work and race have been done since our *Work Trends* research ten years ago, but subsequent studies confirm our findings about the racial divide at work. As the famous line from the Talmud goes, "We see the world not the way it is, but the way we are." Racial identity—a hybrid of family history, personal experience, and cultural mores—affects our perceptions and is also influenced by people's day-to-day experiences.

A survey of active-duty service members in the U.S. Army in 2004 focused on the experiences of Hispanics and examined views on discrimination among all races. On the positive side, the report, supervised by Army Major Jason Dempsey and Columbia University Professor Robert Shapiro, found that enlisted personnel reported less discrimination in the army than in private life. Military personnel in all racial groups expressed faith in the fairness of army leaders and opportunities for all racial and ethnic groups in the army.[27]

In other ways, the racial divide persisted. Among officers, just 3 percent of whites said they encountered discrimination in their unit, compared with 27 percent of black and Hispanic officers. Among the enlisted ranks, 22 percent of whites, 19 percent of Hispanics, and 24 percent of blacks said they had been discriminated against. As reported by Gary Langer of *ABC News*, enlisted whites were as concerned as Hispanics and blacks that their race would be held against them when being considered for promotions. Among white officers, 84 percent believed there was less discrimination in the military than in civilian life. That figure dropped to 52 percent of enlisted whites and 35 and 36 percent of enlisted blacks and Hispanics, respectively.

The authors wrote that the "discrepancy between the opinions of white officers and the opinions of minorities on this issue is particularly important given that whites make up over 80 percent of the senior officer ranks and therefore set policy for the Army." Referring to senior army leaders, they added, "Having had little experience or exposure to discrimination themselves, and believing the Army to have achieved success in the area of racial and ethnic relations, they may not recognize the frequency with which minorities encounter discrimination. In sum, they are colorblind—unaware of the true prevalence of discrimination."[28]

In the past decade, several lawsuits brought by minority workers against their employers have garnered large settlements and received wide media attention. In one noteworthy case, the giant electronics retailer Best Buy settled a discrimination case for over $10 million for damages, legal fees, and costs. The lawsuit, filed in 2005 by eight current and former employees and one job applicant, accused Best Buy of denying desirable job assignments, promotions, and transfers to African American, Latino, and female employees.[29]

Coca-Cola settled a class-action lawsuit for $192.5 million that was filed in 2010 by current and former African American employees for racial discrimination under the U.S. Civil Rights Act. The plaintiffs alleged they had suffered discrimination in pay, promotions, and performance evaluations. A key aspect of their argument rested on the fact that the median salaries for African American workers were about one-third less than those of white employees at the company. The plaintiffs also claimed that "glass-ceiling" and "glass-wall" policies kept African Americans from gaining better jobs in the company. They argued that relatively few African Americans had advanced to senior levels even though there were substantial African Americans in the firm's workforce.[30]

Effective approaches to addressing bias at work are never easy to implement. The Great Recession and its aftermath will make these tasks more challenging. The Equal Employment Opportunity Commission (EEOC) reported a record number of accusations of workplace discrimination on the basis of race, gender, or other protected categories in 2009–2010. The number of complaints climbed to 99,922, an increase of 7.2 percent, which is the greatest year-over-year increase of new discrimination cases in the agency's history.[31]

In the aftermath of widespread layoffs during the Great Recession, more employees who felt they were discriminated against but remained silent out of fear for their jobs may now be filing complaints. According to *New York Times* reporter Catherine Rampell,

> Workers themselves argue that a poor job market has brought out the often hidden prejudicial side of employers who can afford to be especially picky in selecting employees. Women believe they are being passed over in favor of men, blacks believe whites and Hispanics are taking their jobs, and older workers say fresher faces are having better luck in the job market at the expense of their elders.[32]

Some employers assert that unemployed workers are using EEOC complaints in order to try to avert layoffs, to vent their anger after layoff, or to collect generous and unjustified settlements at the employer's expense. And some employment law experts point out that the actual number of EEOC suits that went to trial declined from the previous tracking year.[33] But other experts, such as Michael Zimmer, a professor of employment law at Loyola University, concluded that the rise in complaints reveals a hidden pattern of discrimination—as workers who believed they were discriminated against no longer held back because of fear of reprisals.[34] The EEOC found that sexual harassment complaints from workers still on the job declined, but this may be due to the view that those who have jobs and experience discrimination or harassment are often reluctant to file complaints.

Few corporate leaders or nonprofit institutions have successfully fostered public dialogue or addressed the gnawing truth about race and gender conflicts and discrimination in the workplace. As we have seen in the EEOC data, lingering pain over discrimination can ultimately express itself often years after incidents have taken place.

A WORKFORCE IN TRANSITION

Broad demographic and social trends are transforming the American workplace. As employers make sweeping changes in workplace benefits and practices, jobs are less secure and workers' dissatisfaction is rising. Even in the best economic times, only a third of workers felt secure about their jobs. Today's workers, having been further bruised by the Great Recession, are far less satisfied with their annual incomes, health and medical coverage, retirement and pension plans, and skills and educational opportunities at work than they were a decade ago. American workers understand they need continuing, career-related education, yet most are paying for it themselves as the number of employers offering training declines.

Americans like the work they do and take pride in it. The work ethic is intact: what's missing is job security. For American workers in their late forties, fifties, and sixties—a majority of the nation's workforce—the Great Recession came at a terrible time and savaged their retirement funds and assets at the peak of their earnings potential. Considering the nation's poor national savings rates, dysfunctional politics around Social Security, and American naïveté about the costs of aging, the retirement of the baby boomers was never going to be a smooth transition for individuals, society, or the federal government. Now workers are traveling an even less certain road to retirement than they expected. An examination of the special misery suffered by older, unemployed workers during the Great Recession era is next.

As employers make sweeping changes in workplace benefits and practices, jobs are less secure and workers' dissatisfaction is rising. Even in the best economic times, only a third of workers felt secure about their jobs.

NOTES

1. *Work Trends* interviews, Heldrich Center at Rutgers, The State University of New Jersey, 2011.

2. Shaila Dewan and Motoko Rich, "Public Workers Face New Rash of Layoffs, Hurting Recovery," *New York Times*, June 20, 2012, A1.

3. Carl E. Van Horn and Cliff Zukin, "What a Difference a Decade Makes," in *Work Trends* (New Brunswick, NJ: Heldrich Center at Rutgers, The State University of New Jersey, December 2009).

4. Herb Schaffner and Carl E. Van Horn, eds., *A Nation at Work* (New Brunswick, NJ: Rutgers University Press, 2003); Carl E. Van Horn and Herb Schaffner, *Work in America: An Encyclopedia of History, Policy and Society* (Santa Barbara, CA: ABC-CLIO, 2003).

5. Barton Gelman, *Angler: The Cheney Vice Presidency* (New York: Penguin, 2008); Stephen Labaton, "OSHA Leaves Workers in Hands of Industry," *New York Times*, April 2007; Amy Goldstein and Sarah Cohen, "Bush Forces a Shift in Regulatory Thrust," *Washington Post*, August 15, 2004, A1.

6. "OSHA hosted an 'OSHA Listens' public meeting March 4 in Washington, D.C., to solicit comments and suggestions from OSHA stakeholders on key issues facing the agency. The event, reflecting President Obama's Open Government initiative on inclusiveness and transparency, was broadcast live on the Internet, where it attracted more than 5,000 viewers, and public comments were posted online." "OSHA Quick Takes," March 15, 2010, http://www.osha.gov/as/opa/quicktakes/qt03152010 .html; Jake Blumgart, "Obama's OSHA: Improved, but Still Weak, March 2, 2012, http://www.salon.com/2012/03/02/obamas_osha_improved_but_still_weak.

7. Michelle Conlin, Moira Herbst, and Peter Coy, "The Disposable Worker," January 7, 2010, http://www.businessweek.com/magazine/content/10_03/b41630329 35448.htm.

8. *Work-Life Balance and the Economics of Workplace Flexibility*, White House, President's Council of Economic Advisors report 2010, Current Population Survey data, and the Sloan Foundation.

9. Ellen Galinsky, James T. Bond, and Kelly Sakai with Stacy S. Kim and Nicole Giuntoli, "2008 National Study of Employers," New York: Families and Work Institute, and When Work Works (2008).

10. Kenneth Matos and Ellen Galinsky, "2012 National Study of Employers," New York: Families and Work Institute, SHRM, and When Work Works (2012).

11. Matos and Galinsky, "2012 National Study of Employers."

12. Matos and Galinsky, "2012 National Study of Employers."

13. Matos and Galinsky, "2012 National Study of Employers."

14. Fredric R. Van Deusen, Jacquelyn B. James, Nadia Gill, and Sharon McKechnie, "Overcoming the Implementation Gap: How 20 Companies Are Making Flexibility Work," 2008, http://www.bc.edu/content/dam/files/centers/cwf/pdf/Flex_Ex ecutiveSummary_for_web.pdf.

15. Carl E. Van Horn and Ken Dautrich, "Work and Family: How Employers and Workers Can Strike the Balance," in *Work Trends* (March 1999).

16. Ed Frauenheim, "Training Is Taking a Beating in Recession, Studies Find," *Workforce*, September 15, 2011, http://www.workforce.com/article/20090126/ NEWS01/301269979#; Bersen & Associates, "Another Year of Training Budget Cuts," January 12, 2010, http://www.bersin.com/blog/post/2010/01/Another-Year -of-Budget-Cuts.aspx; "ASTD Study Training Spending Drops but Each Learner Gets More," November 12, 2010, http://www.workforce.com/article/20101112/ NEWS02/311129998.

17. U.S. Department of Labor, Bureau of Labor Statistics, "1995 Survey of Employer Provided Training—Employee Results," December 19, 2006, http://www.bls .gov/news.release/History/sept.txt.

18. Frauenheim, "Training Is Taking a Beating in Recession, Studies Find"; Bersen & Associates, "Another Year of Training Budget Cuts"; "ASTD Study Training Spending Drops but Each Learner Gets More."

19. *2010 Employee Benefits Survey,* Society for Human Resource Management.

20. Kaiser Family Foundation, Health Research and Educational Trust, "Employer Health Benefits, Summary of Findings," 2011, http://ehbs.kff.org/pdf/8226.pdf; Robin A. Cohen and Michael E. Martinez, "Health Insurance Coverage, Early Release of Estimates from the National Health Interview Survey," June 2012, http://www.cdc.gov/nchs/data/nhis/earlyrelease/Insur201206.pdf.

21. Kaiser Family Foundation, "Change in Percentage of Families Offered Insurance at Work," National Center for Health Statistics/Census data, 2010.

22. Noam M. Levey, "More Small Businesses Are Offering Health Benefits to Workers," *Los Angeles Times*, December 27, 2010.

23. U.S. Bureau of Labor Statistics, http://www.bls.gov/cps/demographics.htm.

24. Jennifer M. Ortman and Christine E. Guarneri, U.S. Census Bureau, *United States Population Projections: 2000 to 2050*, http://www.census.gov/population/www/projections/analytical-document09.pdf.

25. Carl E. Van Horn, K. A. Dixon, Duke Storen, and Ken Dautrich, "A Workplace Divided," in *Work Trends* (2002).

26. Diane Hughes and Mark A. Dodge, "African-American Women in the Workplace: Relationships between Job Conditions, Racial Bias at Work, and Perceived Job Quality," *American Journal of Community Psychology* 25, no. 5 (1997): 581–99; Phillip Moss and Chris Tilley, *Stories Employers Tell: Race, Skill, and Hiring in America* (New York: Russell Sage Foundation, 2001).

27. Gary Langer, "Racial Discrimination: An Army Survey," January 6, 2009, http://blogs.abcnews.com/thenumbers/2009/01/racial-relation.html.

28. Langer, "Racial Discrimination: An Army Survey."

29. "Best Buy Settles Class Action Bias Lawsuit," June 17, 2011, http://www.reuters.com/article/2011/06/17/us-bestbuy-bias-lawsuit-idUSTRE75G64M20110617.

30. Ben White, "Black Coca-Cola Workers Still Angry," *Washington Post*, April 18, 2002, E3.

31. Equal Employment Opportunity Commission, "Fiscal Year 2010 Performance and Accountability Report, U.S. Equal Opportunity Commission," http://www.eeoc.gov/eeoc/plan/2010par.cfm.

32. Catherine Rampell, "More Workers Complain of Widespread Bias on the Job," *New York Times*, January 11, 2011.

33. Rampell, "More Workers Complain of Widespread Bias on the Job."

34. Rampell, "More Workers Complain of Widespread Bias on the Job."

Chapter Four

Misery and Bleak Expectations for Older Unemployed Workers

In a powerful *New York Times* article describing the impact of the Great Recession on American workers, journalist Peter Goodman wrote,

> "I just want to get my life back." Different versions of this sentence have landed frequently in my notebook—in Cleveland, where a former homeowner told me of camping in her car after she lost the place to foreclosure; in Newton, Iowa, where a man who had earned middle-class wages turning steel into refrigerators broke into tears as he described his inability to provide medical care for a sick child after he lost his job.[1]

No group of unemployed Americans experienced greater shocks or more difficulties returning to work than older workers. In September 2012, over 1.9 million workers aged fifty-five or older were unemployed and, on average, had been coping with their diminished circumstances for over a year. Another 1.3 million older Americans were working part-time but really wanted a full-time job.[2] For thousands of these older, unemployed workers, prolonged joblessness or underemployment wiped out retirement savings. The collapse of real estate values devalued homes that many thought would secure their retirement. Fewer Americans could count on

No group of unemployed Americans experienced greater shocks or more difficulties returning to work than older workers. In September 2012, over 1.9 million workers aged fifty-five or older were unemployed and, on average, had been coping with their diminished circumstances for over a year.

guaranteed pension benefits. With depleted savings and less valuable homes, older workers needed another job so they could afford essentials, such as food and shelter. Employed workers aged fifty-five and over desperately clung to jobs so they might eventually be able to "afford" retirement.

This chapter explores the rugged experiences and altered expectations of older Americans in the early twenty-first-century labor market. For decades, demographers predicted that the huge baby-boomer population would stop working full-time as soon as they reached the traditional retirement age of sixty-five, if not sooner. Middle-aged workers assumed that retiring colleagues would open paths to enhanced career opportunities. The mass exodus of aging boomers was supposed to create a bonanza of job openings for young workers graduating from high schools and colleges.

The American "Shangri-La" of an early retirement filled with travel and leisure was eroded for many by broad changes in employer benefits and wiped out for millions by the Great Recession. For some, it ended with a lay-off notice. For others, it faded as workers' savings dwindled to nothing. These harsh realities not only made life miserable for millions of older unemployed workers but also reverberated throughout the rest of the American workforce and economy.

LAST FIRED, NEVER REHIRED

The Great Recession punished unemployed citizens in all age-groups. Fifty- and sixty-year-old workers were greatly damaged for the simple reason that they have fewer years left in their careers to recover their losses. One might not immediately grasp the plight of older workers by perusing overall unemployment rates. In September 2012, 5.9 percent of workers aged fifty-five or over were unemployed, whereas 6.8 percent of the twenty-five- to fifty-four-year-old cohort and 15.5 percent of sixteen- to twenty-four-year-olds were jobless.[3] However, when older workers are laid off, they are much more likely to remain unemployed than younger workers.[4] These findings hold up even when factoring in workers' education, health status, job characteristics, and incomes.[5]

According to the U.S. Bureau of Labor Statistics, the average duration of unemployment for older workers in September 2012 was about fifty-six weeks versus thirty-seven weeks for younger job seekers. More than half (54 percent) of the unemployed older workers were classified as long-term unemployed—out of work for more than six months—at the time. Before the recession began, in December 2007, less than one in four (23 percent) of the older unemployed workers fell into this category.[6] An analysis by the Pew

Fiscal Analysis Initiative estimated that over four in ten older workers were jobless for at least a year.[7]

Heldrich Center *Work Trends* surveys of a national sample of workers who lost jobs during the recession found that older workers had the lowest reemployment rate of any demographic group (see table 4.1). Almost twice as many workers *under* the age of fifty-five were able to find another full-time job (28 percent) as workers aged fifty-five or older (15 percent).[8] Just over half of jobless older workers searched for over two years, as compared to about one in three job seekers under fifty-five years of age.

The disappointing experiences of mature workers clouded their outlook for the future. One in five anticipated that another year or two years would pass before they were back at work, compared to one in twenty of the more optimistic younger respondents. One person we interviewed summarized his situation:

> Being unemployed is frustrating, demeaning, and, at this point, frightening. Articles in the paper say we "baby boomers" will have to work for a few more years especially since so many of us have lost half if not more in retirement "funds." Now, you tell me, how can I work for a few more years if I can't even get a job interview?

Fewer than one in four unemployed workers interviewed by the Heldrich Center in 2009 had obtained a full-time job two years later, in August 2011. Just over one in three were still unemployed and looking for work. Six percent were working part-time while they sought full-time jobs; just 7 percent were satisfied with having only a part-time job. Another 4 percent were self-employed. Given the troubled economy, nearly one in four older workers gave up looking and dropped out of the labor market entirely.

Table 4.1. Most Unemployed Workers Could Not Get Another Full-Time Job during the Recession Era

Workers 55 and older	15%
Workers 18–34	41%
Workers 35–54	32%
High school education or less	33%
Some college	28%
Bachelor's degree or higher	43%
Black, non-Hispanic/other, Hispanic	29%
Income less than $30K	27%
$30K–$60K	29%
More than $60K	56%

Source: C. Stone, C. Van Horn, and C. Zukin, "Out of Work and Losing Hope: The Misery and Bleak Expectations of American Workers," Heldrich Center for Workforce Development, Rutgers University, September 2011.

Of those workers who eventually returned to work, most searched for at least a year before they succeeded. Four in ten got new jobs that were "very different" from their previous one, with one in two describing their new jobs as a "step down" in income and opportunity. Only one in five felt their new occupations represented an improvement. Nearly one in two regarded their new positions as insecure and expected to be back on the job market soon.

A staggering number of the *unemployed* over-age-fifty group that we tracked from 2009 to 2011 had been jobless a very long time. Eighty percent had been searching for over a year, including almost half who had been job hunting for over two years. More were pessimistic than optimistic about soon finding a job by a margin of two to one. Nearly two-thirds doubted they would ever obtain full-time work in their preferred occupation. A sample of what these unemployed workers told Heldrich Center researchers about their frustrating quest follows:

The longer you are unemployed, the less employable you are. . . . The credit is close to being maxed out, so the credit score is good but not great . . . this complicates employers' interest in you.

I continue to leave advanced degrees off applications with the idea I can at least get a foot in the door. However, most applications state to fill it out in completion, and you sign it saying so.

I have a master's degree and cannot find a job. Full-time jobs don't want to hire me because they say they cannot afford me. Part-time jobs tell me I am overqualified.

I've been through one plant closure and two mergers and have been laid off from all three positions through no fault of my own. There has been a lot of consolidation in the industry, and since I'm usually the new person on the block, I'm the first to go.

Older workers' inability to find full-time employment was not due to lack of effort. The vast majority of those interviewed by the Heldrich Center reported that they regularly applied for jobs, scoured newspaper job advertisements, examined online job boards, contacted friends or family members, and e-mailed and called potential employers. Older workers are less likely than younger workers to use social media in their job search, but this is by no means the principal explanation for the difficulties in the labor market.[9] Less than half of mature workers were invited for interviews; many complained that their applications were not even acknowledged by prospective employers.

Older workers were not without jobs because they refused to accept lower-paying positions, according to several studies.[10] Two out of three unemployed respondents told Heldrich Center researchers that they would accept reduced pay to land a position. As one respondent put it, "I'd gladly drive a UPS delivery truck, but I'm fifty something and have two college degrees, so they don't want me—too old and too educated, and it's the same thing every place I look." Another commented,

> I know I have talent and skill in the profession I am trained in. It is a blow to my self-esteem that I know I have this skill and it is just so difficult to compete for work in my field. I have already moved to another state in an attempt to find work, and it's still a struggle.

The vast majority of older displaced workers simply could not find work because of the depressed demand for workers in a weak economy.

Six in ten of the reemployed older workers earned less than they had in their prior job, according to the respondents in the Heldrich Center's surveys.[11] Fourteen percent reported that their new job paid *less than half* than their last job. Roughly one in three workers saw their pay reduced between 31 and 50 percent. Another 29 percent said the incomes from their new jobs were between 21 and 30 percent lower. The typical reemployed older worker lost far more in earnings than the typical reemployed younger worker.

In addition to earning less, one in two older workers described their new positions as something to "get by" while looking for a better job. Some workers started their own businesses, but they too were frustrated. One person we interviewed commented, "I will be trying to start my own business, but there is no credit available. All the banks reduced credit lines without warning, even though all bills [were] paid on time. It makes it even harder to get by."

Other analysis confirms that reemployed older workers endured significant wage losses. According to the Survey of Income and Program Participation,[12] men between the ages of fifty and sixty-one lost 20 percent of median hourly wages when switching or finding new jobs after a period of unemployment. For men sixty-two or over, new median wages were 36 percent below their prior earnings. Younger men, ages thirty-five to forty-nine, experienced only a 4 percent drop in wages, and twenty-five- to thirty-four-year-olds lost only 2 percent in wages at their new jobs. Older displaced women workers also endured significant wage losses but not as severe as for men. Workers with the most experience prior to their dislocation are likely to lose $220,000 or more in lifetime earnings.[13]

Regaining a toehold in the troubled economy was especially hard for workers who were fifty years old or older. Experiences and seniority gained with previous employers often were not valued by potential new employers. Occupational skills obtained years ago may no longer be in high demand or be competitive with younger workers' skills. Dislocated workers in regions with declining industries may need to move to find work, something that is extremely difficult for home owners with deep roots in their communities.[14]

Large numbers of the long-term unemployed workers hoped to enroll in an educational or training program to prepare for a new career. Yet few were able to do so, and when they did, about half paid for it themselves. According to Heldrich Center *Work Trends* surveys, the percentage of the unemployed workers enrolled in skills upgrading declined from 23 percent in 2009 to 14 percent in 2011. Of this small percentage who managed to enroll in an education or training program, less than half (38 percent) got financial help from a government agency.

Large numbers of the long-term unemployed workers hoped to enroll in an educational or training program to prepare for a new career. Yet few were able to do so, and when they did, about half paid for it themselves.

Diminished job prospects for older job seekers may also be the by-product of employers' negative perceptions about mature workers.[15] Some employers assume that older workers are more expensive and less productive and deliver lower-quality work than younger employees. Employers often worry that absenteeism and health care costs will be higher for older workers. Another common employer complaint is that older workers are inflexible about adapting to new circumstances in the workplace. Employers are concerned that workers' skills atrophy when people are out of work for months or years. Yet companies may be reluctant to train people who have less than a decade left in their careers because the company will not receive an adequate return on its investment. Other employers are concerned about being vulnerable to age discrimination lawsuits if they subsequently lay off recently hired older employees.[16]

Mature workers had a lot to say to Heldrich Center researchers about their disappointing experiences:

Even though age discrimination is illegal, I do believe age puts people off from hiring. That is why I took a temporary job on my last job. . . . I've always worked, so this is very depressing. At age sixty, I never believed I would be unemployed unless I chose to be.

I have seen many cases of job discrimination. I can't prove it, but I know it exists.

My age (fifty-nine) leaves me feeling worthless, *very* old, and isolated from the workforce—with little chance of finding employment.

Very few employers are willing to hire someone at my age because they are afraid of possible health concerns down the road and that I may decide to retire too soon to make me a good risk.

Our own experience in the workplace, confirmed by plenty of good social science, tells us that older workers are often as productive and effective as anyone. The aging process affects hearing, vision, memory, and processing speed, but for millions these changes are quite minor. Employees in their fifties and sixties may not be well suited to every job, but neither are younger workers. Stereotyping older workers makes no more sense than does stereotyping women, minorities, people with disabilities, or any other groups. It is also against the law: the federal Age Discrimination Act of 1967 prohibits employers from discriminating against anyone who is forty years of age or older.

In fact, a worker's age is a poor predictor of performance on the job. Employers who adhere to the notion that older workers cannot learn new skills need to reconsider. A thorough review of the research literature, prepared by Ting Zhang of the University of Baltimore for the Employment and Training Administration at the U.S. Department of Labor in 2011, confirmed that older workers are excellent learners and as productive as any age cohort. For example, General Motors employees in their fifties and older were as productive in the workplace as other age-groups. Older workers also learn computer skills effectively, and there are no discernible differences in job performance for different age-groups receiving training.[17]

Older workers are also valued by their coworkers for their maturity and dependability.[18] They contribute valuable experiences, diversity of thoughts and approaches, and established business ties. They also have a strong work ethic, are loyal, and help mentor younger employees, according to a collaborative survey of human resource professionals commissioned by the Society for Human Resource Management, the National Older Worker Career Center, and the Committee for Economic Development.[19]

First-person testimonies provide compelling evidence about the labor market realities encountered by older workers during the Great Recession era. More than a hundred of these stories have been posted at the website http://www.over50andoutofwork.com by video journalists Susan Sipprelle and Sam Newman. At age sixty-four, senior engineer Gary Sirianni of Portland, Oregon, remained jobless for nearly two years despite a sterling career and savvy job search strategies:

You've probably heard this one before, but every job opening has at least one to three hundred applicants. In total, I go to about eight job groups a month; I also run a job group two Tuesdays a month for people fifty-plus who are out of work. . . . I've had literally ten interviews in two years. I've been runner-up; they've taken the jobs off the market, or I'm still waiting.

Sixty-two-year-old Rick Peterson, an information technology executive at Citigroup before he was laid off in 2007, decided he would relocate away from his wife and family anywhere in the country if he could revive his executive career:

> So I decided if the job was right, I would go by myself, and Millie would keep the house. As long as I could sustain her in the house, I'd be happy to go where I had to go. Two weeks ago I had a headhunter call up all excited about my background and wanted to present me for a CIO position in southern New Jersey. We got all excited; I went through the process of doing everything. Last week he told me his SVP didn't want to present me despite the fact that I'm a perfect fit because I've been out of work for three years.

Lab technician Kimberly Giles of Las Vegas lost her job, suffered a devastating back injury, and receives disability payments. However, she enrolled in continuing education to become a sign language specialist and receives some work-study support on her way to what she hopes is full-time work:

> I started taking classes to get my degree in foreign language studies in sign language. . . . I am grateful every day I have some place to go to supplement my disability. Every once in a while, I will borrow from a kid till payday, which is really embarrassing. I want to get a full-time job.

Kathryn Balles, previously a highly successful financial securities executive, told of her roller-coaster experience during the past decade:

> In September, it was 9/11—that was when my career accelerated down. Because the whole thing stopped with MetLife. I was ready to leave California; I was done. Then a headhunter called; a job came in through Lehman Brothers. . . . I had to ask three or four times because I had never heard of Lehman Brothers here in Orange County. Well, it was Lehman Brothers. Now [with this job] I thought this is the end all and be all. I'm employed for the rest of my life. I have a job that is made in heaven. The man that I'm working for is absolutely the best, the place is the best. I don't have to worry . . . it was commercial mortgages. There's nothing I can say more. I loved my job. It just took a few greedy people to make the wrong decisions and take the whole company down, like a tsunami that came over everybody. I went from making $150,000 to barely living on $25,000 a year. It destroyed my career, my personal life, and my social life. . . . We don't have any of the benefits; we don't have anything. We have nothing. . . . I feel that work will happen. I'm on the cusp of good things to happen. I feel it in my heart, but it hasn't happened yet.

THE DEVASTATING
CONSEQUENCES OF LONG-TERM UNEMPLOYMENT

One of the most devastating things with becoming unemployed was losing my identity. I was one thing and then I was nothing. —Fifty-eight-year-old woman[20]

Older workers, often jobless for two or more years, endured great difficulties during the Great Recession era.[21] Less able to move than younger workers, they also have less access to job training and are stigmatized as less desirable by some employers. When older workers do get another job, they have fewer years left during their work life to make up for lost income and savings. Most ran out of their unemployment insurance benefits before they found another job or never had them in the first place. They are more likely to be traumatized by prolonged unemployment.

Heldrich Center *Work Trends* surveys documented the financial and emotional consequences that jobless older workers suffered as they struggled to make ends meet. Among the key findings are the following:

- Seven in ten long-term unemployed workers assessed their financial situation as flat-out poor.
- Over three in four said the recession had a major impact on their family.
- The majority are convinced that their lower living standards are permanent.
- Four in ten anticipate that it will take at least six years for their finances to recover.
- One in ten believes they will never find another job.
- Among those who said they will eventually find work, half believe it will pay less.

Without regular paychecks, long-term unemployed job seekers tried various strategies to weather the storm of unemployment. As shown in table 4.2, six in ten borrowed money from family and friends and/or sold possessions. Nearly as many (55 percent) cut back on doctor visits. Significant numbers reluctantly accepted part-time jobs they did not like or jobs below their educational level, borrowed on their credit cards, and/or missed credit card payments. Four in ten relied on food stamps or charities to feed their families. One in five moved in with family or friends to save money. One unemployed worker commented,

We are the cross-section of Americans which used to be middle-class. Many of us . . . were in the last decade or years of our careers. We're 50 and now 60 year olds. We want to work. There's not one thing sexy, positive, or pleasant about accepting benefits.[22]

Table 4.2. Unemployed Workers Forced to Make Tough Choices

	Unemployed More Than Two Years	Other Unemployed Workers
Sold some of your possessions to make ends meet	60%	40%
Moved in with family or friends to save money	20%	18%
Borrowed money from family or friends, other than adult children	60%	45%
Missed a mortgage or rent payment	26%	19%
Taken a job you did not like	40%	27%
Taken a job below your education or experience levels	36%	26%
Missed a credit card payment	28%	20%
Forced to move to a different house or apartment	20%	10%
Increased credit card debt	31%	28%
Used food stamps or received food from a nonprofit or religious organization	38%	32%
Cut back on doctors' visits or medical treatment	55%	42%

Source: C. Stone, C. Van Horn, and C. Zukin, "Out of Work and Losing Hope: The Misery and Bleak Expectations of American Workers," Heldrich Center for Workforce Development, Rutgers University, September 2011.

In the worst case, according to a study by AARP in 2012, more than 3 million workers over the age of fifty were at risk of losing their homes, more than any other age category.[23]

Two or more years of unemployment exacted huge personal tolls on workers and their families. Over nine in ten respondents told Heldrich Center researchers that they experienced stress in relationships with friends and family, with nearly half (45 percent) saying it had caused a good deal of stress. Over one in four also noticed negative developments in their children's behavior. Workers who have been jobless for more than two years reported lost sleep (85 percent) and were ashamed or embarrassed about their circumstance (74 percent). Perhaps because of these feelings, nearly one of every two respondents said they avoided social situations with friends and acquaintances and lost contact with close friends. Isolation or estrangement from people in their social networks made it even more difficult for these workers to find a new job.[24]

Long-term unemployment has immediate and enduring consequences for workers' mental and physical well-being. For example, in the year after an experienced worker is laid off, mortality rates are 50 to 100 percent higher than average. This "implies a reduction in life expectancy of one to one and a half years."[25] According to Heldrich Center *Work Trends* surveys, one in ten unemployed workers sought help from mental health professionals. One Heldrich Center respondent said plainly, "I love to work, so just the fact that I'm not working is depressing to me." Seven percent said they had become more dependent on alcohol and drugs. Interviews with long-term unemployed workers conducted for the Kaiser Family Foundation and National Public Radio, also reported that "one in five say they have sought help from a medical professional for stress or other major health problems, and one in ten started taking new prescriptions for mental health problems since being out of work."[26]

Long-term unemployment has immediate and enduring consequences for workers' mental and physical well-being.

Because of the difficulties caused by their job loss and reduced earnings, roughly a third of older workers no longer have health insurance. Among the rest of the mature workers, one in three was enrolled in Medicare or Medicaid, and another 10 percent were insured by a family member. Ten percent obtained health insurance from a current employer and 4 percent from a prior employer. Even among those who were able to get health insurance, about one in two older workers went without needed medical care for themselves or family members.[27]

ENDING RETIREMENT AS WE KNEW IT

As with most of my friends, we were ready and had saved for retirement until the market crashed, and then the housing market crashed. We now live from day to day without a job, depleting our meager savings, and watching it slip through our fingers. (unemployed older worker, Heldrich Center interview, 2011)

Beyond the immediate financial and emotional blows, older workers harbor deep concerns about having enough money to help their children or grandchildren pay for college and enjoy a secure retirement. Eighty-five percent of employed and unemployed respondents told Heldrich Center researchers that they had less in savings and income than before the recession. A disturbingly high 62 percent reported having a *lot* less in their savings accounts. Unemployed older workers' savings declined by more than half. To adjust to these new financial circumstances, nearly a third of the older respondents cut spending on essential items. Six in ten gave up something that, while not essential, was desirable, such as family vacations and entertainment.[28]

Further clouding the retirement outlook is the fact that millions of workers who could afford to set aside funds for their retirement did not save enough during the late 1990s and 2000s. They may have believed financial experts who advised them that home ownership was a secure investment. But the collapse of real estate values and fluctuating stock prices in the 2001–2002 and 2008–2012 periods reduced retirement accounts for millions of middle-class workers. Through the first decade of the 2000s, the inflation-adjusted income of the average American worker did not increase.[29] Without real wage gains, the typical workers had less available to save. Millions "borrowed a wage increase" by tapping into credit cards and home equity loans, which hampered them when they were suddenly laid off.

Workers' new outlook about retirement has major implications for the economy, the federal budget, social well-being, health care costs, and private sector competitiveness. The causes of their insecurity are familiar. Despite federal laws meant to safeguard worker contributions and pension benefits, the value of so-called guaranteed pensions have either declined or disappeared because of mergers, restructurings, and bankruptcies. Less than half of those working have any form of employer-sponsored retirement plan. The share of Americans covered by "traditional" defined benefit pension plans that pay a lifetime income, based on years of employment and final salary, declined sharply over the past thirty years, according to the Bureau of Labor Statistics. Fewer than one in five private sector workers in 2008 were enrolled in guaranteed pension plans, compared with nearly two in five in 1980.[30]

During the mid- and late 2000s, federal investigations conducted by the independent U.S. Government Accountability Office discovered that many employers "froze" the value of defined benefit plans.[31] In other words, current participants would receive retirement benefits based on their accruals up to the date of the freeze but would not receive additional benefits. New hires in many firms would no longer be covered by pensions. Experts at McKinsey & Company and the Social Security Administration predict that most private sector plans will be frozen in the next few years and eventually terminated,[32] with substantial financial impacts on baby-boomer retirees. According to the Social Security Administration's Office of Retirement and Disability Policy,

> These trends threaten to shake up the American retirement system as we know it because of vast differences between defined benefit and defined contribution pension plans, including differences in coverage rates within a firm, timing of accruals, investment and labor market risks, forms of payout, and effects on work incentives and labor mobility.[33]

The percentage of Americans covered by defined *contribution* retirement plans soared from 8 percent in 1980 to 31 percent in 2008. These so-called 401k plans, established by many employers, give workers the opportunity to set aside tax-deferred retirement savings. Each employee is responsible for making his or her own investment decisions, choosing from options offered by their employer. If a worker loses his or her job, they can take their 401k earnings with them and either cash it out—with a penalty—or "roll it over" into a new plan. Employers are not required to contribute toward the employee's 401k plans, but many do so.[34] Companies vary in how much and when they make contributions to individual employee retirement. Workers' savings are more vulnerable because of market fluctuations: past performance is "no guarantee for future investment returns," as the financial commercials always note.

The shift from a guaranteed pension check from a company (partially insured by the federal government's Pension Guarantee Benefit Corporation) to investment accounts that do not produce guaranteed returns has been especially widespread in the nation's manufacturing sector. As noted in the discussion of outsourcing and downsizing in chapter 2, Americans realize the implications of U.S. manufacturing and industrial firms—and jobs—moving to other countries. During interviews, workers pointed to the decline of manufacturing as one of the most significant effects of the recession. One worker summed this trend up in the most pessimistic terms: "Manufacturing jobs are leaving this country in droves—we are going to become a third world country due to unbridled greed."

Living in a rapidly evolving economy and dealing with the Great Recession altered the expectations of older workers about retirement. The overall financial status of workers aged fifty-five and older deteriorated for seven in ten respondents between 2009 and 2010. More than half (58 percent) said the recession brought about major, permanent, and negative changes in their lifestyle.[35] Retirement plan professionals, surveyed in 2012 by Deloitte Consulting, agreed: more than eight in ten of these firms judged that "some or very few employees would be financially prepared to retire."[36]

Older workers have a bleak outlook for the country's economic future. Many predicted that the legacy of the Great Recession will include permanently higher unemployment and alter when and how Americans will retire. One unemployed banker wrote me in January 2011,

> I have been unemployed for over two years. It shames me to even type those words on a keyboard. . . . Two years ago I would have never thought it possible I would be in my current circumstance. Today, I have very little hope for my future. My biggest concern is what will the future hold for my seven year old daughter?

Because of the nation's dire economic circumstances, Americans view retirement differently than they did when the Heldrich Center first queried workers in 2000. Then, with the stock market booming and unemployment at post–World War II lows, a majority of American workers expected to retire from full-time employment before reaching the age of sixty.[37] At the dawn of the twenty-first century, most regarded "retirement" as an opportunity to pursue their passions for travel and recreation or find a new fulfilling avocation. Four in ten workers thought they would work part-time but principally for "enjoyment" rather than because they had to. Only 10 percent said they would work part-time for income.[38]

In 2000, only four in ten younger workers were confident that Social Security and Medicare would be available on their retirement. Survey respondents in their fifties and sixties were far more sanguine about the prospects for these pillars of the social safety net. In 2005, well before the Great Recession, one in two workers felt comfortable that they had properly prepared for retirement. More than six in ten were certain they would have enough funds to support a "comfortable" retirement.[39]

American workers have fretted about their employer's pension and retirement programs since our first surveys. In 2002, less than a quarter of Americans were very satisfied with the retirement and pension plans offered by their employer. Most workers, at that time, preferred defined benefit plans—pensions—over a defined contribution plan.[40] They doubted the security of their retirement investment funds, particularly those based on their employer's stock. Unfortunately, these concerns were realized when some large firms, such as Enron, engaged in fraudulent and criminal conduct that destroyed the firm's stock value and their employees' savings. Millions of Americans—particularly workers with low and moderate incomes—are able to save only small amounts of money for retirement. Most of these individuals will rely on Social Security benefits for a substantial portion or all of their retirement income.

The severe economic trauma of the recession sent retirement fears soaring and expectations crumbling. By 2010, nearly seven in ten of the Heldrich Center panelists over age fifty were reconsidering their retirement plans. In the aftermath of tough times during the recession, four in ten expected to work longer than they had anticipated but worried they could not hold on to their jobs. For others, the grim economy convinced them that they had no choice but to retire early.

Two-thirds of older workers said they would file for Social Security benefits earlier than they wanted to; one in five had already done so.[41] Early filing for Social Security benefits, generally at age sixty-two, reduces monthly and lifetime benefits below what one would receive if a worker waited until reaching age sixty-seven or seventy. Weak prospects for reemployment contributed to a 6 percent increase in workers filing for Social Security benefits over what would have occurred in the absence of the recession, according to the Social Security Administration. The recession also led to a 12 percent jump in disability benefit applications.[42]

Other workers concluded they could not afford to retire because they had reluctantly drained their savings during long unemployment spells. According to a survey conducted by AARP in 2011, more than half were not confident they would have enough money to live comfortably in retirement.[43] Evidence from 2011 demonstrates that workers, aged sixty-two years or older, are postponing their retirement in order to build up their savings. In fact, only three-quarters of those eligible to apply for Social Security payments did so, the lowest rate in thirty-five years.[44]

In a study of older workers during the recession, the Government Accountability Office calculated that a fifty-five-year-old worker with $70,000 in retirement savings who used up to half of those savings during a spell of unemployment would need to work another six and a half years in order to fully rebuild his or her retirement account.[45] Little wonder, then, that so many older workers worried that they will never be able to retire.

In the wake of the Great Recession, older workers are pessimistic about the labor market for workers of all ages (see table 4.3). Nearly three in four believe the U.S. economy is undergoing fundamental, permanent changes that have all but eliminated secure, well-paying jobs. Two of three mature workers do not think they will be able to retire when they want to.

Table 4.3.   Older Workers Are Pessimistic about Their Futures and the U.S. Economy

The U.S. economy is experiencing fundamental and lasting changes.	72%
The Great Recession represents a temporary downturn.	27%
The elderly will not be able to retire when they want to.*	67%
It will be many years before the unemployment rate will return to where it was before the Great Recession.	53%
The unemployment rate will never return to the way it was.	40%
Job security will return to what it was before.	35%
Job security will not return to pre–Great Recession levels.	55%
The availability of good jobs at good pay for those who want to work will return to pre–Great Recession levels.	46%
The availability of good jobs at good pay for those who want to work will never return to pre–Great Recession levels.	46%
It will be many years before workers will not have to take jobs below their skill level.	54%
Going forward, workers taking jobs below their skill level will be the norm.	40%

Source: D. Borie-Holtz, C. Van Horn, and C. Zukin, "No End in Sight: The Agony of Prolonged Unemployment," Heldrich Center for Workforce Development, Rutgers University, May 2010.
*This question represents all survey respondents over age fifty.

In many ways, older workers believe the labor market will never be the same. The following are typical of the many comments older workers made during interviews with the Heldrich Center:

The unemployed will not recover from their earnings, savings, and retirement fund losses.

The rich will get richer and the poor will get poorer—I panic if I consider that the middle class will cease to exist, but that does look like where we are heading.

I think our retirement won't be as comfortable as we thought it'd be, mostly because of health care costs. I expect to be working longer, to make up for the lost time working and to pay for the increased healthcare expenses on top of being unemployed!

Policy experts are also concerned that an aging U.S. population, with longer life spans, will not have enough retirement savings. Alicia Munnell of Boston College summarized, "At the same time the need for retirement income is increasing, the retirement income system is contracting."[46] Without adequate savings, millions of retired Americans will experience substantially diminished living standards or even poverty. The burden of supporting older Americans will fall heavily on their children and on the society as the costs of social service programs increase. Munnell concluded that the "solution to the retirement income challenge is straightforward . . . people should remain in the workforce longer, make better use of retirement assets, and save more."[47] While no doubt this is sound advice, it is unfortunately not realistic for millions whose careers were abruptly cut short by the Great Recession.

WHAT OLDER WORKERS NEED

What do older, unemployed workers want employers and policymakers to do? Older Americans believe that unemployment insurance is the most essential benefit that government provides to jobless workers. Speaking to researchers from the Government Accountability Office, many workers said they would have been forced to give up their homes had they not received unemployment insurance checks.[48] Unemployed workers, especially older ones, also need more than cash assistance if they are going to land another job. Seven in ten said they must prepare for new careers by updating their skills. However, only about one in ten were enrolled in retraining programs, according to Heldrich Center surveys.

The gap between older workers' preferences and what they get can be explained by several factors. Older job seekers are underserved by publicly funded training programs.[49] The Workforce Investment Act, a program intended for job seekers of all ages, has seen a vast increase in the numbers of adults seeking help during the Great Recession. Yet adults fifty-five and older made up 12.6 percent of Workforce Investment Act clients, or just over 200,000 individuals, in 2009. At the same time, more than 2 million older adults were unemployed.

Only two government-funded programs are exclusively dedicated to serving older workers: the Senior Community Service Employment Program (SCSEP), which is authorized by Title V of the Older Americans Act, and the Alternative Trade Adjustment Assistance (ATAA) Program under Trade Adjustment Assistance. SCSEP annually provides part-time, subsidized community service employment opportunities to roughly 100,000 low-income workers who are fifty-five years of age or older. The Government Accountability Office estimated that SCSEP serves approximately 1 percent of the eligible population. Some observers question whether SCSEP is a viable model that is appropriate for a broader population of today's older job seekers, especially given its focus on very low-income (125 percent of poverty) older people.[50]

ATAA serves workers who are fifty years old or over who were displaced by foreign competition. These individuals receive a temporary wage subsidy for program participants who find a job that pays less than what they earned previously and is under $50,000 per year. In calendar year 2006, the latest year for which data are available, only 6,352 individuals participated in ATAA.[51]

Many workers forgo training programs because they assume that their next job will come along quickly. They are therefore reluctant to enroll in educational and training courses before attempting to reconnect with their former employer or with another employer in their industry. The unemployed also typically cannot afford to pay for educational and training programs.

Patricia Reid, a laid-off Boeing auditor profiled by reporter Motoko Rich in a September 2010 *New York Times* front-page story, devoted four years to job hunting and training without a single offer; one of her biggest challenges was staying current with software.[52] She lost one opportunity because an auditing position at the Port of Seattle required skills in financial software she had never used. She redoubled her efforts at mastering new skills, according to the story:

> In order to qualify for accounting posts, she is taking an online course in Quick-Books, a popular accounting software used by small business. She recently signed up for a tax course at an H&R Block tax preparation office in Seattle.

And she is plugging ahead with her current plan: to send 600 applications to accounting firms in the area, offering her services for the next tax season.[53]

Contemporary workforce development policies are not well suited to serve the needs of the long-term unemployed as the experiences of Patricia and millions like her illustrate, according to separate reports by the Government Accountability Office and the Council on Adult and Experiential Learning.[54] This is especially true for older workers who endure longer unemployment and can get another job only after longer and more expensive retraining programs. The federal government's primary strategies for assisting unemployed workers consist of partial income replacement through unemployment insurance, job placement services, or short-term training programs more appropriate for younger adult workers. While unemployment insurance payments are highly valued by those who receive it, long-term cash transfer payments without education and training will not transition people into new careers. Unless they can obtain appropriate retraining services, older workers who are too young or financially unable to retire will struggle to find jobs in new career fields.[55] Maria Heidkamp of the Heldrich Center at Rutgers University summarized older workers' needs in the volatile economy:

> Access to training and education, including vocational and other postsecondary education, is increasingly important to all workers, and particularly vital to older individuals who need to change industries and occupation or gain new skills because of job loss, age-related health issues, family and personal circumstances, and/or geographic displacement.[56]

The urgent need to reform policies for unemployed and underemployed older workers is underscored by the nation's changing demography. Older workers, as detailed below, are going to make up a larger portion of the workforce than they did just a few decades ago.[57] Moreover, birthrates in the United States have declined so much that there may not be enough younger workers to fill the positions held by those who do retire or are forced out by employers. The prospect of millions of Americans taking early Social Security because they have no viable alternative could exacerbate the fiscal and political headaches of funding Social Security and Medicare.

It is unwise for employers and policymakers to ignore the potential contributions of older workers. With their experience and skills, mature workers are a valuable asset to the U.S. economy that will be needed in the coming decades. Also, if these workers extend their careers, the costs of Social Security and disability benefits will also be more manageable. While some companies, such as Marriott International and CVS Caremark, are adopting strategies to recruit and retain older workers, they are far from the norm.[58]

Millions of older workers are resilient and devoted to remaining in the workforce, no matter how steep the challenge. This attitude was well captured by Jose, a sixty-four-year-old former printer and unwilling retiree who lost his full-time job in 2008:

> For my age, they can put me against a thirty-year-old guy. I can beat him on doing the job. That's printing, roofing, or laying tile. Society doesn't look at it that way. You are old, you're sixty-four—you're old, you're old. That's people's way of thinking. But I'll never give up. I don't give up. I'll keep on looking for a job until I find one.

NOT SO GOLDEN YEARS

For older workers, retiring from full-time work is supposed to be a time to enjoy family and leisure. Elder Americans expected that Social Security and Medicare would shelter them from the poverty and despair visited on early generations. While these programs are still in place, the restructuring of the U.S. labor market over the past several decades and the Great Recession have lessened the likelihood that older Americans will be able to achieve a reasonable retirement.

Greater challenges are ahead for meeting the needs of an aging workforce in the coming decades. In 2010, there were 30 million workers who were fifty-five years and older, representing 19.3 percent of the total, according to the Bureau of Labor Statistics. By 2020, it is projected that there will be 41.4 million older workers, with their share of the total labor force reaching 25.2 percent, or one in four people. In contrast, the number of workers aged twenty-five to fifty-four will only increase from 103 million to 104 million, an increase of less than 2 percent.[59]

In the best of circumstances, we would like older workers to remain in the workforce as long as they desired and not because they were forced to in order escape poverty. Whether the millions of older workers will achieve their ideal retirement scenario is very much in doubt. In large and small ways, the decisions members of the baby-boom generation make about work and retirement will have enormous implications for young workers after they graduate from high school or college. The next chapter examines how young workers are struggling to find jobs and begin their careers in a volatile labor market.

NOTES

1. Peter Goodman, "The Great Rupture," *New York Times*, July 2, 2010, 1.

2. U.S. Department of Labor, Bureau of Labor Statistics, "Monthly Job Report," October 5, 2012, http://bls.gov/news.release/empsit.nr0.htm.

3. U.S. Department of Labor, Bureau of Labor Statistics, "Monthly Job Report."

4. Jessica Godofsky, Carl E. Van Horn, and Cliff Zukin, "American Workers Assess an Economic Disaster," in *Work Trends* (New Brunswick, NJ: Heldrich Center at Rutgers, The State University of New Jersey, September 2010), and "Shattered American Dream," in *Work Trends* (December 2010).

5. Richard W. Johnson and Corina Mommaerts, "Age Differences in Job Loss, Job Search, and Reemployment," Urban Institute, January 2011.

6. U.S. Department of Labor, Bureau of Labor Statistics, "Monthly Job Report."

7. Scott S. Greenberger and Douglas Walton, Pew Fiscal Analysis Initiative, "A Year or More: The High Cost of Unemployment," April 2010, http://www.pewtrusts.org/uploadedFiles/wwwpewtrustsorg/Reports/Economic_Mobility/PEW-Unemployment%20Final.pdf.

8. Godofsky et al., "American Workers Assess an Economic Disaster," and "Shattered American Dream."

9. Maria Heidkamp, Nicole Corre, and Carl E. Van Horn, "The New Unemployables: Older Jobseekers Struggle to Find Work during the Great Recession," Sloan Center on Aging & Work, Boston College, Issue Brief 25 (October 2010).

10. Jessica Collison, "Older Workers Survey," Society for Human Resource Management, National Older Worker Career Center, and Committee for Economic Development (2003).

11. Godofsky et al., "American Workers Assess an Economic Disaster," and "Shattered American Dream."

12. Johnson and Mommaerts, "Age Differences in Job Displacement"; U.S. Census Bureau, 2011, Survey of Income and Program Participation.

13. The Hamilton Project, "Policies to Reduce High-Tenured Displaced Workers' Earnings Losses through Retraining," Policy Brief 2011-11 (November 2011), 3.

14. U.S. Department of Labor, Employment and Training Administration, *Report of the Task Force on Aging of the American Workforce* (February 2008).

15. Joanna Lahey, "Do Older Workers Face Discrimination?," Boston College Center for Retirement Research (July 2005).

16. Francine M. Tishman, Sara Van Looy, and Susanne M. Bruyere, "Employer Strategies for Responding to an Aging Workforce," NTAR Leadership Center at Rutgers University (March 2012); U.S. Government Accountability Office Forum, Office of Comptroller General (February 2007).

17. Ting Zhang, "Workforce Investment Act Training for Older Workers: Toward a Better Understanding of Older Worker Needs during the Economic Recovery," U.S. Department of Labor/Employment and Training Administration, Research & Publication, No. ETAOP 2011-10 (2011).

18. Zhang, "Workforce Investment Act Training for Older Workers."

19. Collison, "Older Workers Survey."

20. Government Accountability Office, "Unemployed Older Workers," GAO-PUB No. 12-445 (April 2012), 26.

21. Greenberger, Walton, and Pew Fiscal Analysis Initiative, "A Year or More: The High Cost of Unemployment," Pew Charitable Trusts (April 2010).

22. "The Data and the Reality," comment from PeppersDad in response to Bob Herbert column, *New York Times*, December 28, 2010.

23. Robbie Brown, "Facing Foreclosure after 50," *New York Times*, July 19, 2012, A14.

24. Cliff Zukin, Carl E. Van Horn, and Charley Stone, "Out of Work and Losing Hope: The Misery and Bleak Expectations of American Workers," in *Work Trends* (September 2011).

25. Michael Greenstone and Adam Looney, "Building America's Job Skills with Effective Workforce Programs: A Training Strategy to Raise Wages and Increase Work Opportunities," The Hamilton Project (November 2011), 11.

26. Kaiser Family Foundation/National Public Radio, "Long Term Unemployed Survey," December 2011, 2.

27. Godofsky et al., "American Workers Assess an Economic Disaster," and "Shattered American Dream."

28. Scott Reynolds, Neil Ridley, and Carl E. Van Horn, "A Work-Filled Retirement," in *Work Trends* (May 2005); Godofsky et al., "American Workers Assess an Economic Disaster," and "Shattered American Dream"; Debbie Borie-Holtz, Carl E. Van Horn, and Cliff Zukin, "No End in Sight: The Agony of Prolonged Unemployment," in *Work Trends* (May 2010).

29. Employment Policy Institute, "Wages and Compensation Stagnating," December 2010, updated January 24, 2011, http://stateofworkingamerica.org/charts/hourly-wage-and-compensation-growth-for-productionnon-supervisory-workers-and-productivity-1947-2009.

30. U.S. Bureau of Labor Statistics, "National Compensation Survey: Employee Benefits in the United States," Bulletin 2715, March 2008, http://www.bls.gov/ncs/ebs/benefits/2008/ownership/private/table02a.pdf; Department of Labor, "Private Pension Plan Bulletin," No. 11, Winter 2001–2002, http://www.dol.gov/ebsa/PDF/1998pensionplanbulletin.PDF.

31. Alicia H. Munnell, Jean-Pierre Aubrey, and Dan Muldoon, "The Financial Crisis and Private Defined Benefit Plans," Boston College Center for Retirement Research (2008); Government Accountability Office, "Plan Freezes Affect Millions of Participants" (July 2008).

32. "The Coming Shake Out in the Defined Benefit Market," 2007, http://ww1.mckinsey.com/clientservice/bankingsecurities/pdf/coming_shakeout_in_defined_benefit_market.pdf.

33. Barbara A. Butrica, Howard M. Iams, Karen E. Smith, and Eric J. Toder, "The Disappearing Defined Pension Benefit and Its Potential Impact on the Retirement Incomes of Baby Boomers," *Social Security Bulletin* 69, no. 3 (2009), http://www.ssa.gov/policy/docs/ssb/v69n3/v69n3p1.pdf.

34. Butricia et al., "The Disappearing Defined Pension Benefit and Its Potential Impact on the Retirement Incomes of Baby Boomers."

90

Chapter Four

35. Godofsky et al., "Shattered American Dream"; Borie-Holtz et al., "No End in Sight."

36. Gail Belsky, "Retirement Programs Keep Employers on Track," June 22, 2012, http://www.cnbc.com/id/47907842/Retirement_Programs_Keep_Employers_On_Track.

37. Carl E. Van Horn and Ken Dautrich, "Second Wind: Workers, Retirement and Social Security," in Work Trends (New Brunswick, NJ: Heldrich Center at Rutgers, The State University of New Jersey, Center for Survey Research and Analysis, University of Connecticut, September 2000); Reynolds et al., "A Work-Filled Retirement."

38. Van Horn and Dautrich, "Second Wind"; Reynolds et al., "A Work-Filled Retirement."

39. Van Horn and Dautrich, "Second Wind"; Reynolds et al., "A Work-Filled Retirement."

40. Van Horn and Dautrich, "Second Wind"; Reynolds et al., "A Work-Filled Retirement."

41. Godofsky et al., "Shattered American Dream"; Borie-Holtz et al., "No End in Sight."

42. Government Accountability Office, "Unemployed Older Workers," 35.

43. Sara Rix, "Recovering from the Great Recession: Long Struggle Ahead for Older Americans," May 2011, http://assets.aarp.org/rgcenter/ppi/econ-sec/insight50_recovering.pdf.

44. Richard W. Johnson, "Social Security Claims Edged Down in 2011," Urban Institute Retirement Security Brief, No. 5, 2011, http://www.urban.org.

45. Government Accountability Office, "Unemployed Older Workers," 1.

46. Alicia H. Munnell, "Income Security for an Aging Population," in Grand Challenges of Our Aging Society, Workshop Summary (Washington, DC: National Research Council of the National Academies, 2010), 31.

47. Munnell, "Income Security for an Aging Population."

48. Government Accountability Office, "Unemployed Older Workers," 22.

49. Government Accountability Office, "Unemployed Older Workers," 22.

50. Government Accountability Office, "Employment and Training: Most One-Stop Career Centers Are Taking Multiple Actions to Link Employers and Older Workers," GAO-08-548, 2008, http://www.gao.gov/new.items/d08548.pdf.

51. Government Accounting Office, "Trade Adjustment Assistance: Most Workers in Five Layoffs Received Services, but Better Outreach Needed on New Benefits," GAO-06-43, January 2006.

52. Motoko Rich, "For the Unemployed over 50, Fears of Never Working Again," New York Times, September 19, 2010, A1.

53. Rich, "For the Unemployed over 50, Fears of Never Working Again."

54. Government Accountability Office, "Unemployed Older Workers," 27; Council on Adult and Experiential Learning, "Tapping Mature Talent: Policies for a 21st Century Workforce, Executive Summary," May 2012, http://www.cael.org/pdfs/TMT_Summary_Policy_Recs_2012.

55. Carl E. Van Horn and Maria Heidkamp, "Older and Out of Work: Employer, Government and Non-Profit Assistance," Sloan Center for Aging and Work, Boston College (October 2008).

56. Maria Heidkamp, "Older Workers, Rising Skill Requirements, and the Need for a Re-envisioning of the Public Workforce System," Heldrich Center at Rutgers, The State University of New Jersey, 2012.

57. Council for Adult & Experiential Learning, "Tapping Mature Talent: Policies for a 21st Century Workforce, May 2012, http://www.cael.org/pdfs/TMT_Summary_Policy_Recs_2012.

58. "Innovative Practices, Case Study Number 5: Flex Strategies to Attract, Engage, and Retain Older Workers," Sloan Center on Aging & Work, Boston College, 2012.

59. Dixie Sommers and James C. Franklin, "Overview of Projections to 2020," *Monthly Labor Review* 135, no. 1 (January 2012): 12, http://www.bls.gov/opub/mlr/2012/01/art1full.pdf.

Chapter Five

Unfulfilled Expectations for Recent College and High School Graduates

> I graduated with my bachelor's degree over two years ago and I am still unable to gain full-time employment. It is not for lack of trying or too much pride. I just finished working for UPS as a driver helper. I made $9.50 an hour, sweated for every penny, and was lucky to get thirty hours a week. The crazy thing is—I am sad that it is over.
>
> —Joshua, an unemployed college graduate
> interviewed by the Heldrich Center, March 2011

Just as millions of older American workers suffered during the Great Recession and its aftershocks, a new generation of high school and college graduates is also facing an uphill battle for their first full-time job. Students graduating during the recession era are encountering historic obstacles in achieving the foundations of the American Dream. With unemployment rates soaring and remaining high for over four years, it has been difficult for young workers to get full-time jobs in part because they are also competing with slightly older, unemployed adult workers. College graduates are settling for jobs once held by those with no more than a high school education. These and other troubling trends have led many Americans to wonder what's wrong with an economy when even our most talented young people struggle.

It has also spawned a debate about whether our nation places too much emphasis on going to college or not enough. According to economists Claudia

Goldin and Lawrence Katz, Americans' overall level of education stopped rising in the 1970s, after nearly a century of steady and consistent gains.[1] In the early 1980s, following decades of educational progress, the United States led the world in the proportion of adults with postsecondary education. By 2009, the United States had slipped behind fourteen other countries, according to the Organisation for Economic Co-operation and Development. More than half of all college students drop out before earning a degree or a credential. The United States fell from first to eighth place among developed nations in the proportion of twenty-five- to thirty-four-year-olds who graduate from high school. More troubling, only 72 percent of those who begin high school eventually graduate. By 2006, 37 percent of U.S. adults had an associate's degree or higher compared with 55 percent in many of the nations with which we compete for economic growth.[2] What are the implications of such a sharp decline in educational attainment in comparison with the economic competitors of the United States?[3]

HIT HARD BY THE GREAT RECESSION

What are the labor market experiences of young people who graduate from high school? How do their experiences compare with young college graduates? Despite withering and often justified critiques of American higher education, there is no doubt that college graduates are better off economically than those who do not obtain a college degree.[4] During the recession-era economy, however, graduating from high school or college does not guarantee either a full-time job or one that is commensurate with one's education and skills. Three scientific surveys of recent high school and college graduates from the classes of 2006 through 2011 who were interviewed for the Heldrich Center's *Work Trends* series capture the frustrations and disappointments they endured during the recession era.[5]

Left Out of the Labor Market

In 2010, seven in ten high school graduates, more than 20 million people ages eighteen to twenty-four, did not have a college degree according to the American Community Survey (ACS). In this age-group, only 4 million people completed college.[6] The employment status of recent high school graduates not enrolled in college is bleak, as shown in table 5.1, and they are much worse off than recent college graduates. Overall, only three in ten high school graduates were employed full-time in the spring of 2012. College graduates were employed full-time at nearly twice that rate. Of those graduat-

Table 5.1. Recent High School and College Graduates Struggled to Find Full-Time Jobs during the Recession Era

Employment Status	College	High School
Unemployed and looking for work	6%	30%
Unemployed and not looking for work	5%	14%
Working part-time, not looking for full-time work	6%	8%
Working part-time, looking for full-time work	6%	15%
Employed full-time	51%	27%
Attending graduate school, not employed	6%	—
Attending graduate school, employed part-time or full-time	14%	—
Military	3%	2%
Self-employed	0%	3%
Volunteer	3%	1%
Total	100%	100%

Sources: C. Van Horn, C. Zukin, and C. Stone, "Chasing the American Dream: Recent College Graduates and the Great Recession," Heldrich Center for Workforce Development, Rutgers University, May 2012; C. Van Horn, C. Zukin, M. Szeltner, and C. Stone, "Left Out. Forgotten? Recent High School Graduates and the Great Recession," Heldrich Center for Workforce Development, Rutgers University, June 2012.

ing high school in 2006, 2007, and 2008—before the nation's labor market was pummeled by the recession—37 percent had full-time jobs in April 2012 when the Heldrich Center survey was conducted. Only 16 percent of the recession-era high school graduates from the classes of 2009, 2010, and 2011 were employed full-time. Recent college graduates are also experiencing a "recession hangover" as they compete for jobs with slightly older and still unemployed college graduates who have a bit more experience.

Nearly half of high school graduates from the classes of 2006 through 2011 were still trying to land a full-time job in mid-2012, including 30 percent who were unemployed and 15 percent who were working part-time. About one in six left the labor market altogether. High levels of joblessness among young high school graduates, ages seventeen to twenty, is common in good and bad economic times. However, current levels of joblessness in the Great Recession era are far higher than a decade ago, when

Nearly half of high school graduates from the classes of 2006 through 2011 were still trying to land a full-time job in mid-2012, including 30 percent who were unemployed and 15 percent who were working part-time.

around 15 percent of young workers were jobless, according to research from the Economic Policy Institute.[7]

Young high school graduates surveyed by the Heldrich Center who had full-time jobs earned, on average, $9.25 per hour—just $2.00 above the federal minimum wage in 2012. Three-quarters of these full-time jobs were temporary, and only one in ten provided an annual salary with benefits, such as health care. Even if these young people managed to work full-time (thirty-seven-hour weeks) for an entire year, their annual earnings would amount to less than $18,000. While that exceeds the official federal poverty level for a single person, it is barely sufficient to afford a modest lifestyle, let alone purchase a home. The nearly six in ten who were working part-time were unlikely to earn even a poverty-level income. Over the past decade, the average wages of young high school graduates declined by 11 percent. They were 5.4 percent lower for college graduates over the same period.[8]

Given these grim realities, high school graduates were dissatisfied with their high school education. Half said their high school education had not equipped them "very well" or "not well at all" to get their first jobs. Fewer than one in ten thought their high school education had prepared them "extremely well" to succeed in the labor market.

When they started high school, approximately two of every three high school graduates interviewed by the Heldrich Center anticipated attending college, including much larger proportions of blacks and Hispanics than whites. Their hopes were derailed by financial barriers and family responsibilities. Rob, a twenty-seven-year-old high school graduate from New Jersey, explained the difficulty of attending community college:

> How am I going to balance going to school, just a couple of courses even, and try to work and pay for school? If I just do school full-time, it's not like I just came out of high school. I have been out working and I have bills to pay. It's a struggle to start over. You have to work to go to school, but you need school to get a job and I don't have time for both.[9]

Despite increases in the availability of federal student loan programs, four in ten high school graduates could not afford the cost of full-time college but instead sought jobs to support themselves and their families. Recent high school graduates overwhelmingly believe that they will need additional education to be successful in life. Seven out of ten high school graduates said that getting more education is the only way they will ever enjoy a successful career. Kim, a twenty-six-year-old high school graduate from Missouri, offered this perspective:

I always planned to go to college, but I haven't set a time to do that. As I got into restaurant management jobs, I was 22 and thought it was a good job and I was making good money. Now that I am older, I'm realizing that starting out in restaurant management is not a great job. You have to be there all the time and I do not want to do that. If you go to school and get a degree then you're not the one mopping the floors.[10]

One-fifth of the Heldrich Center's survey respondents said they will need at least an associate's degree, one in three believe a bachelor's degree will be necessary, and one in ten want to go on to graduate or professional school. Only one in twenty does not think a college education is essential. Evidence from previous studies of high school graduates conducted in 2002, 2003, and 2004 by Peter Hart Associates found that eight out of ten who were not currently in college believed more formal education or training would enable them to achieve their personal goals.[11]

Recent high school graduates also do not regard themselves to be as well prepared for work as the generation that came before them, by a lopsided margin of 56 to 14 percent. They are concerned that their generation will be less successful than the one that preceded them: the number expecting their generation to do less well financially outnumber those who expect to do better by a margin of four to one (see figure 5.1). Perhaps more surprisingly, recent college graduates hold similar views, a topic we will return to later in the chapter.

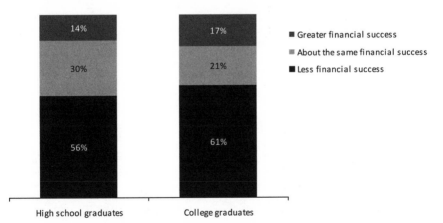

Figure 5.1. Young Americans Doubt They Will Do Better Than the Previous Generation

Sources: C. Van Horn, C. Zukin, and C. Stone, "Chasing the American Dream: Recent College Graduates and the Great Recession," Heldrich Center for Workforce Development, Rutgers University, May 2012; C. Van Horn, C. Zukin, M. Szeltner, and C. Stone, "Left Out. Forgotten? Recent High School Graduates and the Great Recession," Heldrich Center for Workforce Development, Rutgers University, June 2012.

The prevailing anxieties of recent graduates are not limited to expectations about their generation but extend to their own financial futures as well. Not even half of high school graduates (44 percent) expect to be more successful than their parents, even though just 11 percent of their fathers and 15 percent of their mothers obtained a bachelor's degree. Nearly a third anticipates having less success than their parents, and many feel powerless to do anything about it. Thirty-eight percent agreed that "hard work and determination are no guarantee of success."

In a troubled economy, large percentages of recent high school and college graduates—seventeen- to twenty-nine-year-olds—remained heavily dependent on their parents' financial support (see figure 5.2). Among high school graduates, three in five resided with their parents or relatives, twice as many as recent college graduates of the same age. Another quarter is living with their spouse or significant other, leaving only 15 percent of high school graduates living on their own. Fully half of these young people got help from their families for essentials, such as groceries. Roughly one in three recent high school graduates depended on family members to pay bills for their utilities, phones, or health care.

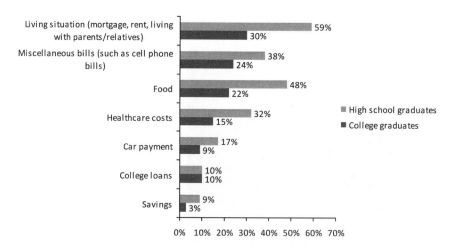

Figure 5.2. Recent High School and College Graduates Are Still Very Dependent on Their Parents

Sources: C. Van Horn, C. Zukin, and C. Stone, "Chasing the American Dream: Recent College Graduates and the Great Recession," Heldrich Center for Workforce Development, Rutgers University, May 2012; C. Van Horn, C. Zukin, M. Szeltner, and C. Stone, "Left Out. Forgotten? Recent High School Graduates and the Great Recession," Heldrich Center for Workforce Development, Rutgers University, June 2012.

A Disappointing Start for College Graduates

Parents, young people, and policymakers have long believed that getting a college degree was the sure path to successful careers and the economic rewards that follow. Attending college was and still is an uplifting dream for millions of American families. Unfortunately, millions of recession-era college graduates and their families are wondering if that vision was just a mirage. Len, a twenty-nine-year-old college graduate from Ohio who majored in marketing, commented, "The old adage of you go to school, get good grades, get a good job and career is a falsehood . . . I have friends with MBAs and graduate degrees and that has helped them, but in my business of marketing, my undergraduate degree didn't help."[12] After finishing their college education—and in most cases borrowing the money to pay tuition bills—only one in two graduates from the classes of 2006 to 2011 had been able to get a full-time job at the time the Heldrich Center interviewed them in April 2012. More than one in ten recent graduates was either jobless (6 percent) or working part-time and seeking a full-time job (6 percent) (see table 5.1, on p. 95).

Remarkably, four in ten recent college graduates said their current job did not even require a college degree. Even fewer—two in ten—think they are on the way to a satisfying career. The unanticipated difficulties in the labor market convinced one in five college graduates to enroll in graduate or professional schools. According to an analysis of the federal government's Current Population Survey conducted by Northeastern University researchers, the combined unemployment and underemployment rate for college graduates under the age of twenty-five reached 53.6 percent in 2011, the highest level in more than a decade. With young college graduates "more likely to be employed as waiters, waitresses, bartenders and food service helpers than as engineers, physicists, chemists and mathematicians combined," Andrew Sum, director of the Center for Labor Market Studies at Northeastern University, concluded, "Simply put, we're failing kids coming out of college."[13]

Understandably, these young graduates were terribly disappointed by this twist of economic fate. Commenting on a *New York Times* column about the Heldrich Center's research by Bob Herbert, a recent college graduate from Oregon said:

> This pessimism does not surprise me. I'm no economist, but I just don't see where a recovery would come from. Why won't the recession be permanent? Jobs don't just materialize and people can't spend money they don't have. Especially for young people like myself, who remember little beyond the boom years immediately preceding the recession, there doesn't seem to be any logical reason for the economy to magically improve. Instead, I feel as if the relatively flush times in which I was raised were a fluke, a lucky golden decade that has disappeared and been replaced by a return to a dour, grinding norm.[14]

Many graduates interviewed for the Heldrich Center's surveys in 2011 and 2012 echoed these frustrations. "There are an unbelievable number of people seeking work," one graduate remarked. "I have submitted over 250 applications and not heard a call back." Another graduate told us, "I have had temporary gigs that aren't all that poor, but in general I know that there are ten people underemployed for every open position." Another graduate remarked, "My field is not hiring due to budget cuts. There are simply no jobs, and if one should come up, they have their pick of anyone they want, and I don't have any experience that counts with them." Thousands of unemployed graduates who prepared for teaching careers when that seemed like a sure bet a few years ago either could not find a teaching position or were laid off. "With school budget cuts it is increasingly difficult to find full-time teaching jobs," one young graduate commented.

Among the graduates working full-time, median earnings at their first postcollege job were $30,000 for those from the classes of 2006 and 2007 before the recession hit. Graduates entering the labor market in 2009, 2010, or 2011 earned $3,000 less on average. Incomes were higher by an average of $5,000 for graduates who got jobs that actually required job holders to have a college degree. Students who completed an internship while in college— about 40 percent of our respondents—earned nearly 15 percent more on average—$30,000 versus $26,000—than those who did not because they already have built up work experience that may prepare them to be more productive employees as soon as they start work.[15]

Mountains of Debt

Over the past decade, the net cost of a college education—after factoring in grants and tax deductions—rose far more rapidly than the rate of inflation.[16] By 2016, unless tuition and fee increases moderate, "the average cost of a public college will have more than doubled in just 15 years, according to the U.S. Department of Education."[17] As a result, college student debt soared at public and private institutions, approaching $1 trillion by 2010, more than the amount Americans owe in credit card debt.[18] This compounded the difficulties of recession-era graduates who were obliged to begin paying off their loans. Roughly two in three students interviewed for the Heldrich Center study borrowed funds, typically from the federal student loan programs, which funds about 85 percent of borrowing. The majority of new college graduates owed $20,000, measured in median terms. Graduates' median public college or university debt was $18,680, whereas private college debt was $24,460. College graduates whose annual earnings were $30,000 owed the same amount as those who earned up to $60,000.

Most students surveyed for the *Work Trends* research reported scant progress in paying down their debt. Only 13 percent had wiped out their college debt; one in four had not paid off any of it. Adding to their financial challenges, nearly half have other financial obligations, including paying off credit card balances. Moreover, most of the one in five recent college graduates enrolled in graduate and professional schools are borrowing more to pay for tuition and living expenses and already owe, on average, an additional $10,000. More than six in ten students enrolled in graduate and professional school have yet to pay off any of their debt.[19]

Student loan indebtedness profoundly affects the lifestyles of young people. More than one in four (27 percent) resided with parents or family members in order to save money. Significant numbers of students (25 percent) accepted any available job just to help them pay off their loans. More than one in four postponed further education until they made progress on retiring their debts. Nearly one in five recent graduates worked a second job to help pay their bills. The debt burden also influenced 40 percent of our respondents to delay major purchases such as a car or house. Another 14 percent even delayed marriage plans because of their loan obligations.

MORE GRINDERS THAN SLACKERS

In countless books and articles, sociologists, human resource experts, and management consultants portray Millennial (Generation Y) graduates entering the workforce in the 2000s as motivated principally by personal fulfillment. Jean Twenge, coauthor of *Generation Me*, argues that these young people commonly "work to live," whereas older workers from the baby-boom generation "live to work."[20] Millennials were said to have a sense of entitlement and be more likely to be disloyal to their employers, skeptical of authority, and in need of constant praise at work.[21]

While some recent graduates and younger professionals may reflect these attributes, our *Work Trends* data offered solid evidence that the newest batch of college graduates do not hold these views. In fact, they are grateful for the jobs they have, are inclined to stay at their jobs, like their work, and are no less committed to their jobs than older workers.[22] Based on the evidence gathered in our surveys, young graduates entering the labor market are much more likely to be "grinders"—people who work hard to get ahead—than "slackers"—people who are lazy and feel entitled. A remarkably high 82 percent of college graduates worked at least part-time during the school year. More than seven in ten managed one to three part- or full-time jobs while enrolled in college. Of these, over a third (36 percent) juggled full-time work and college studies. Nearly all—more than nine in ten—recent college graduates earned money at summer jobs and/or between semesters at school.[23] Large numbers of students, four in ten in our surveys, used their savings to pay for their college education.

Based on the evidence gathered in our surveys, young graduates entering the labor market are much more likely to be "grinders"—people who work hard to get ahead—than "slackers"—people who are lazy and feel entitled.

Given the apparent weaknesses in the U.S. labor market in the recession era, recent graduates who did find work are not likely to move to another job anytime soon. Six in ten of the graduates who obtained a job between 2006 and 2008 remained in that position at least two years, including nearly half (46 percent) who are still working at their first job. Sixteen percent stayed at their first job for between one and two years. For 2009–2010 graduates, nearly seven in ten (68 percent) remain at their first job, and another 9 percent have been there over one year. Nearly seven in ten said they were gratified to have a job. More than half were satisfied with their job duties, and six in ten were pleased to have health coverage. Graduates were somewhat disappointed with the availability of education and training opportunities at work, with less than half expressing approval. Similarly, they were less happy with advancement opportunities and income.

ARE HIGH SCHOOL AND COLLEGE GRADUATES PREPARED FOR WORK?

College and high school graduates in the early twenty-first century enter the labor market with deep feelings of insecurity. Many do not think they are prepared to succeed, and only 28 percent feel they are better prepared than prior generations. Tellingly, almost two-thirds of bachelor's degree recipients either think they need more education (39 percent) or have already gone back to school for more education (26 percent). Seven in ten high school graduates who are not enrolled in college full-time say they must go to college in order to get ahead in the U.S. economy.

College graduates from the classes of 2006 to 2011 are more confident about their career prospects than high school graduates during that era. By a margin of 62 to 23 percent, recent college graduates are more likely to say their education prepared them "extremely or pretty well" to succeed than not. High school graduates not enrolled in college were far less sanguine about their opportunities. Fewer than one in ten high school graduates felt they were "extremely well prepared" to get a job.

College graduates were less enamored with but still positive about how well prepared they were to get their first postcollege job. About one in two was dissatisfied with their school's effectiveness in preparing them to search for a job (see figure 5.3). Fewer than one in ten said they were extremely well prepared for that task. Internships were positively regarded by most college graduates. Those who completed internships during college felt better prepared to succeed at work, with 65 percent saying their college experiences prepared them to get a job, compared to just 44 percent of graduates who did not take an internship. Forty percent of those taking internships said their college experiences helped them find a job, compared to 31 percent of those not doing internships.

In numerous surveys conducted over the past few decades, detailed below, employers have consistently identified several core skills that they want entry-level employees to acquire before entering the workforce. We asked college graduates to comment on how well their colleges educated them on

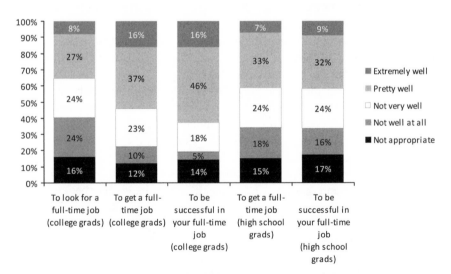

Figure 5.3. Young Graduates Are Not Sure They Are Well Prepared for Work
Sources: C. Van Horn, C. Zukin, and C. Stone, "Chasing the American Dream: Recent College Graduates and the Great Recession," Heldrich Center for Workforce Development, Rutgers University, May 2012; C. Van Horn, C. Zukin, M. Szeltner, and C. Stone, "Left Out. Forgotten? Recent High School Graduates and the Great Recession," Heldrich Center for Workforce Development, Rutgers University, June 2012.

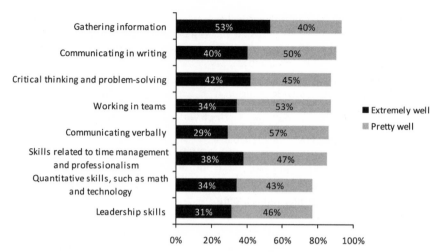

Figure 5.4. Recent College Graduates Uncertain They Have Mastered the Skills to Succeed at Work
Source: C. Van Horn, C. Zukin, and C. Stone, "Chasing the American Dream: Recent College Graduates and the Great Recession," Heldrich Center for Workforce Development, Rutgers University, June 2012.

the eight skill sets listed in figure 5.4. The combined categories of "extremely well" and "pretty well" paint a picture of the graduates' overall satisfaction with these basic competencies. Nine in ten or more believed they acquired sufficient information gathering and communicating skills. More than eight in ten felt reasonably well prepared to think critically, work in teams, and communicate verbally. About three-quarters were satisfied with the quantitative and leadership skills gained in college.

Another way to look at this, however, is to focus on those who complete college feeling fully capable in each area—those who consider themselves extremely well prepared. Applying this higher standard, the 50 percent barrier was exceeded only once when graduates reported that their college did an "extremely good job" teaching them how to gather information. Fewer than half (40 percent) think they acquired top-level writing, critical thinking, problem-solving, and time-management skills. Just one in three believed they graduated with high-level competencies in quantitative skills, including math and technology, verbal communications, and leadership skills.

Having an internship made a modest contribution to skills development in four of the eight areas, proving that all internships are certainly not alike. College interns were about ten percentage points more likely to say they have extremely well-developed leadership, communications, and quantitative skills. There was very little difference between those who did and did not do internships in the areas of time management and professionalism, working in teams, and problem-solving.

Recent graduates are pleased they attended college by a margin of nine to one, and just 3 percent would not have gone to college. Yet more than two of three graduates, with the benefit of hindsight, wished they had done things differently. Just under 30 percent said they would have arranged for more internships, and one-quarter would have visited their career development office earlier and more often so they get their job search under way. Another one-fifth would have taken more career-related classes. Just 14 percent would have chosen a different college to attend. Responding to an article on SmartMoney, a website managed by the *Wall Street Journal*, about the job experiences of recent college graduates, Alex had this advice for his fellow graduates:

> As an employed graduate of the class of 2012, I know exactly what the job market is like. College students need to escape their naivety and realize that applying for jobs is a contact sport. Parents aren't on campus to guide their son or daughter to the right track . . . students need to take it upon themselves and make employment a priority. Relevant extracurriculars, a high GPA (3.5+), and solid internship experiences are prerequisites for employment. Students are employable, no matter their degree. America is dynamic and students need to be the same. Swapping a night at the campus bar for a night applying for jobs shouldn't be so barbaric. Working exceptionally hard from the day you step on campus will yield positive results; that's the conversation you need to have with your students. It worked for me. Hard work beats talent, when talent doesn't work.[24]

Based on the Heldrich Center's survey findings, students must devote more effort, and colleges must bolster advising to help college students select their academic majors and courses. In response to students' frustration, several colleges and universities, though by no means the majority, are initiating strategies to better prepare their students for the labor market. Summarizing some of these new approaches, Lauren Webber of the *Wall Street Journal* wrote,

> Some schools are beginning to make career development a mission-critical aspect of the college experience, with everything from ramped-up career services to academic programs emphasizing real-world applications and efforts to engage faculty in practical mentoring. "We're seeing the emergence of a new model of education that blends liberal and applied learning," said Debra Humphreys, head of public affairs at the American Association of Colleges and Universities.[25]

Recent college graduates told us they would most like to "do over" their choice of academic major. Nearly four in ten had second thoughts. It is apparent that very little job or career-oriented thinking went into the selection of college majors. When choosing among academic majors, which often exceed one hundred at large universities, less than half (39 percent) of the respondents considered postcollege job opportunities. Fewer than one in ten graduates considered long-range earnings potential in their chosen fields. Even fewer—only 3 percent—had factored in entering salaries in their field.

Recent college graduates told us they would most like to "do over" their choice of academic major. Nearly four in ten had second thoughts. It is apparent that very little job or career-oriented thinking went into the selection of college majors.

Asked what they might have done to improve their labor market success, more than four in ten recent college graduates would have pursued a professional major, such as business or health care. Nearly a third would have selected a science, technology, engineering, or math major. A majority of recent college graduates also regretted they had not taken more computer and technology courses. One-third would have enrolled in more business, finance, or quantitative skills classes. Roughly one of every four college graduates also would have taken more writing courses.

High school graduates not attending college also expressed regrets about how they managed their education, with about two-thirds wishing they had done some things differently. Some young graduates blamed themselves for not paying enough attention to their economic futures, while others faulted the secondary school advising system. Overall, about one in four would have been more careful about their elective courses; similar numbers would have taken more classes directly related to career preparation. Twice as many blacks and Hispanics than whites (43 vs. 21 percent) said they should have been more careful in selecting their electives. Nearly a third felt they were not sufficiently prepared for college, including two in ten whites and four in ten nonwhites.

Employers' Views

It is instructive to compare employers' expectations about new hires with the perceptions of recent high school and college graduates about whether they are ready to meet those expectations. In survey after survey, employers urge colleges and high schools to equip students with academic and applied skills, including the ability to work in teams, communicate effectively, and complete complex tasks. For example, a 2010 survey conducted by Hart Research Associates for the Association of American Colleges and Universities reported that nearly eight in ten employers expect colleges and universities to develop their students' ability to apply skills to real-world settings through internships or other hands-on experiences.[26] Nearly nine in ten employers want colleges to teach students how to communicate effectively orally and in writing. Three-quarters of employers believe graduates should be able to connect choices and actions to ethical decisions. Seven in ten employers called for a strong educational foundation in teamwork skills and the ability to collaborate with others in diverse settings.

When assessing new entrants to the workforce, employers said they are not getting what they want and need. A survey of employers by the Conference Board, the Society for Human Resource Management, the Partnership for 21st Century Skills, and Corporate Voices for Working Families reported that they valued applied skills, including professionalism, teamwork, oral communication, and ethics and social responsibility.[27] While these employers said college graduates were "adequate" in fundamental knowledge and applied skills, less than one-quarter regarded the young graduates as excellently prepared. Employers offer far more negative evaluations of high school graduates. One employer summarized his reactions:

> In our industry most of the people that I talk to that are in management, they're discouraged with not only the higher education part, but just coming out of high school, the quality of people, the students that are coming to potential employers. That they may have a high school diploma, but they can't even fill out an application correctly. They can't spell. They can't read and write. But, yet they got this diploma.[28]

The findings from the Conference Board survey of employers, highlighted below, demonstrate that many employers no longer regard the high school diploma as sufficient for workforce preparation. Rather, they expect individuals to complete at least two years of postsecondary education. Because not enough high schools offer robust career and technical education programs, the burden of workforce preparation has shifted to public and private colleges and universities.[29]

These are among the main findings from the Conference Board's survey of employers about the abilities of high school graduates:

- Over 40 percent of employers evaluated high school graduates as deficient in their overall preparation for entry-level jobs; about the same proportion viewed high school graduates as adequately prepared.
- While about half of employers considered "writing in English" as a very important skill for entry-level job performance, nearly three-quarters of them graded high school graduates deficient in this basic knowledge.

• Nearly two-thirds of employers ranked reading comprehension as very important for a high school graduate's first job, but one-third of employers ranked high school graduates as deficient.
• About one-third of employers viewed mathematics as a very important basic skill, and about four in ten employers rated these graduates as deficient in mathematics.
• In applied skills, about eight in ten employers regarded professionalism and work ethic as very important, but eight in ten employers assessed high school graduates as deficient.
• More than half of employers assessed critical thinking and problem-solving as very important applied skills, and seven in ten employers rated high school graduates as deficient.

Two- and four-year college graduates received better assessments from employers:

• Nearly half of employers graded new workforce entrants with a two-year college degree as deficient in writing in English, and one in four employers rated graduates with a four-year degree as deficient in writing in English.
• Nearly half of employers reported two-year college graduates were deficient in written communications, while over one-quarter of college graduates were viewed this way.
• About four in ten employers regarded graduates of two-year degrees as deficient in leadership; another one-quarter of employers rated four-year-degree graduates as deficient in leadership—an applied skill rated as very important by employers for graduates with a four-year degree.[30]

Employers' laments about the quality and quantity of job applicants are common whether the economy is skimming along with low unemployment or slogging through a recession. For example, a recent study released by the large temporary services company, Manpower, reported that "one third of employers worldwide cannot find qualified talent." ManpowerGroup President Jonas Prising observed, "Being a college graduate doesn't mean you're work-ready."[31] When job openings occur, employers are impatient to fill them quickly and at the lowest wage or salary possible. Given the intense competitive pressures that many firms endure, they are not willing to allocate resources to train entry-level workers. Rather, they prefer to shift those responsibilities to individuals and educational institutions. Employers have an even greater advantage in a struggling economy because job applicants are more bountiful and the incumbent workforce is much less likely to jump ship and move to a competitor.[32]

Just because companies may be exaggerating their recruitment problems to deflect criticism about compensation levels does not mean their concerns should be dismissed. To begin with, employers—whether in the private or the public sector—always have more power in the labor market. Employers have the jobs; only job applicants with unique skills and experience are in strong negotiating positions. Moreover, many companies can either relocate to a different region of the United States or move their operations to a country where wages and benefits are more to their liking. Companies can and will go elsewhere to find qualified workers.

DOES EDUCATION SERVE THE NEEDS
OF EMPLOYERS? HOW MUCH SHOULD IT?

Clearly, there are major differences in the perceptions of educators and employers about the quality and purposes of education. Educators believe they have prepared their students to succeed in the workplace and in life. Most employers are not convinced that students learn in high school or college to properly perform their job responsibilities. Written communications in the workplace (say, a PowerPoint presentation) may encompass different rules and goals than college students learn in classroom assignments. College courses test students in many ways but not necessarily the ones that matter most to employers.

Employers are voicing their dissatisfaction and ratcheting up pressure on educators to do a better job of preparing work-ready graduates. Although far from a coordinated, coherent strategy, employers' concerns goaded governors and legislators into raising high school graduation standards throughout the nation. Educators are reconsidering how they educate the next generation of students for careers. In response to employer complaints, colleges and universities are expanding internship and cooperative education programs, creating new academic majors and research institutes, and forming employer advisory committees to shape college and university curricula.

It is the accepted wisdom of economists, employers, and politicians that a college and high school education should be better aligned with labor market needs. American citizens agree with this conclusion. In a 2011 Gallup poll, half of adults (including younger people) said that earning money is the main reason students should get education beyond high school. One in three said the main purpose of education was "to get a good job."[33] No other reason polled by the researchers was even close. Only 5 percent of adults said that the value of a postsecondary education was "to become a well-rounded person." In an era of stubborn, long-term unemployment and global economic competition, the purposes and performance of high school and postsecondary education will and should be reassessed.

For nearly forty years, beginning most notably with the publication of *A Nation at Risk: The Imperative for Education Reform* by the National Commission on Educational Excellence of the U.S. Department of Education, a broad consensus has developed around the notion that the education system must be improved so it can graduate better prepared knowledge-economy workers. At this juncture in American history, there is little controversy over the need to strengthen the K–12 education system through higher standards and rigorous assessments of students, teachers, and institutions.

Although the task of improving high school education is far from complete, greater scrutiny from government, private employers, and scholars is now focused on American colleges and universities. In 2006, for example, a commission appointed by U.S. Secretary of Education Margaret Spellings issued a highly critical report about American higher education that contained dozens of recommendations for improvement.[34] With costs rising and millions of college graduates either unemployed or working in jobs that do not require a college degree, questions are being raised about the effectiveness of colleges and universities in delivering an education that results in acceptable results for individuals and for U.S. competitiveness.

Colleges and universities and their students cannot do much to affect the demand for new workers, but new approaches can be implemented to improve the preparation of new college graduates for the workforce. Students will benefit from more information and advice about how to achieve their personal and professional goals in a daunting labor market. Millions of college and high school graduates and military veterans retiring from active duty make critical education choices without reliable, independent advice from government agencies or educators. These young people—and older working adults, too—must be able to obtain accurate, unbiased information about the potential value of a bewildering array of academic specializations. Students and their families want to know more about the return on investment for private and public universities and "elite" name-brand colleges as well as community colleges. They would like a better understanding of how the educational path they are considering might help them get a job and career. Congress is beginning to consider these issues. Several versions of draft legislation would require colleges and universities to publicize detailed information on postgraduation earnings, average costs, and debts, including one introduced in 2012 by Senator Ron Wyden of Oregon, known as the Student Right to Know before You Go Act.[35]

High school and college educators are likely to face additional pressures and significant new challenges in the early decades of the twenty-first century. As high school and college graduates enter the workforce, many are profoundly disappointed and angry. Educational institutions cannot simply absolve themselves of responsibility by complaining about a volatile economy characterized by the "creative destruction" of jobs and businesses. As policymakers recalibrate the value of public investments in higher education, they are demanding greater efficiency and performance from colleges while simultaneously shifting greater responsibility for paying tuition fees to students and their families.

A recurrent theme of the recession-era labor market is that graduates are not getting the jobs they want and businesses are not getting the talent they need. Pressures will intensify on higher-education institutions to prepare students for the world of work not only by engaging employers but also by responding to their needs. Colleges and universities will be expected to acknowledge that their institutions are part of—not apart from—global economic competition. As summarized by the National Governors Association in its 2011 report, *Degrees for What Jobs?*,

> A large part of ensuring a fertile environment for new and innovative industries and the well-paying jobs they bring is for universities and colleges to strategically match students, degrees, skills, and research to an innovation economy, as well as to state and national economic development efforts to develop and revitalize key industry clusters. . . . With globalization encouraging businesses to extend their ties beyond local areas, universities and colleges must contend with the reality that they can attract and hold businesses by offering them worker training, world-class research and flexible relationships in a way that is specific and responsive.[36]

This report for the nation's governors and much commentary probes this central question: in what ways can and should colleges and universities do more to prepare graduates for the labor market?

Better alignment between educational preparation and employers' needs will not grow the economy by itself, but it will help ameliorate structural unemployment. Better matches between supply and demand will not only put more people to work but also make established firms more competitive, which in turn will generate higher and more sustained growth. Many economists and management consultants believe that stronger alignment between the skills workers possess and the skills employers require would lower the U.S. unemployment rate, though there is no consensus by how much.[37] Researchers at the Federal Reserve Bank and other nonpartisan economists have concluded that millions of jobs could be added to the U.S. economy if workers with needed skills were available. For example, economists Harry Holzer and Marek Hlavac in reviewing the literature on this topic concluded,

> From a policy point of view, it is therefore important that the skills obtained by workers match the areas of the labor market where demand is strongest, and that

we give them the credentials sought by employers in well-paying jobs. Potential workers need more career guidance from workforce development systems on where labor market demand is strong, and employers need to be engaged in the process of generating workers' skills to fill their available jobs, through "sectoral" training programs, apprenticeships, and other kinds of incumbent worker training.[38]

There are abundant examples of skills shortages even during the Great Recession economy where millions of people are unemployed. For example, a *Bloomberg Businessweek* cover story in September 2011 noted that "Silicon Valley companies fight over software engineers; Union Health Service and the Harvard hospital system complain it's hard to find nurses and technicians; manufacturers like Caterpillar and Westinghouse can't hire enough welders and machinists to keep their state-of-the-art lathes running."[39]

While thoughtful reporting will uncover these mismatches during most any economic period, the Great Recession spurred insightful researchers and policymakers to focus investments and leadership on training programs that provide real bang for the buck for the workforce. Michigan's *No Worker Left Behind* is one such example. Initiated by Governor Jennifer Granholm in 2007, it had served over 125,000 people by 2010. The program consolidated several funding streams and reimbursed unemployed and dislocated workers for community college and training courses in targeted sectors of Michigan's economy where employers face skilled labor shortages. The program was particularly effective in Michigan's advanced manufacturing clusters around the automotive and defense industries.[40]

Higher-education leaders must manage an intensely competitive environment and balance conflicting demands. They serve their students, employers who hire their graduates, and governors and state legislators who fund public institutions and student aid programs. College and university administrators and faculties also want to protect their historic roles as teachers and creators of knowledge and critical thought. In the new global, competitive marketplace that characterizes the U.S. economy, colleges and universities are being questioned sharply, even by those who work in academia. For example, in a widely cited study that tracked over two thousand students from 2005 to 2009, sociologists Richard Arum and Josipa Roksa concluded that students typically do not invest much time in their studies or take demanding courses. They found that one in three undergraduates had not improved crucial writing and reasoning tasks since their first semester in college.[41]

Another critical assessment was offered by Ohio University Professor Richard Vedder:

> College costs are soaring, and almost certainly the education system is becoming less efficient, at a time when labor productivity is rising elsewhere. The ic-

ing on the cake is the total disconnect between student job expectations, college curricula, and the realities of today's labor market. More college grads are taking low-skilled jobs previously occupied by those with high school diplomas—more than 80,000 bartenders, for example, have at least a bachelor's degree. If students are successful in graduating (a big "if"), they often are saddled with debt and only able to get a relatively low-paying job.[42]

The strong correlation between higher education and higher earnings during America's post–World War II period is an unassailable fact. Up to this point, postsecondary education has paid off for most graduates, but it is not clear if that pattern will hold. Right now the earnings gaps between those with college or advanced degrees and those who do not complete college or who obtain only a high school diploma are substantial and have widened over the past two decades. Thirty years ago, recent college graduates earned about $4,000 more than young high school graduates: by 2010, the gap had tripled to $12,000, in inflation adjusted dollars. According to an analysis of earnings data from the U.S. Census by Adam Looney and Michael Greenstone, "An individual who entered college in 1980 could expect to earn about $260,000 more over the course of her life compared to someone who received only a high school diploma. In contrast, for someone starting college in 2010, the expected lifetime increase in earnings . . . was more than $450,000.[43]

College degree earners often realize other economic benefits, such as greater economic mobility, than those with less formal education. Children who get college degrees do far better in moving out of the economic strata where they were raised. Only 16 percent of children who began life in the bottom income quintile but received college degrees ended up in the same income level.[44] Finally, college graduates are more likely to remain employed during economic downturns and more likely to be reemployed if they are laid off.

Structural transformations in the economy and in higher education threaten the financial and generational promise of higher education. The huge influx of college graduates and the recession-provoked drop in demand for entry-level employees are depressing the market value of a college education. Anticipated retirements by the large baby-boomer generation were supposed to create enough room in the labor market for the large numbers of new college graduates. In 2000, the Bureau of Labor Statistics noted, "For the first time in many years . . . college-level job openings between 1998 and 2008 will nearly equal the number of college-educated entrants to the labor force. And a primary reason is the large number of retirements expected from workers at the edge of the 'baby boom' generation."[45]

Reeling from the Great Recession's impact of the value of housing and retirement portfolios, millions of baby boomers are working longer than expected. Nearly four in ten who are working past the age of sixty-two reported in 2009 that "the bad economy has forced them to delay their retirement plans," according to the Pew Research Center.[46] The growing ranks of college graduates are outpacing forecasted job growth. The share of workers over age twenty-five in the labor force with college degrees has increased from 31 percent in 1999 to 36 percent in 2012, even as employers have slashed millions of jobs.[47]

The rising costs of higher education and associated debt burdens for graduates raise other troubling questions. As the average cost of tuition and fees increased significantly, students and their families became more dependent on loans to finance education. With two in three students borrowing to pay for college, many will enter the job market already in substantial debt. Increases in the cost of a four-year college degree have outpaced the cost of living and growth in family incomes. Between 1998 and 2009, the average cost of a college degree rose 40 percent at public colleges and 18 percent at private institutions. However, the Consumer Price Index increased by only 27 percent, and average compensation increased by less than 1 percent (.5 percent).[48] In 2012, the average college graduate owed 25 percent more than those who graduated in 1998, in constant dollars.[49] Yet real wages for new college graduates have barely budged since 1989.[50]

NEXT-GENERATION EDUCATION REFORMS

Few institutions enjoy such a deep reservoir of national trust than colleges and universities. What should they do to justify and protect that good faith? What will students and families do to ensure their investments are worthwhile? In the early years of the twenty-first century, it is deeply embedded in American culture that all students who want to experience the good life should go to college. As Georgetown University's Anthony Carnevale summarized in his essay "College for All?":

> The American belief in "college for all" arises from deep in our individualistic cultural bias. We welcome an increasing reliance on college as the arbiter of individual career opportunity since, in theory at least, using education to mediate opportunity allows us to expand merit-based success without surrendering individual responsibility. . . . The use of postsecondary education as the gateway to opportunity also complements our other key preferences for an open economy and a limited government.[51]

Attending college is still a lifting dream for millions of young people and their parents. Seven in ten of the recent high school graduates interviewed by the Heldrich Center in 2012 who were not attending college hoped to do so in the coming years. Despite struggling in the labor market, few college

College education remains the American repository of career and personal transformation and the pipeline of talent for major employers. This adds urgency to our debates in the public square about how we measure and improve higher-education outcomes.

graduates regretted their experiences. The nature and quality of a college education is far harder to evaluate and value in a chaotic and unpredictable labor market. College education remains the American repository of career and personal transformation and the pipeline of talent for major employers. This adds urgency to our debates in the public square about how we measure and improve higher-education outcomes.

There is enormous interest in assessing the value of higher education for many reasons, not the least of which is the rising cost of a college degree. It seems inevitable, then, that policymakers, students, and their families will want to mine earnings and employment data to assess the benefits and costs of not only a college education but also specific academic specializations. A more robust portrayal will inform critical decisions made by students and institutions. Among the questions that should be addressed are the following:

- *What's the new graduate first job index?* College graduates' entry-level jobs have major implications for their future salaries and employment prospects in the long run. Potential students want to know about recent graduates' success in getting jobs and their earnings.
- *What are returns on investment from academic majors?* Decades of scholarship and the personal experience of generations have long established that professions such as law, engineering, and corporate management pay better than education, human services, social work, and publishing. When the difference in lifetime earnings potential between one major and another is estimated to be more than 300 percent, stakeholders will demand detailed information on the payoff from undergraduate majors.[52]
- *What is each college's financial return on investment for graduates?* Within a matter of years, colleges and universities will no longer be able to characterize their value by pointing to their selectivity and reputational rankings. Rather, they will be expected to report on their success in educating young people and their alumni's labor market experiences. In 2012, the Obama administration and the U.S. Department of Education asked colleges and universities to provide information on a voluntary basis and then

posted the results on the Web as part of an initiative they called the College Affordability and Transparency Center.[53]

Understanding educational outcomes and making meaningful comparisons across institutions will require answering complex questions. It is relatively easy to determine the return on investments from various colleges or majors. Far more difficult are the tasks of figuring out whether and how colleges and universities can steer, nudge, and support students to graduate ready for work in our knowledge economy and how they can best prepare for the long-term needs in the labor market. Some of these questions include the following:

- How can high schools and colleges ensure that larger numbers of students graduate with high school diploma and college degrees?
- How can educators reduce the amount of time needed to obtain college degrees without compromising quality?
- How can educators prepare students in the core competencies that are demanded in the labor market? Should there be exit exams to prove learning progress?
- How can we link information about high school, college, and labor markets so we can better inform policymakers and institutional leaders about the progress and success of American workers?
- How can we induce universities and colleges to improve performance without diminishing the value of independent research and teaching institutions that succeed by pursuing knowledge creation?

The next two chapters examine the economy into which millions of young people are graduating and the policies that may lead to a brighter future for them.

NOTES

1. Claudia Goldin and Lawrence F. Katz, "The Race between Education and Technology: The Evolution of U.S. Educational Wage Differentials, 1890 to 2005," NBER Working Paper no. 12984, National Bureau of Economic Research, Cambridge, MA, March 2007.

2. Erin Sparks and Mary Jo Waits with Carl E. Van Horn, Maria Heidkamp, and Aaron Fichtner, "Degrees for What Jobs? Raising Expectations for Colleges and Universities in a Global Economy," March 2011, http://www.nga.org/files/live/sites/NGA/files/pdf/1103DEGREESJOBS.PDF.

3. David Wessel and Stephanie Banchero, "Education Slowdown Threatens U.S.," *Wall Street Journal*, April 26, 2012, 1.

4. Adam Looney and Michael Greenstone, "Regardless of the Cost, College Still Matters," The Hamilton Project, October 2012.

5. Jessica Godofsky, Cliff Zukin, and Carl E. Van Horn, "Unfulfilled Expectations: Recent College Graduates Struggle in a Troubled Economy," in *Work Trends* (New Brunswick, NJ: Heldrich Center at Rutgers, The State University of New Jersey, May 2011); Charley Stone, Carl E. Van Horn, and Cliff Zukin, "Chasing the American Dream: Recent College Graduates and the Great Recession," in *Work Trends* (May 2012); Carl E.Van Horn, Cliff Zukin, Mark Szeltner, and Charley Stone, "Left Out. Forgotten? Recent High School Graduates and the Great Recession," in *Work Trends* (June 2012).

6. U.S. Census National Community Survey, "Educational Attainment in the United States, 2011, Detailed Tables," 2011, http://www.census.gov/hhes/socdemo/education/data/cps/2011/tables.html.

7. Heidi Shierholz, Natalie Sabadish, and Hilary Wething, "The Class of 2012, Labor Market for Young Graduates Remains Grim," Economic Policy Institute, Washington, DC, May 3, 2012.

8. Shierholz et al., "The Class of 2012, Labor Market for Young Graduates Remains Grim."

9. Respondent's interview, Heldrich Center for Workforce Development (March 2011).

10. Respondent's interview, Heldrich Center for Workforce Development (March 2011).

11. Peter D. Hart Research Associates/Public Opinion Strategies for Achieve, Inc., "Rising to the Challenge: Are High School Graduates Prepared for College and Work?," survey of high school graduates from the classes of 2002, 2003, and 2004, February 2005, http://www.achieve.org/files/pollreport_0.pdf.

12. Respondent's interview, Heldrich Center for Workforce Development (March 2011).

13. "In a Weak Job Market, One in Two College Graduates Are Jobless or Underemployed," *Huffington Post*, April 22, 2012, http://www.huffingtonpost.com/2012/04/22/job-market-college-graduates_n_1443738.html.

14. Post on *New York Times* website in response to the Bob Herbert column, "The Data and the Reality," December 28, 2010.

15. Godofsky et al., "Unfulfilled Expectations"; Stone et al., "Chasing the American Dream."

16. "Trends in College Pricing," College Board Advocacy and Policy Center, 2011.

17. Andrew Martin and Andrew W. Lehren, "A Generation Hobbled by Soaring Cost of College," *New York Times*, May 12, 2012, 1.

18. Martin and Lehren, "A Generation Hobbled by the Soaring Cost of College," 1.

19. Godofsky et al., "Unfulfilled Expectations"; Stone et al., "Chasing the American Dream."

20. Julie Halpert, "Could Millennials Spawn a Productivity Crisis?," *Fiscal Times*, May 23, 2012, http://www.thefiscaltimes.com/Articles/2012/05/23/Could

-Millennials-Spawn-a-Productivity-Crisis.aspx#page1; Jean Twenge, *Generation Me: Why Today's Young Americans Are More Confident, Assertive, Entitled—and More Miserable Than Ever Before* (New York: Free Press, 2006).

21. Cathy Trower, presentation, Brown University, 2009, http://www.brown.edu/Administration/Provost/Advance/Trower%20Generations%20and%20Mentoring.pdf; Ron Zemke, Claire Raines, and Bob Filipczak, *Generations at Work* (New York: Amacom, 2000).

22. Cliff Zukin and Mark Szeltner, "Net Impact, Talent Report: What Workers Want in 2012," May 2012, http://www.heldrich.rutgers.edu/sites/default/files/content/Net_Impact_Talent_Report_0.pdf.

23. Godofsky et al., "Unfulfilled Expectations"; Stone et al., "Chasing the American Dream."

24. Quintin Fottrell, "The Jobless Class of 2012," Smart Money, Real Time Advice Blogs, July 6, 2012.

25. Lauren Weber, "Colleges Get Career-Minded," *Wall Street Journal*, May 22, 2012, A3.

26. Hart Research Associates, "Raising the Bar: Employers' Views on College Learning in the Wake of the Economic Downturn," January 10, 2010, http://www.aacu.org/leap/documents/2009_EmployerSurvey.pdf.

27. Jill Casner-Lotto, Linda Barrington, and Mary Wright, "Are They Really Ready to Work?," October 2006, http://www.conference-board.org/publications/publicationdetail.cfm?publicationid=1218.

28. Steve Farkas, "Hiring and Higher Education: Business Executives Talk about the Costs and Benefits of College," Committee for Economic Development, Washington, DC, 2001, 10.

29. "Investing in America's Future: A Blueprint for Transforming Career and Technical Education," April 2012, http://www2.ed.gov/about/offices/list/ovae/pi/cte/transforming-career-technical-education/pdf.

30. Casner-Lotto et al., "Are They Really Ready to Work?"

31. Roya Wolverson, "Why Can't College Grads Find Better Jobs?" *Time Business*, May 20, 2011.

32. Shierholz et al., "The Class of 2012, Labor Market for Young Graduates Remains Grim."

33. "Most Americans See College as Essential to Getting a Good Job," Gallup/Lumina Foundation, August 18, 2011, http://www.gallup.com/poll/149045/americans-college-essential-getting-good-job.aspx.

34. "A Test of Leadership, Charting the Future of U.S. Higher Education," 2006, http://www2.ed.gov/about/bdscomm/list/hiedfuture/reports/final-report.pdf.

35. Senator Wyden's Office, "Wyden Bill Takes Guessing Game Out of College," February 9, 2012, http://www.wyden.senate.gov/news/press-releases/wyden-bill-takes-guessing-game-out-of-choosing-a-college.

36. Sparks et al., "Degrees for What Jobs?"

37. Sparks et al., "Degrees for What Jobs?" See, for example, Jinzhu Chen, Prakash Kannan, Prakash Loungani, and Bharat Trehan, "New Evidence on Cyclical and Structural Sources of Unemployment," IMF Working Paper (WP/11/106).

38. Harry J. Holzer and Marek Hlavac, *A Very Uneven Road: U.S. Labor Markets in the Past 30 Years* (New York: Russell Sage Foundation, March 2012), 32.

39. Drake Bennett, "Can Retraining Give the Unemployed a Second Chance?," September 14, 2011, http://www.businessweek.com/magazine/can-retraining-give -the-unemployed-a-second-chance-09142011.html.

40. "Fact Sheet, No Worker Left Behind," May 2010, http://www.michigan.gov/ documents/nwlb/NWLB_Fact_Sheet_Final_203216_7.pdf.

41. Richard Arum and Josipa Roksa, *Academically Adrift: Limited Learning on College Campuses* (Chicago: University of Chicago Press, 2010).

42. "Employers Catch On: Why Look Down on a Business Degree?" *New York Times*, Room for Debate, April 17, 2011, http://www.nytimes.com/roomforde bate/2011/04/17/why-look-down-on-a-business-degree/employers-are-catching-on.

43. Adam Looney and Michael Greenstone, "Regardless of the Cost, College Still Matters."

44. Ron Haskins and Isabel Sawhill, "Getting Ahead or Losing Ground: Mobil- ity in America," Brookings Institution, February 2008, http://www.brookings.edu/ reports/2008/02_economic_mobility_sawhill.aspx.

45. U.S. Bureau of Labor Statistics, "Quarterly Outlook: The Outlook for College Graduates, 1998–2008: A Balancing Act."

46. Pew Research Center, "Recession Turns Graying Office Grayer: America's Changing Workforce," September 2009.

47. U.S. Bureau of Labor Statistics civilian labor force statistic as of the second quarter of 2012.

48. Employment Cost Index, December 2001–December 2010, http://www.bls .gov/web/eci/ecconstnaics.pdf.

49. The Project on Student Debt, National Center for Education Statistics, U.S. Department of Education, 2009 National Postsecondary Student Aid Survey.

50. Economic Policy Institute, http://www.epi.org/publication/bp340-labor-mar ket-young-graduates.

51. Anthony P. Carnevale, "College for All?," *Change*, January/February 2008, 1, http://www.changemag.org/Archives/Back%20Issues/January-February%202008/ abstract-college-for-all.html.

52. Reported in Georgetown University Center on Education and the Workforce, Anthony P. Carnevale, Jeff Strohl, and Michelle Melton, "What's It Worth: The Economic Value of College Majors," May 2011, http://cew.georgetown.edu/whatsit worth.

53. http://collegecost.ed.gov/catc.

Chapter Six

Unfinished Business: Recovering from the Great Recession

Crack down on illegal immigrants who take jobs from citizens of the United States. Stop giving breaks to businesses raking in millions to billions in profit which are yet unwilling to hire US workers or keep their factories in the US.

—Interviews conducted by the Heldrich Center, August 2011

The Great Recession and the economic changes in the first decade of the twenty-first century inevitably give rise to reexaminations of American policies and priorities. Troubling realities about the American workplace raise important questions about the kind of economic future the nation would like or can achieve. To American workers, the answer is simple: create good jobs for everyone who wants to work. They want the public and private sector to invest and rebuild the economy. They expect national leaders to protect workers from the random "economic violence" of globalization and rapid technological change. The U.S. economy must strengthen its ability to successfully compete worldwide with perennial economic powers, such as Europe and Japan, and rising ones, such as China, India, and Brazil.

Millions of U.S. workers are still hurting from the emergency created by the Great Recession. By the fall of 2012, about half of the approximately 9 million jobs that disappeared during the recession had returned to the economy. At the same time, workers continued to struggle with an evolving crisis brought about by decades of rapid globalization and technological transformations. In this chapter, I assess the progress the United States has made in responding to the challenges caused by the Great Recession and the policy disagreements and gridlock that followed when the economy did not recover quickly. I also discuss the need for more effective strategies to combat joblessness and heal a wounded economy. The next and final chapter outlines the major reforms that are essential for building a stronger labor market and restoring opportunities for all American workers.

BOLD ACTIONS BATTLE THE FINANCIAL CRISIS

Before considering the next frontier of policy options, let's review the battle to recover from the Great Recession. During the recession and its aftermath, the United States experienced the highest unemployment rates in over thirty years and the longest period of negative growth since the Great Depression. As many as 20 million Americans collected unemployment benefits in 2009 at the recession's peak.[1]

The nation's economy plunged into deep economic troubles as multi-billion-dollar global investments tanked and financial institutions neared collapse or failed entirely. Financial industry executives exposed their corporations to unprecedented risks, loading their portfolios with high-risk mortgage-backed securities and other derivative instruments or by partnering with funds and companies that specialized in these high-stakes gambles. These financial strategies rested on the shaky foundation of grossly inflated and, in some instances, corrupt real estate and credit industries. Loans were extended to millions of individuals who could not afford to pay them. Investments were predicated on the unspoken assumption that housing prices would always increase. If the purchaser could no longer afford the mortgage payment, financial institutions would just sell the foreclosed property to the next customer.[2]

It is painfully clear that the leaders of many of these large financial institutions either did not believe that real estate prices would fall or did not care. They were collecting fees for the transactions and then selling potentially worthless assets to the next round of investors. The sudden and sharp decline in real estate assets meant that investments previously worth trillions of dollars were suddenly worth practically nothing. Global financial markets were traumatized, and credit was frozen worldwide. Government leaders were forced to take emergency actions in 2008.

Here are some highlights of the financial crisis that almost brought down the entire global financial system:

- In March 2008, JP Morgan Chase paid $236 billion and borrowed $30 billion from the U.S. government to salvage a nearly bankrupt Bear Stearns. The result—over five thousand employees were laid off.
- In April 2008, financial giant Lehman Brothers declared bankruptcy, sold off its assets, and terminated twenty-three thousand workers.
- In September 2008, federal home ownership agencies Fannie Mae and Freddie Mac, with trillions of dollars in their mortgage loan portfolios,

were placed under the conservatorship of the Federal Housing Finance Agency at a cost of $375 billion to U.S. taxpayers.

- Also in September 2008, the U.S. Treasury and Federal Reserve extended over $180 billion in loans to the American International Group (AIG), a global insurance giant, in order to save it from collapsing and bankrupting dozens of financial institutions.
- In October 2008, Congress passed the Emergency Economic Stabilization Act of 2008 with broad bipartisan support. The law established the $700 billion Troubled Asset Relief Program (known conventionally as TARP) to buy back bad loans ("toxic assets") from banks and financial institutions. The law required that banks exchange the purchase amounts for "equity warrants" and pledge to repay the federal government in the future. This bold measure had been championed by President George W. Bush, Treasury Secretary Henry Paulson, and Federal Reserve Chairman Ben Bernanke and supported by Democratic presidential candidate Barack Obama and Republican presidential candidate John McCain.
- In October and November 2008, previously profitable global financial institutions, such as Citigroup, Goldman Sachs, and Bank of America, received TARP monies, along with dozens of other financial firms.
- In late 2008, the U.S. Federal Reserve Bank slashed interest rates to near zero in order to shore up equity markets and encourage lending.
- Automakers Chrysler and GM received over $84 billion in loans and equity investments from the TARP program and U.S. government protection from creditors to enable them to restructure and avoid bankruptcy and massive layoffs.[3]

The federal government's swift actions subsequently became known as a "bailout" of financial institutions that were deemed "too big to fail." Washington policymakers were desperate to prevent a meltdown of the global financial and banking system. By doing so, they protected deposits and savings, recapitalized banks, and created a firewall against catastrophic unemployment, which had already skyrocketed from 5 percent in January 2008 to 7.8 percent in January 2009.[4]

With the global economy teetering on the brink of disaster and little or no time to explain and justify these swift actions, it is not surprising that taxpayers reacted negatively and that these actions subsequently became very controversial.[5] As was noted by the *Democracy in America* blog at *The Economist* in October 2010, the American public had sufficient reasons to distrust programs:

> Much of the public's anger over TARP flows from a sense that it perpetrated a good deal of distributive injustice. The widespread perception that the

relationship between Treasury and Wall Street was suspiciously cozy, and that taxpayer money saved the hides of a good number of especially well-connected multi-millionaire bankers is by no means unreasonable. However, it's certainly plausible that the bank bailout aspect of TARP was necessary to prevent a more catastrophic collapse. I suspect it was. But for many people the argument to this effect sounds a lot like supply-side arguments to the effect that tax cuts for rich people are our only sure path to economic recovery.[6]

Shortly after the November 2008 elections, President-elect Barack Obama, his new economic team, and Democratic leaders in Congress began crafting additional policy responses to the economic and financial emergency. In February 2009, soon after the inauguration of President Obama, Congress passed an $840 billion stimulus package that was unprecedented in its size and scope. Titled the American Recovery and Reinvestment Act (ARRA), the law included provisions that did the following:

• Provided $288 billion in tax cuts and benefits, principally by reducing wage taxes
• Increased federal funds for entitlement programs, such as extending unemployment benefits, by $224 billion
• Made $275 billion available for construction projects, grants to state and local governments, and renewable-energy investments

Institutions and government agencies receiving funds under the programs were required to regularly report on their use of the money. These data have been collected and are available to the public at the government website http://www.recovery.gov.

The enactment of the Emergency Economic Stabilization Act of 2008 and ARRA of 2009 demonstrated that policymakers in the White House, Congress, and the Federal Reserve could act decisively and in a bipartisan coordinated fashion when urgent responses were needed. In a matter of months, two presidential administrations (one Republican, one Democratic), leaders from both parties in Congress, and independent financial regulators, such as the Federal Reserve Bank, reached agreement on a rescue

The enactment of the Emergency Economic Stabilization Act of 2008 and ARRA of 2009 demonstrated that policymakers in the White House, Congress, and the Federal Reserve could act decisively and in a bipartisan coordinated fashion when urgent responses were needed.

plan for the economy. Together, these laws allocated over $1.5 trillion in loans, grants, and tax reductions to combating the economic woes gripping the nation and damaging millions of Americans who were losing jobs, financial assets, and even their homes.

At the time these two landmark bills were under consideration, and immediately after these laws took effect, progressive and conservative politicians and commentators sharply criticized the government's actions. Progressive economists warned that the stimulus package was too anemic to cure the nation's economic ills. Paul Krugman, a Nobel laureate in economics and *New York Times* columnist, wrote,

> You have a negative shock on the order of 6 percent of GDP [gross domestic product] . . . against this you had a stimulus bill of $800 billion—except $100 billion of that was AMT (Alternative Minimum Tax) extension that was going to happen anyway, another $200 billion was other tax cuts of dubious effectiveness, so you were left with $500 billion of spending, spread over more than 2 years—maybe 1.5 percent of GDP or less.[7]

Conservative members of Congress complained that President Obama's approach to reigniting economic growth not only was the wrong medicine but also a dangerous expansion of government power over the economy. Even though over 100 Republican members of Congress voted in favor of the TARP "bailouts" in 2008 when George W. Bush was president, no Republicans in the House of Representatives voted for the economic stimulus plan in early 2009. Economists, such as John Samples from the conservative CATO Institute, accused Congress of acting in a "lawless" manner, failing "to meet its constitutional obligations to deliberate, to check the other branches of government, or to be accountable to the American people."[8] The Center for Fiscal Accountability, led by the antitax conservative Grover Norquist, charged the Treasury

Independent, nonpartisan agencies, such as the Congressional Budget Office and the Government Accountability Office, concluded that the TARP "bailout," aggressive monetary policy by the Federal Reserve Bank, and the economic stimulus package (ARRA) achieved their fundamental objectives—averting a catastrophic global financial crisis and saving or creating millions of jobs.

and Congress of using TARP as a backdoor to "nationalize" financial and auto industries.[9] Despite supporting TARP when she was a vice-presidential candidate in 2008, former Alaska Governor Sarah Palin criticized it as "crony capitalism at its worst" in 2010. Republican presidential candidate and former Massachusetts Governor Mitt Romney praised aspects of TARP in his book *No Apology* but criticized its size and implementation during the 2012 campaign.[10]

While TARP and ARRA generated plenty of criticism as either too small or too large, dispassionate analysts offered more nuanced assessments. Independent, nonpartisan agencies, such as the Congressional Budget Office (CBO) and the Government Accountability Office (GAO), concluded that the TARP "bailout," aggressive monetary policy by the Federal Reserve Bank, and the economic stimulus package (ARRA) achieved their fundamental objectives—averting a catastrophic global financial crisis and saving or creating millions of jobs.[11]

For example, the CBO concluded that TARP will eventually cost the federal government approximately $19 billion, dramatically less than original estimates that exceeded $700 billion. In its March 2011 report on TARP, the CBO wrote,

> CBO estimates that the cost to the federal government of the TARP's transactions (also referred to as the subsidy cost), including grants for mortgage programs that have not been made yet, will amount to $19 billion. That cost stems largely from assistance to American International Group (AIG), aid to the automotive industry, and grant programs aimed at avoiding foreclosures. *Other transactions with financial institutions will, taken together, yield a net gain to the federal government, in CBO's estimation.* CBO's current estimate of the cost of the TARP's transactions is $6 billion less than the $25 billion estimate shown in the agency's previous report on the TARP. . . . The costs directly associated with the TARP, when taken in isolation have come out toward the low end of the range of possible outcomes anticipated when the program was launched . . . *the outcomes of most transactions made through the TARP were favorable for the federal government.*[12]

By and large, the financial institutions that received assistance from TARP paid back their loans, the U.S. Treasury sold its equity shares at a profit, and improvements in the financial services industry meant less demand for TARP funds.

Positive outcomes from the ARRA stimulus package of increased spending and tax cuts were also documented by analysts at the CBO. Without ARRA, the CBO reported, the Great Recession would have endured far longer and with worse consequences for the nation. The CBO reported that ARRA's spending programs and tax cuts had the following positive impacts by the third quarter of 2010[13]:

• Raised gross domestic product by between 1.4 and 4.1 percent after adjusting for inflation
• Lowered the unemployment rate between .8 and 2.0 percentage points
• Added 1.4 million to 3.6 million jobs to the U.S. economy

The GAO concluded that the federal stimulus programs had been efficiently managed, without delays, cost overruns, or fraud. After reviewing dozens of ARRA programs, including building weatherization, transportation and water infrastructure projects, energy-efficiency and conservation programs, and educational initiatives, the GAO identified very few examples of fraud or abuse. Instead, the GAO found that loans and grants under ARRA were effectively and quickly disbursed to their intended beneficiaries.[14] By September 30, 2010, the administration achieved its goal of spending 70 percent of ARRA funds, $551 billion, and committed the remaining stimulus funds to specific projects.

A PAINFULLY SLOW RECOVERY YIELDS DISAPPOINTMENT

The evidence is persuasive that ARRA produced or saved millions of jobs, generated thousands of construction projects, and enhanced the economy. However, the measures taken by U.S. policymakers were either not sufficient to meet the nation's needs or the wrong mix of strategies. After aggressive fiscal and monetary policy interventions by the federal government and the Federal Reserve, unemployment remained above 9 percent for nearly two years and above 8 percent for about four years after modest economic growth resumed—the longest period that unemployment has been that high since the Great Depression. The unemployment rate did not go below 8 percent until September 2012 when it fell to 7.8 percent.

The initial criticisms from the left and right of the political spectrum were reinforced by the fact that the economy has not fully recovered. Elected officials and commentators from the left of the ideological spectrum argued that the slow economic recovery was caused in part by the government's timid response to the crisis. A year after the economic stimulus plan was enacted, *New York Times* columnist Bob Herbert observed,

The crippling nature of the joblessness that has moved through the society like a devastating virus has gotten neither the attention nor the response that it warrants. . . . Right now there is no plan that can even remotely be expected to result in job creation strong enough to rescue the hard-core groups being left behind.[15]

For those on the right, weak economic performance had been caused by excessive government spending and borrowing and regulations that would saddle future generations with unpaid bills. The 2012 Republican presidential candidate, Mitt Romney, commenting on the sustained high levels of unemployment, offered this sharp assessment of the Obama administration's policies: "Badly misguided policies have acted as a severe drag on growth." He further commented that the stimulus package included "a binge of borrowing and spending that set off worldwide alarms about the creditworthiness of the United States" and a "vast expansion of costly and cumbersome regulations of sectors of the economy."[16]

Ordinary Americans were also dissatisfied with the federal government's handling of the economy. After all, hardly anyone working in America during the Great Recession had ever experienced a labor market with the combination of widespread, high levels of long-term unemployment. Economic misery was so expansive that few individuals could reasonably be satisfied with the pace of recovery. Given such widespread suffering and fear about the future, blame was bound to be directed at the nation's leaders. Asked by the Heldrich Center in 2010 whether the president or congressional Republicans could best manage the economy, 45 percent of American workers said they trusted neither. The same year, 31 percent blamed President George W. Bush's policies for high unemployment levels and 33 percent blamed President Barack Obama's policies.

Throughout his entire first term, President Obama and Congress received low marks for their handling of the economy.[17] In April 2010, a national survey conducted by the Pew Research Center for the People and the Press found that:

Many Americans are dubious about the effectiveness of the government's principal economic programs. Just 33% say the economic stimulus passed by Congress last year has helped the job situation and only somewhat more (42%) say the loans the federal government provided to troubled financial institutions prevented a more severe financial crisis. Less than a third (31%) says that the government has made progress in fixing the problems that caused the 2008 financial crisis.[18]

Over three in four voters interviewed in 2012 presidential election exit polls said the economy was still in bad shape. President Obama was re-elected to a second term, yet they trusted him by only 1 percentage point more than they trusted Governor Romney to manage the economy.[19]

Comments about the government's management of the economy, which are representative of the hundreds we received during *Work Trends* interviews conducted in September 2011, reveal the anger, frustration, and cynicism of American workers:

> The politicians should listen to what they say. It is obvious that they are not listening to the people who need help the most. They listen only to their wealthy contributors—businesses, banks, health insurance and gas companies. . . . The politicians work to get re-elected, definitely not for the people.

> Quit spending money, no earmarks, no foreign aid. Keep the money here.

> Stop giving tax breaks to businesses raking in millions to billions in profit which are yet unwilling to hire U.S. workers or keep their factories in the U.S.

> Government regulation and the legislated costs for hiring additional employees are killing the economy. Government needs to get out of the way and allow the market to steam forward.[20]

Americans' assessment of President Obama's administration may have been undermined when he sought a major overhaul of the nation's health care system in the midst of a difficult economic and political environment. The president persuaded Congress to pass a major health care reform law in 2010, known as the Patient Protection and Affordable Care Act. The law emerged after a protracted legislative battle and passed without a single Republican vote in either the House or the Senate. A nasty briar patch of public reactions followed. The major tangible benefit of the law—health care insurance coverage for an additional 30 million Americans—would not occur until 2014. Millions of Americans reacted to the price tag and uncertainties about future health care coverage before the broader populace would experience any tangible benefits.

POLICY GRIDLOCK

Doubts about the efficacy of TARP and economic stimulus spending, criticism from conservatives and liberal commentators, and the controversy surrounding the health care reform further undermined confidence in the Obama administration and Congress. Although the health care reform law was a historic legislative victory, it cost President Obama vital support among American workers. Not only had the president seemed to take his eyes off the economic crisis, but he had championed a law that was neither well understood nor widely supported. Numerous polls showed a divided electorate, tilting slightly against the proposed health insurance reform. In November 2009, Gallup polls found that 49 percent of Americans opposed it. Less than a year after the law was enacted, Gallup reported that 47 percent of Americans wanted it repealed.[21] Voters interviewed in the 2012 exit poll surveys were evenly divided about whether the Affordable Care Act should be repealed or kept in force.[22]

Further blocking bipartisan consensus on economic policy were mounting waves of conservative anger and opposition to government spending. Funding from wealthy activists, such as businessman David Koch, funded gatherings of aggrieved Americans that rapidly grew into a national conservative political movement known as the Tea Party.[23] Focused and well organized, especially in Republican congressional districts, Tea Party activists pressed Republican officeholders to cut or eliminate government programs, halt illegal immigration, and repeal the Affordable Care Act, which its opponents called "Obamacare."[24]

In the 2010 congressional primary elections, the Tea Party successfully challenged dozens of Republican incumbents whom they regarded as too moderate and willing to compromise with President Obama and congressional Democrats. The organizational savvy, funding, and enthusiasm of Tea Party members substantially contributed to a Republican takeover of the U.S. House of Representatives in the 2010 elections and victories in statehouses as Republicans won governorships in Ohio, Pennsylvania, South Carolina, and other states. The Tea Party's success convinced dozens of incumbent members of the House and Senate and governors to strongly endorse reduced government spending and socially conservative policies.[25]

The switch to Republican Party control of the House of Representatives set the stage for partisan confrontations with Senate Democrats and the White House over economic policy. It also foreclosed the possibility of any additional, major job-creating initiatives until after the presidential and congressional elections in 2012. The 2010 election focused attention on the federal deficit and national debt. News media attention to newly elected officials' concerns both reflected and shaped public opinion. Fixing the economy remained Americans' top priority, but surveys taken in 2009 and 2010 reported that reducing the budget deficit had grown in importance by 7 percent. Strengthening the economy, while still important, had fallen by 2 percent; providing health insurance to the uninsured had fallen by 3 percent.[26] The president and leaders in both parties in Congress supported deficit reduction strategies but on very different timetables. House and Senate Republicans wanted to enact immediate budget cuts. The president and his Democratic colleagues in Congress wanted to postpone significant spending reductions, sometimes called "austerity measures," until after the economy fully recovered.

A new conservative Republican majority in Congress in 2010 and rising concerns about deficit spending, however, meant that previously uncontroversial decisions would now generate heated battles. Exhibit A in this realm was the unprecedented conflict over raising the U.S. government's debt ceiling, which is the total amount that may be borrowed by the U.S. government. Traditionally, debt ceiling votes were rather routine affairs because they merely authorized the U.S. government to meet its prior financial commitments and obligations. But during the summer of 2011, the president and Congress wrangled for weeks over whether to meet or ignore this fundamental responsibility. In the worst-case scenario, failure to raise the debt ceiling could cause a federal government "shutdown" and default its obligation to pay holders of U.S. Treasury bonds. The open squabbling and the potential financial risks alarmed Americans and U.S. and foreign investors, especially occurring a few years after the collapse of major financial institutions.

As President Obama and Democratic and Republican leaders engaged in protracted discussions about the debt ceiling, new economic and job-creating actions were sidelined. Seeking a bipartisan compromise, the Obama administration offered to cut discretionary and entitlement spending in return for raising taxes on families earning over $250,000 annually. House Republican leaders, including Speaker John Boehner, were under pressure from newly elected conservative members and rejected any tax increases. Even if their stand risked previously unimaginable outcomes, Republican lawmakers refused to budge.

Eventually, after reaching an impasse in August 2011, the president and Congress agreed to temporary debt ceiling increases that postponed a fiscal and economic "Armageddon." A special "supercommittee" of senators and members of Congress was appointed to craft an agreement that would reduce the nation's debt and deficit. If the committee—and Congress—were unable to reach agreement, across-the-board reductions, half from the defense budget and half from domestic spending and tax increases, would go into effect. Because the debt ceiling compromise included concrete agreements for "automatic" spending reductions but no commitments to tax reform or increases on more prosperous Americans, President Obama was regarded by liberal observers (including those in his own party) as having been outmaneuvered, particularly since he made early concessions to House Republicans. By late July 2011, a Gallup poll found that only 41 percent of Americans approved of the president's handling of the debt ceiling negotiations, but they preferred his approach over that of the Republican leadership.[27]

The inability of Congress and the president to reach agreement further soured many Americans on the federal government's capacity to handle the government's essential responsibilities. The fact that President Obama and his administration could not focus on job creation and economic recovery during and immediately after the 2010 election disappointed many Democrats and plenty of other Americans.

ELECTION-YEAR POLICY AND POLITICS

Less than a month after the debt ceiling brinksmanship ended with a temporary settlement, President Obama pivoted back to the biggest concern for most Americans—creating jobs. The proposals laid out in President Obama's American Jobs Act during a national address in September 2011 highlighted the huge chasm between the preferred policy remedies of the two national parties. In some ways, the president's $500 billion proposal harkened back to the policy strategies he promoted in early 2009—namely, targeted increases in spending and continued tax reductions. But in this round of policy proposals, President Obama called on Congress to enact dozens of policies that had previously enjoyed bipartisan support.

The proposals laid out in President Obama's American Jobs Act . . . highlighted the huge chasm between the preferred policy remedies of the two national parties.

The proposed American Jobs Act included the following:

- Tax cuts to small business
- Payroll tax reductions for individuals and for small and medium-size businesses
- Aid to local and state governments to hire or retain teachers and public safety officers
- A summer jobs program for youth
- Tax credits for hiring veterans and the long-term unemployed
- An infrastructure bank to expand airport and highway construction projects
- Additional unemployment insurance benefits and reforms that would generate more training and "work-sharing" opportunities

Independent analysts concluded that the proposals would grow the economy and create jobs. Moody's Analytics chief economist Mark Zandi, for example, forecast that enactment of the entire jobs bill would add two percentage points to national growth and bring down the unemployment rate by a full 1 percent. The economic forecasters at Macroeconomic Advisers estimated that the president's plan would boost GDP by 1.5 percent by the end of 2012 and add 2 million jobs to the economy by the end of 2013. Other economists were somewhat less positive, but most projected a net gain of at least half a million jobs and a sufficient enough boost to prevent the economy from slipping back into recession.[28]

As soon as the American Jobs Act was announced, Republican congressional leaders pronounced it "dead on arrival." They countered with an entirely different prescription for the ailing economy. It emphasized reductions in government spending, including entitlement programs such as Unemployment Insurance, Medicaid, and Supplemental Nutritional Assistance Programs. Republican lawmakers also insisted that rather than increase taxes on upper-income Americans, Congress should preserve existing tax rates for all Americans and cut taxes for businesses.

During the 2012 primary campaign that eventually resulted in the nomination of former Massachusetts Governor Mitt Romney, Republican candidates denounced President Obama's management of the economy and his proposed solutions. They promised to repeal the health care law, roll back banking and other regulations, cut taxes, and reduce the federal budget. The Republican presidential primary candidates urged Congress to reject the president's second round of stimulus spending, arguing that the 2009 stimulus package had failed miserably. Mitt Romney summarized his view in an economic plan titled *Believe in America*: "Taken cumulatively, the programs in Barack Obama's agenda in his first three years in office have set back the American economy and contributed significantly to the high levels of unemployment we are now enduring."[29]

After months of high-profile campaigning by the president and counter-messaging by Republicans, a handful of politically popular proposals were approved, but none was expected to make a major dent in the lingering high unemployment levels. The new initiatives included tax credits for businesses that hired veterans, extending payroll tax cuts, and additional federally funded unemployment benefits for the long-term unemployed. In July 2012, Congress passed a $120 billion transportation bill that continued funding for highway and mass transit projects, which was projected to create or save up to 2.9 million jobs. Another component of this law included a provision that continued current low interest rates on the nation's largest student financial aid program, known as Stafford loans.[30]

During the presidential campaign in 2012, President Obama and Governor Romney emphasized the importance of job creation and economic growth.

Romney advocated for additional tax cuts, deficit reduction, deregulation of small businesses, and increases in energy production. Obama stressed the need for greater investments in education and training, alternative energy development, scientific research, and infrastructure projects. The president also supported deficit reduction, but said it should be achieved over a longer time period and include raising taxes on higher income earners—those earning above $250,000 annually.

President Obama was reelected to a second term. Republicans won enough seats to maintain solid control of the U.S. House of Representatives and Democrats added members to their majority in the U.S. Senate. Therefore, the balance of power and the ideological differences over the economy that have separated Democrats and Republicans were not altered by the 2012 election.

FRUSTRATION AND PROTEST

During the Great Recession, Heldrich Center surveys captured the frustrations of American workers about the economy. As noted earlier, they were unhappy with the policies of both President Bush and President Obama. There was also plenty of blame leveled by U.S. workers at foreign competition, immigrants, and Wall Street financial institutions. In the fall of 2011, a loosely organized and decentralized protest movement, calling itself Occupy Wall Street (OWS) emerged in New York City, camping in a park near Wall Street. The movement's leaders complained about income inequality and the disproportionate power of the global financial elite. Protesters charged that financial institutions and their leaders should be held accountable for the human suffering brought about by their financial risk taking and misdeeds.

Initially ignored by the mainstream media, the protests expanded through social media and the Internet, spawning protest activities around the country from Boston to Chicago to Oakland, California. Within months, OWS gained greater public attention as students, union leaders, and unemployed workers clashed with police in acts of civil disobedience. Media theorist Douglas Rushkoff characterized the movement in this way:

> [OWS is a] product of the decentralized networked-era culture, it is less about victory than sustainability. It is not about one-pointedness, but inclusion and groping toward consensus. It is not like a book; it is like the Internet. Occupy Wall Street is meant more as a way of life that spreads through contagion, creates as many questions as it answers, aims to force a reconsideration of the way the nation does business and offers hope to those of us who previously felt alone in our belief that the current economic system is broken.[31]

Surveys of Americans in 2011 revealed a surprisingly high level of support for the goals of OWS, considering that it was a mass street movement dominated by leftists, students, and labor unions. An October 2011 CBS News/ *New York Times* poll reported that 43 percent of Americans supported the basic message of the OWS movement. Two in three Americans, including 67 percent of independent voters, agreed that wealth should be distributed more equally in America.[32]

Heldrich Center *Work Trends* surveys found that large shares of the American workforce wanted the nation's political leaders to take decisive action to lower unemployment. One respondent to a Heldrich Center survey in September 2011 sent this note to us:

> IF the government went unemployed for a period of time. Had bills mounting up on them. Looked for work and only could get something way, way, WAY below the payscale they are used to. IF ONLY they would take that job and have to scrape on the bottom of the food chain for a while to see what it's like to have employers walk all over you because they know you are "desperate" for employment. Then and ONLY THEN—will the government come up with a REAL solution to the unemployment situation and realize how URGENTLY it needs to be addressed!!!!!!

About half of the sample of unemployed and employed workers said "it is the responsibility of government to take care of people who cannot take care of themselves." Roughly the same share (54 percent) agreed that the federal government should fund programs that create jobs for the unemployed even if it causes the debt to increase. A slightly smaller number (50 percent) said that tax cuts for businesses were worthwhile if they created jobs, even if the policy added to the deficit. Whether the respondent was currently employed or unemployed, of course, made a big difference in the way they viewed the policy options. Only 28 percent of employed workers concluded that the United States needed another stimulus package to help the economy, while 54 percent of unemployed Americans did not share that sentiment.

According to public opinion polls and Heldrich Center surveys, Americans backed greater investments in the economy, job creation, and entitlement programs; however, they also favored actions to reduce government spending, taxes, and the deficit.

Political leaders correctly claimed that the public supported both political parties' preferred solutions to the economic emergency. According to public opinion polls and Heldrich Center surveys, Americans backed greater investments in the economy, job creation, and entitlement programs; however, they also favored actions to reduce government spending, taxes, and the deficit. For example, a Heldrich Center *Work Trends* survey conducted during August 2011, just before President Obama's jobs speech, asked workers who were unemployed at some point during the previous three years to evaluate policies that might bring down high unemployment. We reminded them that most or all of the proposals would require increased spending by the government that would add to the annual deficit and national debt. Every policy that we tested was supported:

- Eight in ten supported long-term education and training programs to help people change careers.
- Seven in ten supported giving tax credits to businesses that hire new workers.
- Seven in ten supported having government create jobs for unemployed people.
- Six in ten supported requiring people to enter training programs in order to receive unemployment insurance.
- Six in ten supported longer and higher benefits from unemployment insurance.

We also asked unemployed workers to opine about policies that might bring about economic improvements in the short term. Majorities endorsed policies that create jobs through direct government spending (55 percent), provide more unemployment insurance (53 percent), and invest in construction and infrastructure projects (49 percent). Republican budget-cutting prescriptions also garnered very strong support, with two out of three unemployed workers saying that Congress should cut government spending to reduce the deficit—findings similar to national Gallup and the Pew Charitable Trusts polls of the overall American population.[33]

At first glance, it might seem that supporting more spending and more tax cuts while also reducing federal deficit is a logically inconsistent strategy. However, these views reflect the urgent desire for action from Washington's policymakers, to whom American workers are sending a clear message: they want their government to place economic recovery and lowering unemployment as the nation's top priority.

In the real world of fiscal policy trade-offs and politics, balancing the federal budget and simultaneously funding additional job creation programs or tax cuts is nearly impossible in the short run. It also would be counterproductive to sharply cut spending because that would reduce economic demand and drive up unemployment, a phenomenon that is well illustrated by the public sector layoffs caused by state government budget cuts. Nevertheless, the impasse over how to address the nation's economic dilemma continued because the political positions held by the two parties hardened in the wake of the 2010 and the 2012 elections. Nearly all Democrats believe economic recovery and growth will be bolstered by maintaining—if not increasing—government spending. Just about every Republican is convinced that more government spending and borrowing will stymie economic growth. Therefore, the route to economic prosperity and job growth is cutting taxes, reducing regulations, and curbing government spending. Whether President Obama and Republicans in Congress can find common ground on job creation and economic growth strategies remains to be seen.

DIGGING OUT OF THE DITCH

Four years into the nation's worst recession in seventy years and with millions still needing full-time jobs, Americans support a broad range of economic strategies. To the typical unemployed American, the task is conceptually not that complicated: the federal government should create more jobs. Congress, the president, and the Federal Reserve Bank must finish the economic recovery that ran out of steam in 2011 and 2012.

To the typical unemployed American, the task is conceptually not that complicated: the federal government should create more jobs.

Many business leaders, economists, and workforce experts also endorse emergency actions to ease the pain of jobless adults who are absorbing devastating financial and psychological damages, losing confidence in the nation's economic system, and dropping out of the labor force. It is possible to meet their basic needs, restore confidence, and rebuild trust with the right mix of government actions. What should be done to recover from this unprecedented and unrelenting economic disaster in the next few years?

Direct Job Creation

Federal government spending—and borrowing—must be expanded in order to fill the yawning gap between the demand for private sector workers and the supply of unemployed workers. Two effective strategies are available for accomplishing this task. The first strategy, investing in improving the nation's infrastructure of roads, bridges, railroads, ports, water, and energy supply systems, has not been big enough to meet the needs of the economy or the unemployed. The other strategy, public service jobs programs for the long-term unemployed, has not even been tried during this crisis, despite its proven track record during one of the nation's most disastrous recessions in the late 1970s.

Infrastructure and Energy Grid Investments

Close observers of American history know that political leaders in both parties have traditionally cooperated to make essential investments repairing, maintaining, and building transportation, education, water treatment, and other public works projects. Government spending on the nation's infrastructure has played a central role in America's economic growth, including the great canal and rail projects of the nineteenth century, the innovative public works projects of the 1930s New Deal, the construction of the interstate highway system in the 1950s and 1960s, the upgrading of water treatment plants that improved public health, and the space program of the 1960s and 1970s. Leaders in both parties knew that a state-of-the-art infrastructure stabilized communities and made businesses more competitive.

Estimates by the Center for American Progress and other reliable analyses show that the package of infrastructure and transportation spending from the 2009 stimulus package directly created 1.1 million jobs in the construction sector by March 2011. Those 1.1 million jobs represent 17 percent higher construction employment than would have been the case without government action and substantially cut the unemployment rate in the construction trades. As noted in a Center for American Progress paper by Adam Hersh and Kristina Costa, improving infrastructure

> indirectly creates jobs in other sectors of the economy, including manufacturing, because construction projects require sophisticated materials and machines. And the good middle-class incomes earned by those newly employed in infrastructure investment projects fuel spending elsewhere in the economy, thereby maintaining and increasing private-sector employment.[34]

The pressing national needs and economic benefits of infrastructure projects are not only supported by progressive and labor-allied groups. The Milken Institute, an independent and nonpartisan think tank, documented the importance of national infrastructure investments, noting it "has become painfully apparent that U.S. infrastructure, once the envy of the world, is now strained and aging, while other nations are constructing bullet trains, cutting-edge broad band networks, public transit systems, modern ports, and energy delivery systems."[35] The Milken report *Jobs for America* stated that a $425 billion investment in projects ranging from highways to smart energy grids would create 3.4 million jobs in construction and research and development and generate $147 billion in earnings. Also, according to the report, "Accounting for ripple effects across other sectors, the total impact will add up to 10.7 million jobs, $420.6 billion in earnings, and $1.4 trillion in output."[36] While investments of this magnitude are unlikely in the near future, their formula demonstrates that a $1 billion investment would directly and indirectly generate roughly twenty-five thousand jobs.

Governments are better suited to fairly allocate funds for airports, highways, and water treatment plants than private companies. Governments are also likely to do a better job deciding when to grant approval to companies that want to explore for energy deposits on public lands. Government officials are more likely to ensure safe and cost-effective nuclear energy production. Publicly funded investments not only create jobs now but also directly affect America's security, according to former Homeland Security Secretary Tom Ridge.[37]

Further proof that infrastructure should be a bipartisan issue was provided in December 2011 when a high-ranking Chinese official hinted that his country might be willing to pick up the tab for improving America's infrastructure if U.S. policymakers failed to do so. China's Commerce Minister Chen Deming told Commerce Secretary Locke and U.S. business leaders, "China is unwilling to take on too much U.S. government debt. We are willing to turn that money into investment." Chen told the group that he was amazed at the high quality of American subways and other infrastructure when he visited twenty years ago but observed that many roads, railways, and ports now were deteriorating. He said, "U.S. infrastructure in some areas needs rebuilding, for example its electricity grid, railways and transportation networks. . . . This type of investment, even more, can help resolve the unemployment issue in the United States." When our most daunting economic adversary taunts the United States for having substandard energy grids and transportation, it should be a wake-up call for American policymakers.[38]

Notwithstanding the long history of bipartisan cooperation and support from both the U.S. Chamber of Commerce and the AFL-CIO, conservative Tea Party Republicans sidelined President Obama's proposed National Infrastructure Bank, and it has not reached his desk for signature as of late 2012. The National Infrastructure Bank proposal would establish a bank with a modest $10 billion in start-up capital. The fact that a scaled-down transportation bill extending existing programs did get through Congress in 2012 is an encouraging sign of progress.

Public Service Jobs

The federal government should also revive the proven strategy of creating temporary public service jobs for hundreds of thousands of unemployed Americans. Within months, people could be working on community projects in cities and towns around the country—repairing roads and bridges, cleaning up parks and public housing projects, weatherizing homes and apartments, and helping in day care and senior citizen centers. For example, thousands of workers with a wide range of skills could work on the massive cleanup and repair efforts required due to Hurricane Sandy, which devastated a large swath of the northeastern United States in the fall of 2012.

Workers employed by state and local governments or nonprofit agencies there could help the businesses and displaced home owners and renters struggling to rebuild after the natural disaster that compounded economic recovery in the region.

There is nothing novel or radical about this approach, yet it has been neglected during the current public discourse by Democrats and, less surprisingly, Republicans. During the mid- to late 1970s, with the U.S. economy mired in a punishing recession, the federal government, under Republican Presidents Nixon and Ford and Democratic President Carter, mounted a $10 billion emergency employment program. The Carter-era public service employment program was modeled after the successful Works Progress Administration and Civilian Conservation Corps of the New Deal and employed over 730,000 Americans in 1978 and 1979.[39]

Based on the experiences gleaned from similar programs in the 1970s, public service jobs can be deployed rapidly and generate immediate benefits for unemployed workers and the economy. Compared to construction projects that can take months to initiate and often require highly trained workers, public service employment programs provide a complementary and nimble alternative. To control costs, per person public service job salaries and wages could be capped at $25,000 to $30,000 annually and be set aside for those who have been jobless for a year or more. Small-scale community-based projects are also more likely than large construction projects to employ those who are being hit hardest by the recession—namely, people with limited education and skills who live in cities and isolated rural communities. To reinforce the emergency nature of public service employment, no one should be permitted to remain in the public service jobs program for more than eighteen months, and the entire program should be tied to fluctuations in federal and state unemployment rates.

Independent researchers determined that the 1970s-era public service jobs delivered valuable benefits to communities and individuals facing economic hardship, so why was this once-acceptable remedy for high levels of unemployment shunned during the Great Recession? Democrats and Republicans became disenchanted with public service employment in part because of several exposés of poorly chosen projects. As such, public service job programs acquired an unfair reputation as government boondoggles.

Another important critique of public service employment programs is that federal financing substitutes for jobs that state and local governments and nonprofits would have created with their own funds. In other words, no net new jobs are created. Independent analysis of the Comprehensive Employment Training Act public service employment, enacted during the nation's second-worst recession since World War II, concluded that about 15 percent of the jobs would have been created by state and local governments if the federal funds were not available. The same analysis found that substitution of nonprofit jobs was much less prevalent.[40]

The concern about substituting federal dollars for state and local funding resurfaced in connection with President Obama's stimulus program, with some critics questioning whether funds distributed to state and local governments and school systems around the country actually "saved" as many jobs as the administration claims. Considering that devastating layoffs in local and state government workforces, including teachers, firefighters, cops, and sanitation workers, occurred when ARRA funding ran out, it appears there was not much substitution effect at all.

There are no indisputable answers to the question of how many new or saved jobs are created by public service employment programs or, for that matter, any other federal investment. Given pernicious unemployment that has lasted nearly five years, concerns about state and local governments substituting federal funds for theirs seem to have been exaggerated. Using the lessons learned from the 1970s and even the 1930s, a program can be designed as an emergency intervention that creates net new jobs and avoids the abuses that sullied direct public service employment programs' reputation as an effective policy remedy.

Bolster and Refocus the Workforce Development System

A handful of policies to address the lingering effects of the Great Recession have been enacted by Congress since the ferocious partisan gridlock that prevailed in 2011 and 2012. But there is far more that must be done to increase the velocity of job creation now. Just as importantly, serious leaders of both parties—from labor, business, and the nonprofit sector—need to accelerate their work on a long-term reform of our workforce system that is the emergency room for an ailing economy.

To begin with, the president and Congress need to increase funding to bolster the capacity of public workforce agencies and particularly the nationwide network of One-Stop Career Centers (now known as the American Job Center) funded under the Workforce Investment Act (WIA) of 1998. Staff at these public agencies are charged with providing information about local job opportunities and about training options for job seekers. During the Great Recession, these centers were overwhelmed registering people for assistance, helping them find jobs, and arranging education and training. With overburdened staff and facilities, confusion and delays inevitably meant that potential job–worker matches were missed. Between 2000 and 2008, funding for these frontline agencies was cut by 14 percent. While ARRA reversed these shortsighted decisions, One-Stop Center funding declined again in 2011 and 2012. More resources are needed to keep up with demand and provide effective services. When someone has been looking for months to get a job, that person should not have to wait for days to see a career counselor.

While greater resources are essential, the workforce system also needs to undergo significant reforms. Positive example of innovative and effective state and local workforce programs are evident, but they are no means widespread. Heldrich Center colleagues Kathy Krepcio and Michele Martin point out,

> WIA was fundamentally a response to the question: How do we reduce fragmentation and duplication of services and bring together disparate programs in an environment of heavy job growth? While a reasonable question for 1998, it is no longer the question we should be asking in 2012. Not only is this question too small and limiting, it also assumes a job environment that no longer exists.[41]

They and others correctly argue that a significantly reformed workforce development system that serves unemployed workers in the contemporary economy must better connect workers with employer needs, target services that create new jobs, integrate training and Unemployment Insurance, and customize help for their "customers" when and where they need it.[42]

As the One-Stop Career Centers are reformed and strengthened, the U.S. Department of Labor should also deploy the best-in-class online information technology and communications tools for job seekers. The job centers should provide reliable and timely information to the full range of job seekers, including professional and white-collar workers. The centers must also collaborate more closely with employers and industry clusters where job demand is the highest, acting as true brokers between employers and job seekers. They must also build a stronger culture of accountability and performance measurement, identify their weaknesses, and build on their strengths so that they can better serve America's job seekers.

SHIFTING TO TOP GEAR

Shifting America's job-creating engine into higher gear will not be accomplished without great difficulty. American political leaders profoundly disagree about the appropriate remedies, but the nation's progress depends on their ability to find common ground. Restoring confidence and creating jobs are essential so that the economy can get out of neutral and produce sufficient jobs for all the Americans who need to work.

It remains to be seen whether the policy differences separating Washington politicians will deepen in the years following the 2012 election. What is clear, however, is that Americans want their government's policymakers to build a consensus for policies that not only address this existential job emergency but also build a stronger economy and workforce for the coming decades, the challenge I consider in the next chapter.

NOTES

1. Associated Press and *Daily News* staff writer, "A Record 20 Million-Plus People Collected Unemployment Benefits at Some Point in 2009," http://articles.nydailynews.com/2009-12-31/news/29436857_1_national-employment-law-project-jobless-benefits-unemployment-benefits

2. William D. Cohan, *House of Cards* (New York: Doubleday, 2009); Bethany McLean and Joe Nocera, *All the Devils Are Here* (New York: Viking Penguin Portfolio, 2010).

3. "History of US Government Bailouts," April 15, 2009, http://www.propublica.org/special/government-bailout; Matthew Goldstein, "JP Morgan Buys Bear on the Cheap," *BusinessWeek*, March 16, 2008, http://www.businessweek.com/stories/2008-03-16/jpmorgan-buys-bear-on-the-cheapbusinessweek-business-news-stock-market-and-financial-advice; Francesco Guerrera, "JP Morgan Seeks Jobs for Sacked Bear Staff," *Financial Times*, May 18, 2008, http://www.ft.com/cms/s/0/5ea65688-2509-11dd-a14a-000077b07658.html#axzz2B4lV0tW5; Douglas McIntyre, "The Layoff Kings," August 8, 2010, http://www.dailyfinance.com/2010/08/18/the-layoff-kings-the-25-companies-responsible-for-700-000-lost; Committee for a Responsible Federal Budget, http://stimulus.org; Krishna Guha, Michael Makenzie, and Nicole Bullock, "Fannie and Freddie Bailout Hits Public Finances," *Financial Times*, September 10, 2008, http://www.ft.com/intl/cms/s/0/db2fcc5a-7ecf-11dd-b1af-000077b07658.html#axzz1iU8Z2luV.

4. U.S. Bureau of Labor Statistics, Labor Force Statistics from the Current Population Survey, Series LNS14000000, http://www.data.bls.gov.

5. Dennis Jacobe, "Six in Ten Oppose Wall Street Bailouts," March 3, 2008, http://www.gallup.com/poll/106114/six-oppose-wall-street-bailouts.aspx.

6. "How Effective Was TARP, Really?," October 8, 2010, http://www.economist.com/blogs/democracyinamerica/2010/10/public_opinion_and_bailouts.

7. Paul Krugman, "On the Inadequacy of the Stimulus," *New York Times*, September 5, 2011.

8. John Samples, "Lawless Policy," February 4, 2010, http://www.cato.org/pub_display.php?pub_id=11183.

9. "TARP Is on Its Way to Failure," 2009, http://www.fiscalaccountability.org/index.php?content=cog09-12#.

10. "Quick Fact: Despite Her Previous Support, Palin Bashed TARP as 'Crony Capitalism at Its Worst,'" February 7, 2010, http://mediamatters.org/research/201002070013; Mitt Romney, *No Apology* (New York: St. Martin's Griffin Press, 2011).

11. Congressional Budget Office, "CBO Report on TARP," March 11, 2011, http://www.cbo.gov/ftpdocs/121xx/doc12118/03-29-TARP.pdf; Daniel W. Drezner, "Hazards of Policymaking in a Fact-Poor, Pundit-Rich World," September 15, 2010, http://drezner.foreignpolicy.com/posts/2010/09/15/the_hazards_of_policymaking_in_a_fact_poor_pundit_rich_world; Sewell Chan, "In Study, 2 Economists Say Intervention Helped Avert a 2nd Depression," *New York Times*, July 27, 2010; "TARP: The Successful Orphan," *Economist*, September 25, 2010.

12. Congressional Budget Office, "CBO Report on TARP."

13. Congressional Budget Office, "Estimated Impact of the American Recovery and Reinvestment Act on Employment and Economic Output," November 2011, http://www.cbo.gov/sites/default/files/cbofiles/attachments/11-22-ARRA.pdf.

14. Government Accountability Office, "Following the Money, GAO's Oversight of the Recovery Act," http://www.gao.gov/recovery/bimonthly/programs/energy.php, http://www.gao.gov/recovery/bimonthly/programs/education.php, http://www.gao.gov/recovery/bimonthly/programs/transportation.php, http://www.gao.gov/recovery/bimonthly/programs/water.php, and http://www.gao.gov/recovery/bimonthly/programs/head-start.php.

15. Bob Herbert, "A Different Creature," *New York Times*, April 13, 2010, A25.

16. Romney for President, Inc., "Believe in America," Mitt Romney's Plan for Jobs and Economic Growth, 2011, 3.

17. "Views about the Economy, Budget Deficit and Health Care," April 21, 2011, http://www.nytimes.com/interactive/2011/04/21/us/nat-poll.html; "ABC News/*Washington Post* Poll: Dissatisfaction with Washington Hits 19-Year High," July 19, 2011, http://abcnews.go.com/blo; Jessica Godofsky, Carl E. Van Horn, and Cliff Zukin, "Americans Assess an Economic Disaster," in *Work Trends* (New Brunswick, NJ: Heldrich Center at Rutgers, The State University of New Jersey, September 2010); Cliff Zukin, Carl E. Van Horn, and Charley Stone, "Out of Work and Losing Hope," in *Work Trends* (September 2011), http://www.heldrich.rutgers.edu/news-updates/all/out-work-and-losing-hope-misery-and-bleak-expectations-american-workers.

18. Pew Research Center for People and the Press, "Pessimistic Public Doubts Effectiveness of Stimulus, TARP," April 28, 2010, http://www.people-press.org/files/legacy-pdf/608.pdf.

19. Gary Langer, "A Draw on the Economy, a Win on Empathy—and the Face of a Changing Nation," November 7, 2012, http://abcnews.go.com/blogs/politics/2012/11/a-draw-on-the-economy-a-win-on-empathy-and-the-face-of-a-changing-nation.

20. "Voices of the Unemployed: Survey Respondents' Views on What the Government Should Do to Help the Unemployed and What One Thing Would Be Helpful in Finding a Job," http://www.heldrich.rutgers.edu/sites/default/files/content/Work_Trends_Verbatim_Responses_September_2011.pdf; *Work Trends* (New Brunswick, NJ: Heldrich Center at Rutgers, The State University of New Jersey, September 2011).

21. "Americans Still Leaning against Health Care Legislation," November 30, 2009, http://www.gallup.com/poll/124496/Americans-Leaning-Against-Healthcare-Legislation.aspx.

22. Langer, "A Draw on the Economy, a Win on Empathy."

23. Frank Rich, "Billionaires Bankrolling the Tea Party," *New York Times*, August 28, 2010, http://www.nytimes.com/2010/08/29/opinion/29rich.html; "Romney Campaign Memo: Koch Brothers Financial Engine of the Tea Party"; http://thinkprogress.org/politics/2011/11/03/360433/romney-koch-tea-party/?mobile=nc; Jane Mayer, "Covert Operation," September 1, 2010, http://www.newyorker.com/reporting/2010/08/30/100830fa_fact_mayer.

24. "Contract from America," assorted Tea Party groups, January 8, 2012, http://www.contractfromamerica.com/Idea.aspx; "Freedom Works Key Issues," January 8, 2012, http://www.freedomworks.org/issues 1-8-2012.

25. See David E. Campbell and Robert D. Putnam's important *New York Times* essay, "Crashing the Tea Party," August 16, 2011.

26. Pew Research Center for the People and the Press, "The Public's Political Agenda," January 25, 2010, http://pewresearch.org/pubs/1472/public-priorities-president-congress-2010.

27. "Obama Rates Higher Than Boehner," July 28, 2011, http://www.gallup.com/poll/148718/Obama-Rates-Higher-Boehner-Reid-Debt-Situation.aspx.

28. Jackie Calmes and Binyamin Appelbaum, "Bigger Economic Role for Washington: Jobs Bill Could Help Economic Growth," September 13, 2001, http://www.nytimes.com/2011/09/14/us/politics/jobs-bill-could-help-economic-growth-some-forecasters-say.html.

29. http://www.scribd.com/ncc1701m/d/94594527-Believe-in-America-Plan-Mitt-Romney-2012-Presidential-Campaign-Official-Document.

30. Jonathan Weisman, "Congress Approves a $127 Billion Transportation and Student Loan Package," June 29, 2012, www.nytimes.com/2012/06/30/us/politics/congress-approves-transportation.

31. Douglas Rushkoff, "Think Occupy Wall St. Is a Phase? You Don't Get It," October 5, 2011, http://www.cnn.com/2011/10/05/opinion/rushkoff-occupy-wall-street/index.html.

32. "Poll: 43 Percent Agree with Views of 'Occupy Wall Street,'" October 25, 2011, http://www.cbsnews.com/8301-503544_162-20125515-503544/poll-43-percent-agree-with-views-of-occupy-wall-street.

33. Zukin et al., "Out of Work and Losing Hope."

34. Kristina Costa and Adam Hersh, "Infrastructure Spending Creates American Jobs," September 8, 2011, http://www.americanprogress.org/issues/2011/09/jobs_in frastructure.html.

35. Ross DeVol and Perry Wong, "Jobs for America: Investments and Policies for Economic Growth and Competitiveness," January 2010, http://www.milkeninstitute .org/jobsforamerica.

36. DeVol and Wong, "Jobs for America: Investments and Policies for Economic Growth and Competitiveness."

37. Peter Whoriskey, "Ridge Report Warns U.S. on Trade, Infrastructure," *Washington Post*, July 25, 2012, A15.

38. Associated Press, "Infrastructure Was Impressive . . . 20 Years Ago," http:// articles.businessinsider.com/2011-12-02/news/30466479_1_beijing-and-washington -chen-deming-clean-energy.

39. Donald C. Baumer and Carl E. Van Horn, *The Politics of Unemployment* (Washington, DC: CQ Press, 1985).

40. Richard Nathan, *Public Service Employment: A Field Evaluation* (Washington, DC: Brookings Institution, 1981).

41. Kathy Krepcio and Michele M. Martin, "The State of the U.S. Workforce System: A Time for Incremental Realignment or Series Reform?," Heldrich Center at Rutgers, The State University of New Jersey, June 2012, 2.

42. See, for example, Ed Strong, "One-Stop Career Centers Must Be Re-invented to Meet Today's Labor Market Realities," Corporation for a Skilled Workforce, March 2012, and Peter Edelman, Harry Holzer, Eric Seleznow, Andy Van Kleunen, and Elizabeth Watson, "State Workforce Policy: Recent Innovations and an Uncertain Future," Georgetown Center on Poverty, Inequality, and Public Policy and National Skills Coalition, June 2011.

Chapter Seven

Restoring the Shattered Dreams of American Workers

Digging out of the nation's worst recession in seventy years—completing the task begun in 2008 and 2009—would get millions of Americans back to work, boost their living standards, and restore the confidence of Americans who have been struggling for half a decade. No matter how successful, however, these emergency actions will not adequately address the enduring crisis gripping the American labor market. The citizens of the United States and the country's political, business, and educational leaders face fundamentally new challenges in a global, competitive, technology-driven environment where economies, entire industries, and companies are transformed with lightning speed. How does America, through its laws, and private and public institutions, build a productive and competitive workforce and restore the promise of upward mobility? How can we achieve a productive balance of powers among workers, employers, and capital so that those who work hard can get ahead and that they and their children will be better off?

How can we achieve a productive balance of powers among workers, employers, and capital so that those who work hard can get ahead and that they and their children will be better off?

The broad forces shaping the U.S. labor market did not originate with the Great Recession but have been coursing through the labor market for the past thirty years. Unlike a summer storm that comes and goes, the new realities of work in the twenty-first century are more like a hurricane that altered the economic landscape, creating a still evolving, uncomfortable new "normal" for American workers. The immense

disruptions of globalization, deindustrialization, outsourcing, and deunionization give employers enormous leverage over American workers who are competing in a buyer's market. Because many large employers view outsourcing
and contingent work as preferable human resources strategies, employer-
based investments in workers' education and training diminished or disappeared. During the 2000s, Congress also weakened its support for innovative
workforce learning programs, blaming the programs for failing to counter
the recession. Congress did extend federal unemployment insurance funding
for up to ninety-nine weeks and then pulled back, but there was little or no
progress achieved on enacting proposals to substantially reform workforce
development programs that would better assist the long-term unemployed.

The Great Recession unleashed a flood of warnings that the nation's failure to invest in workers will ultimately undermine its competitive position in
the rugged global economic terrain. Unless significant reforms are adopted,
the way the U.S economy functions and employers dominate the American
workplace will prevail for the foreseeable future. Although a small number
may benefit, the status quo will not be a positive in the long run for the nation's businesses, workers, social health, or economy. Tectonic shifts of this
magnitude require responses that are truly "all in" not only for policymakers
but also for businesses and citizens.

There is an urgent need to address the long-simmering crisis in the American workforce that has become less equitable, and tougher on those without
advanced education. Unless the economy rebounds in the next decade, it is in
danger of becoming less competitive. Strengthening the American workforce
and the educational institutions that prepare people for work and reemployment must be a top national priority, not an afterthought. The underlying
problems will not be solved by the passage of time. If the United States delays
in tackling these challenges, it will lag in the global competition for economic
growth and will lose societal cohesion. The case for profound change is compelling from economic, political, and social perspectives.

Long before the Great Recession inflicted severe pain, *Work Trends* surveys revealed American workers' serious misgivings about our public policies. Americans consistently ranked improving the quality of elementary and secondary education as the most important action government could take to improve jobs and competitiveness—outranking tax breaks or health care insurance. Well before the Great Recession, older workers worried about their ability to retire early and maintain their standard of living.[1]

Heldrich Center surveys taken before and after the Great Recession also revealed American workers' doubts about the federal government's ability to manage the economy and lower unemployment. Trusting neither President Obama nor Congress, the prevailing view, held by 45 percent of American workers in our 2011 survey, was that neither political party would be able to improve the country's economic prospects. While public confidence in President Obama improved substantially in 2012, Americans' assessment of the economy continued to be negative following the November 2012 election.[2] Even though Americans have low expectations about public officials and government institutions in general, there are still more than half of the unemployed and one in three employed Americans who regard government as principally responsible for helping workers during recessions, according to Heldrich Center surveys. Although workers are skeptical about the ability of elected officials to deal effectively with unemployment, they are convinced that government must play a stronger role during hard times. Safety net programs, such as Unemployment Insurance and training opportunities for the unemployed remained highly popular across the spectrum of public opinion during and after the recession. Most Americans strongly support unemployment insurance benefit programs and do not believe these programs have been abused by the unemployed.

Americans want the federal government to take action to create jobs directly or indirectly. Over three-quarters (77 percent) of the jobless and half (51 percent) of all workers supported government-funded job creation programs to stimulate the economy. Over half (57 percent) of the jobless and 49 percent of all employed workers supported cutting taxes for business that create jobs, even if these actions increase government deficits and debt.[3]

A NEW WORKFORCE PARADIGM

Addressing this altered economic landscape requires a fundamentally new paradigm for workforce development policy—animated by new ways of thinking and acting. At the core of this new paradigm is the challenge of how to educate, train, and retrain people so that they can achieve their full potential and offer employers valued skills. The entire society—workers and political, business, and educational leaders—must rally around several central goals.

First, we must strive for greater equity and opportunity by developing a better-educated and more competitive workforce. A society in which only the top 1 percent (or only the 30 percent that have a college education) succeeds will not be sustainable. America is growing apart as those with the most val-ued skills and those employed in growth industries prosper while those on the other side of the ledger fall further behind. Such deep disparities in income cannot be solved solely by raising taxes on those who are well off or cutting the taxes of low-income workers. While such redistribution of the tax burden may be desirable, it will not be sufficient to lift low-income workers into the middle class. Rather, greater equity will be achieved by helping workers get the high-quality education and training they need to be competitive in the labor market.

The United States faces stiff competition from developed and developing nations for economic growth. Advanced developed nations, such as those in Europe, and Japan and South Korea, are investing more per capita in the preparation and continued education of their workforce than the United States. Developing countries, such as Brazil, India, and China, are also making huge investments in educating and training their citizens, and that includes sending them to American colleges and universities.

Advanced developed nations, such as those in Europe, and Japan and South Korea, are investing more per capita in the preparation and continued education of their workforce than the United States.

The United States must develop a more aggressive pro-growth policy and reject zero-sum politics. Greater effort must be devoted to enlarging the nation's economic pie rather than fighting over the best way to divide it. The notion of enhancing Ameri-can competitiveness and generating faster growth garnered wide support in the 1980s and 1990s. To this end, the Council on Competitiveness brought together corporate CEOs, university presidents, and labor leaders in 1986 to advance policies that would enable the U.S. economy to prosper in a global economy. (For example, see the Council's twenty-fifth anniversary report published in May 2011.[4]) While this point of view still has numerous supporters among the country's business and education elite, too often U.S. politicians and business and labor leaders are more concerned about how they can secure or enlarge their corner of the economy.

A broader vision of growth that embraces the notion that a rising tide lifts all boats is sorely missing from the American dialogue. Maintaining and ex-panding a globally competitive workforce is a central component in achieving economic progress in the coming decades. The United States cannot win a "race to the bottom" in wages and benefits, but it can win the race to the top of value-added economic growth in both manufacturing and services.

The policies outlined here—growing the economy and providing economic opportunity for those willing to work for it—used to be less controversial. In our nation's recent history, neither progressives nor conservatives dominated politics and policy for more than brief periods. Only during the early stages of the New Deal in the 1930s and the first two years of Lyndon Johnson's presidency did progressives push through fundamental changes in domestic policy. While there are glimmers of hope on the horizon, the past few years of partisan wrangling in Congress have been discouraging and unprecedented in modern times. Whether the partisan gridlock will diminish in Washington, D.C., after the 2012 election remains to be seen.[5] Most likely, it will take a decade or more to develop and implement a new workforce development paradigm. The devastating consequences of the Great Recession must be addressed by providing immediate relief to long-term unemployed workers thus far left out of the anemic recovery, as noted in chapter 6. But the nation also must move forward with large-scale transformations of its workforce and education policies to improve the prospects for workers and the economy in the twenty-first-century, globalized, technology-driven economy. The new realities of work in the twenty-first century are not going to change. American workers and policymakers must adapt or American workers and the nation will suffer further pain and economic decline.

ASSUMPTIONS, EXPECTATIONS, AND HOPES

Before delving into the specifics, it is important to articulate several assumptions, expectations, and hopes that form the foundation of my recommendations for transforming workforce development policies and practices. Building a new workforce development paradigm requires more than overcoming partisan gridlock in Washington, D.C. Indeed, too much emphasis has been placed on having the federal government shoulder the entire burden. Building a broad consensus in the private sector, among educational and nonprofit institutions and the nation's citizens, is essential. Private companies, state governments, schools and colleges, and community-based organizations must continue to experiment with new approaches and strategies, as they always have in the American experience.

Enduring strategies must be based on traditional American values and expectations. In other words, government policies and programs are important components of the overall strategy, but they are not the exclusive force that builds a better workforce. Private enterprise and entrepreneurs and educators will determine, in large measure, the shape of the economy and workforce development strategies. Workers should be given every opportunity to advance through hard work and self-improvement, not guaranteed success. Workers, employers, and educators will be free to enter into mutually beneficial arrangements, subject to basic government protections against discrimination and unsafe working conditions.

Throughout the Heldrich Center's fifteen years of surveys, American workers affirmed their expectation that workers, employers, and governments all have significant roles in making the workforce and economy successful. American workers believe that government policies and educational institutions are essential elements in preparing people for the labor market and helping the unemployed get back to work. Yet workers also are convinced that they and their employers are principally responsible for success. A system that depends too heavily on one component of this tripartite arrangement is out of balance and will not succeed. In the past decade, the pendulum swung too far in the direction of employers, in the opinion of most American workers.

The strategies outlined in this chapter assume it is unlikely that substantial expansions in government spending will be forthcoming. To avert a larger economic disaster, federal policymakers already bailed out the nation's financial institutions and giant automakers. To assist the Great Recession's victims, federal spending on entitlement programs, such as food stamps and Medicaid, skyrocketed. To get the economy moving again, lawmakers authorized nearly a trillion-dollar federal stimulus package that included tax reductions, infrastructure projects, and renewable energy programs.

While there is still much controversy over whether the government's recession-fighting policy efforts were too large or not large enough, there is no doubt that they were expensive. The federal government stimulus package, the loans to automakers, and the bailout of financial institutions amounted to approximately $1.5 trillion in new spending and loans. Increased spending coupled with declining revenues meant that inevitably the national debt would grow rapidly. By the middle of 2012, the national debt exceeded 100 percent of the nation's gross domestic product for the first time since World War II.[6]

For the next decade, at least, the government's postrecession fiscal situation will be further hampered by rising costs for social services and perhaps flat or diminishing revenues. Pressure will be intense for deficit and debt reduction. Together, these forces may thwart most proposals for expanding government discretionary spending. A realistic and feasible policy agenda will begin with the assumption that the first and perhaps only option is to make better use of the resources that are now available or find more efficient ways of delivering needed services with less or no government support.

Educating Americans has never been regarded as a purely public good, financed entirely by governments. Individuals, companies, and taxpayers contribute time and money to the development of a productive workforce. However, given limited resources, those who can afford to pay should be expected to contribute more toward their postsecondary education so that those who cannot afford to will pay less. To some extent, this already occurs. However, in the coming decades, with less available government resources, assistance must be more precisely targeted to help low- and moderate-income workers and students.[7] Education and workforce development programs must also skillfully blend high-tech delivery strategies with personal assistance from well-trained teachers and advisers. Twenty-first-century technologies have made education widely available at modest cost to anyone who has a smart phone with Wi-Fi or a computer with broadband access. As never before, students and workers are better positioned to navigate their careers or bolster their education from a coffee shop or their living room. One can research companies, search job listings, upgrade skills, and get a degree or certificate without ever going to a building or meeting another classmate or the instructor.

While these new technologies create unprecedented opportunities, they also have limitations and bring new perils. As everyone who has ever searched for information or taken online instruction already knows, the Internet is simultaneously a cornucopia of useful services and an open pit of misleading claims that can lure the unsuspecting down a useless and expensive path. Internet-based workforce development services, such as job searches and training courses, represent the best and the worst of commerce. The opportunity to generate revenues—either for nonprofit organizations or for-profit companies—is the reason that these services have proliferated. In the hands of the unscrupulous, however, the profit motive can result in the exploitation and abuse of learners and job seekers.

If we are to realize the full potential of delivering services on the Internet, students and workers will need assistance sorting out the good from the bad, the great from the mediocre. In short, they will need an "umpire" to call the "balls and strikes." That neutral umpire might come from the nonprofit sector, but it is far more likely that states and the federal government should assume that responsibility because they are, at least in theory, able to "call them as they see them." Markets function best when consumers have access to good information to make choices. Government agencies are well positioned not only to compel organizations to make that information available but also to publicly distribute it without favoritism. The Obama administration took some steps in this direction in 2012 by requesting that higher-education institutions release more information about costs and the success of graduates (see chapter 5 for a discussion of the college experience). Several states, including New Jersey and Oregon, offer consumer report cards that help individuals sort through training and education options and report on program performance.[8]

Transparency benefits not just the consumer, student, and/or job seeker but also companies and institutions that play by the rules and provide high-quality services. American governments have long applied these principles to the financial markets and health care products and services, albeit not with uniform success. We have only begun the first, tentative steps to harness the power generated by the information-technology revolution to improve education and workforce services. At the same time, we must ensure that those powerful new tools serve the learner and not only the firm or government agency marketing those services.

While robust, transparent, and regulated Internet-based learning can provide efficient services and open up opportunities for millions, these technologies have limits. One-on-one, personal, "high-touch services" are essential for those who cannot navigate through the difficult transitions in the labor market from school to work and from one job to another or from working to retirement. The free-agent, entrepreneurial economy may be just fine for the affluent, savvy, well-educated worker or student. It does not work nearly as well for the less-well-educated older worker or those with disabilities or those who lack English literacy. These individuals are less likely to have the personal networks, resources, and financial support that will help them figure out how to manage the complex world of work let alone get through tough times.

While more education and workforce services should migrate to the Internet, it is also imperative to keep personal counseling in the equation. It is unrealistic to expect that individuals can find jobs, get an education, and manage financial problems on their own by just tapping into the World Wide Web. Expecting people to cope with personal crises on their own may even have tragic consequences.

It is still true that most jobs are found through personal networks—a finding reinforced each time the Heldrich Center surveyed American workers. Whether it is friends and family or the references from a school or government agency counselor, more than two-thirds of all jobs are obtained through personal networks, according to the thousands of unemployed workers and recent college and high school graduates we interviewed for the *Work Trends* project. The playing field can be leveled for those without extensive personal networks by professionals working in nonprofits, educational institutions, or government job placement agencies.[9]

That being said, it is unrealistic and unwise to expect that teachers, parents, professors, or the Internet will have all the information a person needs to cope with let alone master the confusing labor market and bewildering education and training enterprise. Instead, we must develop a well-trained cadre of counseling professionals—in educational, governmental, and social institutions—to help people decipher the labor and education markets when they inevitably encounter vexing transitions.

Prolonged unemployment brings not only economic hardship but also serious psychological and health consequences. The unemployed are more likely to experience significant health problems, divorce, spouse and family abuse, and even early death than those who are employed, as noted by Dean Baker and Kevin Hassett in a *New York Times* column in May 2012.[10] Assisting workers wrecked by joblessness is a task for highly trained professionals and cannot be accomplished by reading lists of job search "dos and don'ts" on a website.

FOUR NATIONAL PRIORITIES

In order for the United States to build a sustainable, globally competitive economy that provides good jobs and wages for Americans, policymakers, business, labor, community, and education leaders and citizens must mobilize around four national priorities:

- Reform high school and college education to prepare all students for careers
- Expand learning opportunities for workers throughout their careers
- Replace Unemployment Insurance with Reemployment Insurance
- Establish a twenty-first-century worker–employer compact.

Reform Education to Prepare Students for Careers

This country needs a well-educated population to compete in an increasingly technological world economy. Free public education should be provided not just for K–12, but also beyond, at least for the first four years of college . . . being able to obtain a no-cost or low-cost quality education through college should be a major goal of our government. (Heldrich Center interview, August 2011)

America's high schools are raising standards and innovating in the classroom, usually in response to state laws requiring them to do so. Although secondary school administrators and teachers and policymakers have raised standards and innovated in the classroom, progress has been disappointing for millions of young students. Since 1970, economists Henry Levin and Cecilia Rouse point out, the United States has dropped from leading the world to twenty-first in high school completion, and

now only 7 of 10 ninth graders today will get high school diplomas. A decade after the No Child Left Behind law mandated efforts to reduce the racial gap, about 80 percent of white and Asian students graduate from high school, compared with only 55 percent of blacks and Hispanics.[11]

The nation's vast array of educational institutions and training programs must do a much better job of preparing young people to be successful in the workforce. (For an excellent report on this topic, see the National Center on Education and the Economy's "Tough Choices or Tough Times, the Report of the New Commission on the Skills of the American Workforce," published in 2007.) Accomplishing that goal means, among other things, that secondary school educators understand and respond to employers' labor market needs. High school educators must enable their students to acquire the crosscutting skills, discussed in chapter 5, that employers value. Young workers will be better able to secure desired jobs if they have these foundational skills on graduation from high school.

These perspectives should animate reforms in secondary schools—and in higher-education institutions, which is addressed below. Aggressive actions will be required to narrow the persistent and growing gap between highly educated, highly skilled professionals and the lagging skills and technological proficiency of high school graduates—and those who don't even get that far in their formal education. Significant demand will continue for jobs in health care science, technology, and engineering fields as well as professionals in every field who have those skills and disciplines.[12]

America's high schools devote so much time advising young people to attend college that they have neglected their mission to prepare people for work. These educators must recognize and act on the simple fact that the majority of high school graduates either do not attend college or do not obtain a degree. By embracing the college-for-all strategy, educators are doing a great disservice to the seven in ten young people who do not obtain a bachelor's degree. As a result, the responsibility for preparing the workforce has been all but abandoned by most high schools. Career and technical education—what used to be called vocational education—has either been eliminated entirely or become an educational backwater in America's high schools.[13] High school educators have given up on preparing young people for work. Unfortunately, colleges and universities have not embraced that mission either. Whether a student is headed to college or not, high school students should begin exploring the world of work. They need to understand what will be expected of them in the workplace and develop their work ethic—namely, showing up on time, respecting one's coworkers, and dressing appropriately.

Important academic requirements must also be communicated clearly, early, and often to middle school and high school students. A young woman who aspires to be an engineer, physician, or scientist, for example, will have difficulty doing so unless she completes foundational math and science courses, including advanced placement classes, in high school. According to an influential report issued by the Center for American Progress and subsequently endorsed by the Obama administration,

> By any reasonable measure, our current education and workforce training system is not meeting the demand for better-educated workers. Right now our workforce is too concentrated at the low end of the education spectrum. To maintain our economic competitiveness, we need to provide more opportunities for workers to advance from low-skill and middle-skill careers into middle-skill and high-skill careers.[14]

American high schools and colleges are not producing enough workers who have mastered advanced technical skills. Even as the nation emerges from the Great Recession, employers report major shortages of skilled workers, including engineers and software developers, according to 2012 data published by the U.S. Commerce Department and the National Economic Council.[15]

Meeting these challenges should begin in high school, if not sooner. The United States must do more to develop young people's skills and help them develop a commitment to lifelong learning. Several steps should be taken in the coming years:

- Align high school curricula and assessments with the expectations of postsecondary educational institutions and employers
- Provide feedback to educators by creating a system for tracking high school graduates' experiences in the workplace and postsecondary education
- Hold high schools accountable for increasing the percentage of graduates who complete curricula that prepare them for a postsecondary education and the twenty-first-century workforce, by tying funding and evaluations to these goals
- Expand internships, apprenticeships, and job shadowing through industry/agency/school collaborations
- Establish high expectations and standards for all students, whether they are graduating to a four-year university, seeking additional training, or plan to enter the workforce right away[16]

Preparing young people for careers as adults is the shared responsibility of families and high school educators.[17] To meet those responsibilities, teachers, counselors, and administrators must deepen their sophistication about careers and the labor market. High school students should have access to information and advice that will help them make better decisions about career goals and postsecondary education. Given staff cutbacks, many high school guidance counselors are no longer able to provide these essential services. Additional resources should be made available to career counseling functions so that professionals can help students move from school to work. Students who are not ready for college should be offered a wider array of high-quality alternatives after high school, including industry-recognized certificate programs. National service programs could be expanded for high school (and college) graduates, a strategy that would help them gain experience and prepare for college and/or careers. (See, for example, the Corporation for National and Community Service for details about a variety of current programs, http:// www.nationalservice.gov.)

American higher education also has been enormously successful on many levels over the past several decades. The percentage of eighteen- to twenty-four-year-olds enrolled in college rose from 25 percent in 1967 to 42 percent in 2009.[18] Needs-based financial aid and loans have put a high-quality education within reach of students from low- and moderate-income families. For example, see http://www.finaid.org, a website containing a wealth of information on student financial aid available from governments, higher-education institutions, and other sources.

The story is much less encouraging when we examine the progress that higher-education institutions have made in ensuring that young people complete their degrees. Nearly eight in ten students who enter community colleges do not obtain associate's degrees, and more than half of entering students quit college before getting a bachelor's degree. Colleges are also not doing enough to prepare their students for labor market success, according to employers and a significant percentage of the recent graduates, as chronicled in chapter 5.[19]

When critics challenge the performance of American higher education, all too often faculty and administrators complain that colleges are not "factories" designed to produce well-trained robots for employers.[20] It is no doubt true that there is a subset of higher-education leaders who want to go on doing things the way they have always been done. Most college and university educators, however, genuinely do not understand how rapidly and radically the labor market has changed since they attended college decades ago. They want to help their students succeed, but they are not sure how to accomplish that.

Employers do not want their entry-level college hires to be "human robots," but they do expect students to contribute at work more quickly than ever before. Moreover, students deserve better advice about how to get the most from their college education and a helping hand to get ready for employment or graduate and professional school. As the Heldrich Center's reports on recent college graduates revealed, students do not regret attending college, but they do yearn for better advice about the connections between what they learn at school and how their education can lead to successful careers.[21]

Higher-education leaders cannot make predictions about where the labor market is headed because no one knows exactly what it will look like in four years. Nor should they channel students into a narrow range of undergraduate specializations. They should, however, ensure that college graduates have acquired the essential skills required for success in a global knowledge economy driven by innovation, technical skills, and entrepreneurial discovery. The focus of college and university educators should be on educating students in these core skills that they will need throughout their careers.

Improving educational outcomes is not just about deciding on a major and field of study, although students still too often make these choices based on fads or after a chat with their favorite uncle. Not many academic majors translate directly to jobs. Strengthening undergraduate education is more about making sure that graduates are able to communicate in writing and orally, think critically, solve problems when confronted with new circumstances, evaluate quantitative evidence, and work effectively with diverse teams of coworkers. Such skills and abilities are demanded in just about every job and can be taught in just about every academic major, from accounting to comparative literature. The nation's colleges and universities should overhaul their curricula so that their graduates are better prepared for the twenty-first-century labor market.

A better understanding of financial opportunities and responsibilities of paying for a college education is also essential for students and families. Among other things, students should consider the returns on their higher-education investment and which institutions offer the best opportunities. In 2012, the U.S. Department of Education urged colleges to be more transparent about the cost of attending, graduation rates, and labor market outcomes. The new Consumer Financial Protection Bureau worked with the department to develop a model for a financial aid shopping sheet that colleges can provide parents and students to help them understand the complexities of financing college.[22] Commenting on the department's strategy, *Washington Post* columnist Michelle Singletary asked pointedly, "Why are we begging these schools to follow a standard format that everyone would get so they can determine what they can afford? Please, let's not plead. It's pitiful."[23] Legislation requiring financial disclosures in a standard format is an important next step toward providing baseline, comparable information for students and their families.

The United States still leads the world in top-flight institutions of higher learning, but it has fallen behind other countries in college graduation rates. After leading the world for many years in the percentage of young people with college degrees, the United States ranked twelfth in 2011 among thirty-six developed nations.[24] Thirty percent of new entrants to college leave before or after completing their first year, and half never graduate. Millions of recent high school graduates are accepted to colleges every year, yet one in five freshmen must enroll in at least one remedial course because they are not prepared for college-level courses. When students take longer to finish college, they pay more for their degrees and incur more borrowing costs.

Colleges and universities are supplementing the domestic supply of young adults with students from economic competitor nations, including China, India, and Korea. Between 2000 and 2010, higher-education exports of U.S. education services to foreign students doubled to reach $21 billion in tuition and services.[25] Hundreds of public higher-education institutions are replacing revenues that previously were provided by state government by accepting substantial numbers of "full tuition payers" from abroad.

Higher-education institutions are making progress in several states, but these reforms are by no means widespread. A 2011 National Governors Association report, "Degrees for What Jobs?," highlights successful strategies undertaken by governors and universities in Minnesota, North Carolina, Ohio, and Washington to "align postsecondary education with the state's economic goals." Some of these promising practices that could be replicated around the country include the following:

- Governors and legislatures set clear expectations for higher education's role in economic development in building a competitive twenty-first-century workforce.
- Universities adapt rigorous use of labor market data and other sources to define goals and priorities.
- State policymakers target incentives and publicity to reward universities that seek and use state and regional employers' ideas and data about the types of skills and workers they will need in building their workforce.
- Policymakers require that institutions of higher education collect and use outcome data on students' employment outcomes, workforce gaps, employer satisfaction, and state economic growth.
- Funders and agencies tie funding and other incentives to meeting innovative program goals such as developing industry-oriented curricula.[26]

Without a doubt, students must take more personal responsibility for obtaining the education they need for a successful career. Few recent college graduates will have a job waiting for them as they exit the graduation ceremony. Also, they should expect that they will need to work hard at convincing employers to hire and retain them in good jobs. The postrecession global economy is characterized by widespread contingent employment and unpredictable labor markets and companies. From high school through entry into the labor market and for their working lifetimes, Americans must get better at preparing and learning, reacting and adapting to the new realities at work. Most of us, especially young workers, live in a "do-it-yourself" career world. American educators and policymakers must accept greater responsibility for providing advice and assistance to young workers as they transition from the relative calm of schools and colleges to the rough-and-tumble world of work in the modern era.

Expand Lifelong Learning Opportunities for Workers

> I think that the government should make it easier for those who are unemployed to go back to school and get a better education, by absorbing some of the school costs or by providing training programs that will help those who want to move ahead in their careers. (Heldrich Center interview with unemployed worker, August 2011)

No matter how successful our high schools and colleges become or how well prepared graduates are to begin working, additional skills training and education will be required throughout their careers. It is no longer sufficient to complete most, if not all, of your formal education by the age of eighteen for high school graduates or age twenty-two for college graduates. The idea that education is a "one-and-done" matter does not fit the realities of a volatile economy. Successful individuals must be lifelong learners. American workers know this already: seven out of ten told us that learning new skills at work is extremely or very important in Heldrich Center surveys conducted between 1999 and 2009.[27]

In fact, the United States currently has two distinct and unequal lifelong learning tiers for its citizens. Formal continuing education is not only expected but also required for professionals, such as doctors, lawyers, teachers, and accountants. For the vast majority, however, there are neither expectations nor clear pathways to further learning. If you work at a company that invests in its workers, tuition aid and learning on the job are available. Most workers, however, either pay for their own education and training or are left behind. The federal government provides limited financial incentives to assist adult learners: the United States ranks no better than average among advanced industrial nations in supporting its workers' continuing education.[28] Such an underfunded and haphazard approach to developing Americans' talent is not sufficient for either societal or individual progress, and it is devastating for people who cannot afford skills upgrading courses when they are trying to transition from unemployment to reemployment.

In a do-it-yourself career world, workers need an integrated high-quality system of continuing education. American employers will never win a race to the bottom with less developed nations where millions are willing—or forced—to work for low wages. As illustrated in groundbreaking articles in the *New York Times* on Apple's factories in China, their workers and engineers can deliver a high-quality product—an Apple iPhone.[29]

If the United States wants to be globally competitive, it must ensure that its workers obtain excellent, just-in-time training in leading technologies and processes. "America must never compete in the battle to pay workers least— and it will take sustained innovation to ensure we don't have to," remarked Bruce Mehlman of the U.S. Commerce Department in 2003.[30] Nearly a decade later, the White House Conference on Innovation concluded,

> Our long-term economic competitiveness depends on boosting the education and technical skills of millions of middle-skill workers for careers in emerging and high-growth industries such as healthcare, biotech, nanotech, clean energy, and advanced manufacturing. . . . We are currently on pace to encounter a shortage of nearly 5 million workers with postsecondary credentials—such as welders and nursing assistants—by 2018.[31]

These findings were confirmed by the McKinsey Global Institute, whose massive analysis on labor disparities concluded that 71 percent of U.S. workers are in jobs for which there is weak employer demand, an oversupply of eligible workers, or both. Researchers at this global management consultancy reached an unambiguous conclusion:

> Unless the mass of America's workers can develop new skills over the next ten years, the nation risks another period in which growth resumes but income dispersion persists, with Americans in the bottom and middle-earning clusters never really benefiting from the recovery. The redevelopment challenge is enormous. But the country has met such challenges before.[32]

In the early decades of the twenty-first century, it is imperative to transform the loosely organized, haphazard American system of continuing education. In the global knowledge economy, job training can no longer be just an emergency response for a small percentage of unemployed workers. Rather, it must be a core element of each worker's personal plan for career advancement. Access to high-quality training must be as well engineered and accessible as shopping on Amazon.com or using an online bank account.

In the global knowledge economy, job training can no longer be just an emergency response for a small percentage of unemployed workers. Rather, it must be a core element of each worker's personal plan for career advancement.

Congress, the executive branch, and industry should collaborate and fund flexible lifelong learning accounts and other opportunities for incumbent workers. One promising approach, developed principally by the Council on Adult and Experiential Learning, would establish employer-matched portable accounts, similar to 401k retirement accounts, that people could use as needed to finance education or training courses. (See an online guide showing employers and workers how to use these accounts at http://www.lifelong learningaccounts.org.) Although legislation creating these accounts has been introduced with bipartisan support, it is yet to gain support in Congress.

The U.S. community college system is well prepared to be the backbone of a national system. As described in a Center on American Progress report, *Building a Technically Skilled Workforce*, "Community colleges serve a more diverse student body than four-year colleges. And they also have experience working directly with private-sector employers to design and adapt programs to address specific labor market needs." The Center on American Progress proposed Community College and Industry Partnership Grants to fund new programs that "would combine public and private resources to create alternative college education programs. . . . These programs [would] ensure that academic credentials are directly linked to current job requirements and that program expansion is based on future job openings."[33]

Academic and business partnerships that foster skill development have been endorsed by Democratic and Republican policy leaders for decades. It's time to revive these bipartisan, commonsense policies around a national workers' "GI Bill" to sharpen our competitive edge and restore greater employment opportunities for middle-class workers. An influential report issued by the National Commission on Skills of the American Workforce concluded in 2007, "Enabling everyone to get the continuing education they will need throughout their work lives is . . . the single most important investment we can make in our economic future. No other step the nation could take would have a higher payoff in economic agility and competitiveness."[34]

In the decade ahead, leaders from both parties should make good on President Obama's declaration in his 2012 State of the Union speech: "I want to cut through the maze of confusing training programs, so that from now on, people . . . have one program, one website, and one place to go for all the information and help they need."[35] Although the president and Republicans may struggle to reach compromises over fiscal policies, prospects should be better for reaching agreement about the organization and delivery of more effective workforce development programs.

Replace Unemployment Insurance with Reemployment Insurance

The government should give unemployed people free job training or education to qualify for a better job or different jobs and unemployment benefits to support them until they finish and find a good job in their new field. (Heldrich Center interview with unemployed worker, August 2011)

For over seventy years, Unemployment Insurance (UI) has been a financial lifeline for millions of unemployed Americans. Workers received over $300 billion in benefits at the depth of the recession in 2008, 2009, and 2010.[36] The monies not only sustained nearly 20 million unemployed workers and their families but also stimulated the economy because UI recipients immediately spent the money they received to buy goods and services.

Despite its many positive features, the contemporary U.S. unemployment insurance system should be overhauled. The UI system was designed for an economy that no longer exists. In 1935, UI was geared to serve employers and workers who experienced short spells of unemployment. Job loss in the contemporary labor market is more likely to be permanent. More than half of the unemployed never receive unemployment checks because of complex UI eligibility standards that favor full-time workers with higher earnings and stable work histories.[37]

In order to return to work, laid-off workers in the contemporary economy often need not only cash assistance but also new skills training. Many European countries have adopted so-called flexicurity strategies that actively intervene when a worker loses his or her job. Summarizing the approach in Denmark, Professor Per Kongshoj Madsen commented,

> A further important feature of Danish labor market policy is the emphasis on early intervention . . . that after one month of unemployment all unemployed enter a regime of mandatory activities, such as interviews, counseling, and monitoring of active job seeking. After six or nine months, depending on age, the unemployed must . . . take part in some form of active measure (like job training or labor market education).[38]

While such reforms might be controversial among some Washington policymakers, six in ten unemployed workers interviewed by the Heldrich Center in 2011 supported the concept of requiring workers receiving unemployment insurance to enroll in skills training programs.[39] This can be accomplished either by subsidizing employers who conduct the training on the job or by giving unemployed workers training vouchers that can be applied at educational institutions. Making more UI recipients eligible for federal student financial aid under the Pell Grant program would also be an important component of the new reemployment system.

The severity of the recession exposed weaknesses that may finally generate long-overdue reforms of the outdated UI program. President Obama, in his 2012 State of the Union address, called on Congress to take action: "It's time to turn our unemployment system into a reemployment system that puts people to work."[40] A bipartisan presidential commission should review the UI system and the lessons learned from the dozens of pilot projects in states that were funded by the Recovery Act. A new UI system should build on these promising reforms and extend them nationwide. The commission should recommend strategies for covering more part-time and self-employed workers and connecting unemployed workers to reemployment services and retraining. Specific recommendations for consideration include:

UI should be more flexible and cover more workers for shorter periods of time. While workers receiving formal layoff notices may apply for state-funded benefits, typically lasting up to twenty-six weeks, those who have not worked long enough or earned enough before losing their jobs are ineligible, including millions of low-wage workers. Many workers whose employers have made payments on their behalf never access UI benefits when they need them.

Expand UI to cover part-time workers. Nineteen states and the District of Columbia grant benefits to people who are laid off from part-time jobs. Part-time workers who live elsewhere in the United States are ineligible for benefits. As noted by the Center on Budget and Policy Priorities in a 2009 analysis,

> All other states require UI applicants to look for a full-time job, even if they were working part-time before being laid off, are parents raising very young children, and meet all other eligibility requirements—including having a sufficient earnings history. This outdated requirement particularly disadvantages women, who are much more likely to work part-time than men.[41]

UI benefit levels are based on how much they earned before being laid off; therefore, since part-time workers generally earn less than people who work full-time, they would receive smaller benefits.

Cover more contingent, freelance, and independent workers. The UI system was designed to cover short-term periods of job loss in a manufacturing-driven economy. It does not adequately serve a twenty-first-century workforce where millions of Americans work as freelancers, contingent workers, independent contractors, or consultants or operate home-based businesses. Congress should consider establishing tax-free UI savings accounts where individuals make contributions with a matching federal formula. Howard Rosen and Lori Kletzer of the Hamilton Project at the Brookings Institution, among others, have advocated this approach:

> allowing self-employed workers, and perhaps others, to contribute up to 0.25 percent of annual income, up to $200 per year, into Personal Unemployment Accounts (PUAs). These contributions would be matched by the federal

government and could be withdrawn later to cushion severe income losses or to finance training or job search.[42]

Encourage work-sharing models. American policymakers should also provide stronger incentives for work-sharing programs in lieu of cash transfers to the unemployed. Following a practice that is more common in Europe, more workers would be able to remain on the job. Their employer would allocate the unemployment benefits their employees would have received as wages or salaries. This approach also benefits employers who lower their personnel costs and avoid layoffs for workers and thus enables them to earn more. It is also cost-neutral to the government. In 2012, the Obama administration encouraged states to experiment with these approaches.

Critics of the UI system must also recognize that slashing UI benefits for the long-term unemployed is not the medicine that will force people back to work.[43] Not only is UI unavailable to millions of unemployed workers, its payments are too low to replace prior earnings. Heldrich Center survey results confirmed that almost half of unemployed workers receiving UI benefits described their financial condition as flat-out "poor," with most reporting reduced spending on essentials such as food, health care, and transportation. Getting unemployment insurance is not a "paid vacation" because payments are too small to stave off financial stress. Most long-term unemployed workers have exhausted other strategies, such as borrowing money or drawing down savings.

> *The UI system was designed to cover short-term periods of job loss in a manufacturing-driven economy. It does not adequately serve a twenty-first-century workforce where millions of Americans work as freelancers, contingent workers, independent contractors, or consultants or operate home-based businesses.*

In addition, receiving UI does not discourage its beneficiaries from looking for work or accepting job offers. Two out of three (69 percent) unemployed respondents in the *Work Trends* surveys and 80 percent of those who received benefits said they would be willing to take a pay cut to get a new job. While state-funded unemployment benefit programs permit job seekers to pass up job offers if they are unrelated to their past work experience during the first few months of unemployment, they set time limits on the recipient's ability to reject lower-paying job offers. Those receiving extended support from the federal government are required to accept reasonable offers of employment.

Establish a Renewed Worker–Employer Compact

Instability and uncertainty are likely to characterize the U.S. labor market for years to come. However, a number of policy and practice reforms could renew workers' confidence that the rules of the free market are being applied fairly and that they are protected from the worst excesses of global competition. Workers do not expect a "free lunch," but they do expect employers to stop viewing their employees as disposable costs and instead value them as assets.

Politicians cannot legislate massive and promising cultural changes. Instead, greater trust and collaboration must be nurtured by employers and employees. As a first step, business must open the doors to establishing mutually beneficial policies for sustainable productivity with good jobs and skilled workers.[44] Together with the reforms in UI and education, a new twenty-first-century employee–employer compact would ensure that workers not only succeed with their current employers but also smoothly transition to another job when necessary. As a starting point in building trust and employee loyalty, advance-warning notices about layoffs should be expanded and enforced. Worker confidence, recruitment, and retention would also be enhanced by expanding family-friendly policies that meet the needs of stressed-out American workers.

Strengthening Advance Warning of Layoffs and Assistance

Workers deserve more advance warning of job cuts from their employers. The federal Worker Adjustment and Retraining Notification Act protects workers, their families, and communities by requiring most employers with one hundred or more employees to provide notification sixty calendar days in advance of plant closings and mass layoffs. While a handful of municipalities and states have expanded WARN requirements to include mass layoffs and plant closings affecting smaller workforces, the time has come to revise national standards and better enforce current law. California, for example, requires advance notice for plant closings, layoffs, and relocations of fifty or more employees, which is far more comprehensive than the federal law. Employers should be fined if they do not comply with state and federal notice rules. When companies do not warn their employees of impending layoffs, costs rise for families, communities, and society.

The nation's programs that are supposed to help the unemployed transition to new jobs are unnecessarily complex and confusing. They also provide widely different levels of assistance, depending on whether workers lose jobs because of foreign trade or the service or government sectors. As noted above, long-term unemployed workers should be given access to education and training so they can move into new careers and employment.

Reinvigorate Workplace Family-Friendly and Flextime Policies

Through more than fifteen years of survey research, workers consistently and highly ranked policies that would enable them to balance work and family responsibilities. Their desire for progressive work and family policies is on par with their desire for employer-supported health insurance, retirement plans, and even job security. Yet, as we have learned through our research, only half of U.S. workers were very satisfied with what their employers offer.

Working Americans are deeply concerned about getting more flexibility in their work schedule to take care of family needs. While only one in three American households has young children living at home, far greater numbers are feeling the work–life time crunch. With a growing elderly population, longer commutes, time-intensive medical treatments, and technologies, workers in every type of family face new time and money pressures.

Only the largest and most profitable firms support generous work–life policies. But, as the economy improves and the baby-boom generation retires, smaller businesses, high-tech firms, and larger corporations should also address workers' long-simmering frustrations. The so-called Millennial generation works hard, but all the research indicates they will take nothing on faith from employers. If corporations want to retain talent and particularly retain women in their thirties and forties, they must have workplace policies that are more responsive to their workers.

RESTORING BALANCE AND SHARED SACRIFICE TO ACHIEVE GREATER PROSPERITY

To ameliorate the damage caused by a lost economic decade, political, business, and education leaders should heed the urgent pleas of American workers documented in nearly twenty-five thousand interviews conducted by the Heldrich Center. One unemployed worker surveyed in August 2011 summed up the feeling of many frustrated workers this way: "Basically, in plain English: the government needs to get its act together and quit arguing among themselves like spoiled children." American workers want their government to adopt more aggressive and creative policy responses than it has so far been able or willing to deliver. Workers understand that the basic realities of the postrecession twenty-first-century workforce are radically different from those of the late twentieth century. They know that job insecurity is to be expected in a globally competitive economy that is experiencing rapid innovations in technology. Workers understand they must become lifelong learners. They also realize that retirement has been redefined. American workers stand the most to gain or lose in the fierce competition with other nations to "win the future" or at least avoid a future where India or other countries outsource their "bad jobs" to the United States.

No matter whether they are working or unemployed, Americans hold similar views about what ails the economy and what should be done about it. Republican and Democratic policymakers in Washington are far more divided along partisan and ideological divides than are American workers, including Independents and people who identify with political parties. While many political and business leaders continue to promise that the U.S. economy can and will re-create the post–World War II economy without making any major policy changes or sacrifices, most working Americans are skeptical. Nearly two-thirds of all respondents to our *Work Trends* surveys—Republicans, Democrats, and Independents—were frustrated with government, and they want action.

The profound challenges of developing effective policies for unemployed workers have vexed policymakers and experts for a long time. Writing in the mid-1980s after a particularly severe recession, Donald Baumer of Smith College and I commented in *The Politics of Unemployment*,

> Government strategies for reducing unemployment are as numerous as the causes of the problem. . . . Government sponsored training measures tackle an enormously difficult task. In simple terms they seek to transform chronically unemployed people into steady, productive workers. Most of the people served by the current job training system have not been successful in school, have only limited skills, and may exhibit personal characteristics that make them unattractive to employers. Their jobless status may be just one manifestation of a broad and deeply rooted set of problems.[45]

In the post-2012 economy, however, there are many more highly qualified workers who have felt the sting of unemployment. The consequences of sticking with outmoded approaches to workforce development are even greater for individuals, families, business, and the nation.

American workers fundamentally agree that the nation must not yield to the threat of economic decline caused by globalization and technological change. Americans know they are fighting for jobs and opportunity in a global marketplace bursting with millions of workers willing to accept far less pay. American workers harbor few illusions about the sobering realities of globalization. The sea change in how Americans view globalization was revealed in a January 2011 *Washington Post* poll.[46] The percentage of Americans who believed the global economy is "a good thing" declined from 60 percent in 2001 to 36 percent in 2011. This same poll found that more Americans in 2011 saw "instability in the global economy" as a bigger threat to stability than terrorism.

Similar concerns lie at the heart of the Tea Party and Occupy Wall Street movements. Americans holding widely different political views were expressing anger that they were being left behind in a global economy run for and by the elites. How can we restore more fairness and common sense to our economics, labor, and trade policies without alienating blocs of voters and ending up in gridlock? Can we rebuild the opportunity society that made the United States the economic superpower in the latter decades of the twentieth century?

One overarching theme that emerges from fifteen years of *Work Trends* studies is that American workers expect everyone to make sacrifices and play by the same rules. The nation must help its workers, businesses, and educational institutions meet the challenges of globalization in the postrecession era. To accomplish those critical goals, the United States must first fix its disjointed, inefficient workforce and education policies. I do not underestimate how difficult it will be to develop a consensus and implement policies based on the goals outlined above. Nearly thirty years ago, Donald Baumer and I wrote,

The issues of long-term economic growth, competiveness, productivity, and job security are receiving more attention now than at any time since the end of World War II. Despite all this attention, the federal government's basic strategies for addressing unemployment problems so far have remained essentially unchanged. Are we on the verge of a major breakthrough in unemployment policy?[47]

In the second decade of the twenty-first century, I am not certain that the nation is "on the verge" of major positive changes or will remain

American workers need help, and they are ready for big policy changes. Will our nation's business, government, education, and community leaders rededicate themselves to embracing these principles and restoring the American dream for all Americans?

mired in partisan rankling and gridlock. Cobbled together through decades of hyperpartisanship, U.S. labor market policies are like a house built by two carpenters who hate each other and are put in charge of construction on alternating weeks. A successful policy agenda that produces a sustainable, opportunity society must build consensus around principles that have bipartisan appeal. American workers need help, and they are ready for big policy changes. Will our nation's business, government, education, and community leaders rededicate themselves to embracing these principles and restoring the American dream for all Americans?

NOTES

1. Scott Reynolds, Neil Ridley, and Carl E. Van Horn, "A Work-Filled Retirement," in *Work Trends* (New Brunswick, NJ: Heldrich Center at Rutgers, The State University of New Jersey, 2005).

2. Jeffrey M. Jones, "Improving National Outlook Key to Obama Victory in 2012," November 8, 2012, http://www.gallup.com/poll/158567/improving-national -outlook-key-obama-victory-2012.aspx.

3. Reynolds et al., "A Work-Filled Retirement"; Jessica Godofsky, Carl E. Van Horn, and Cliff Zukin, "American Workers Assess an Economic Disaster," in *Work Trends* (September 2010); Jessica Godofsky, Carl E. Van Horn, and Cliff Zukin, "Shattered American Dream," in *Work Trends* (December 2010); Carl E. Van Horn, Cliff Zukin, and Charley Stone, "Out of Work and Losing Hope," in *Work Trends* (September 2011).

4. Council on Competitiveness, "Raising the Competitive Bar for America since 1986," 25th Anniversary Report, May 2011.

5. Thomas Mann and Norman Ornstein, *It's Even Worse Than It Looks: How the American Constitutional System Collided with the New Politics of Extremism* (New York: Basic Books, 2012).

6. "National Debt Graph by President," September 20, 2012, http://zfacts.com/ p/318.html.

7. Lesley McBain, "State Need-Based and Merit-Based Grant Aid: Structural Intersections and Recent Trends," American Association of State Colleges and Universities, September 2011.

8. Carl E. Van Horn and Aaron Fichtner, "Eligible Training Provider Lists and Consumer Report Cards," in *The Workforce Investment Act—Implementation Experiences and Evaluation Findings*, eds. Phoebe H. Cottingham and Douglas J. Besharov (Kalamazoo, MI: W. E. Upjohn Institute, 2011).

9. Jessica Godofsky, Cliff Zukin, and Carl E. Van Horn, "Unfulfilled Expectations"; Charley Stone, Carl E. Van Horn, and Cliff Zukin, "Chasing the American Dream: Recent College Graduates and the Great Recession," in *Work Trends* (May 2012); Carl E. Van Horn, Cliff Zukin, Mark Szeltner, and Charley Stone, "Left Out. Forgotten? Recent High School Graduates and the Great Recession," in *Work Trends* (June 2012).

10. Dean Baker and Kevin Hassett, "The Human Disaster of Unemployment," *New York Times*, May 12, 2012.

11. Henry M. Levin and Cecilia E. Rouse, "The True Cost of High School Drop-outs," *New York Times*, January 25, 2012, http://www.nytimes.com/2012/01/26/opinion/the-true-cost-of-high-school-dropouts.html.

12. Claudia Goldin and Lawrence F. Katz, *The Race between Education and Technology* (Cambridge, MA: Belknap Press of Harvard University Press, 2008).

13. U.S. Department of Education, Office of Vocational and Adult Education, "Investing in America's Future: A Blueprint for Transforming Career and Technical Education," April 2012, http://www2.ed.gov/about/offices/list/ovae/pi/cte/transforming-career-technical-education/pdf.

14. Louis Soares and Stephen Steigleder, "Building a Technically Skilled Workforce," Center for American Progress, January 2012, http://www.americanprogress.org/wp-content/uploads/issues/2012/01/pdf/dww_sp_scitechworkforce_execsumm.pdf.

15. U.S. Department of Commerce, National Economic Council, "The Competitiveness and Innovative Capacity of the United States," January 2012, http://www.aspet.org/uploadedFiles/Advocacy/Policy_Updates_News/Dept%20of%20Commerce%20Report.pdf.

16. Michael Bangser, "Preparing High School Students for Successful Transitions to Postsecondary Education and Employment," 2008, http://betterhighschools.org; U.S. Department of Commerce, National Economic Council, "The Competitiveness and Innovative Capacity of the United States."

17. Carl E. Van Horn, Denise Pierson-Balik, and Herb Schaffner, "The 70% Solution: Five Principles for Helping Young People Make Better Choices during and after High School," Heldrich Center at Rutgers, The State University of New Jersey, June 2004.

18. National Center for Higher Education Management Systems, http://www.nchems.org/services/infosvc/reports.php#Enrollment.

19. Godofsky et al., "Unfulfilled Expectations"; Stone et al., "Chasing the American Dream: Recent College Graduates and the Great Recession."

20. Lauren Webber, "Colleges Get Career-Minded," *Wall Street Journal*, May 22, 2012, A3.

21. Webber, "Colleges Get Career-Minded."

22. U.S. Consumer Financial Protection Bureau, U.S. Department of Education, "Know before Your Owe," 2012, http://consumerfinance.gov/students/knowbeforeyouowe.

23. Michelle Singletary, "No More Begging: Legislation Would Help Families Shop Around," *Washington Post*, July 25, 2012, A15.

24. John Michael Lee Jr., Kelcey Edwards, Roxanna Menson, and Anita Rawls, "The College Completion Agenda," 2011 Progress Report, College Board, July 2011.

25. U.S. Department of Commerce, National Economic Council, "The Competitiveness and Innovative Capacity of the United States," 4–6.

26. Erin Sparks and Mary Jo Waits, with Carl E. Van Horn, Maria Heidkamp, and Aaron Fichtner, "Degrees for What Jobs? Raising Expectations for Colleges and Universities in a Global Economy," National Governors Association, NGA Center for Best Practices, March 2011.

27. Carl E. Van Horn and Cliff Zukin, "What a Difference a Decade Makes," in *Work Trends* (December 2009).

28. Organisation for Economic Cooperation and Development, "Better Skills, Better Jobs, Better Lives: A Strategic Approach to Skills Policies," 2012, doi: 10.1787/9789264177338-en.

29. Charles Duhigg and David Barboza, "In China, Human Costs Are Built into I-Pad," *New York Times*, January 25, 2012, A1.

30. David F. Shaffer and David J. Wright, "A New Paradigm for Economic Development," Nelson A. Rockefeller Institute of Government, University at Albany, March 2010, http://www.rockinst.org/pdf/education/2010-03-18-A_New_Paradigm .pdf.

31. Soares and Steigleder, "Building a Technically Skilled Workforce."

32. Diana Farrell, Martha Laboissiere, Iman Ahmed, et al., McKinsey Global Institute, "Changing the Fortunes of America's Workforce: A Human Capital Challenge," June 2009, http://www.mckinsey.com/insights/mgi/research/labor_markets/ changing_the_fortunes_of_us_workforce.

33. Soares and Steigleder, "Building a Technically Skilled Workforce," 2.

34. National Center on Education and the Economy, "Tough Choices or Tough Times," Report of the New Commission on the Skills of the American Workforce, 2007, 18.

35. Transcript of President Barack Obama's 2012 State of the Union Message to Congress, January 24, 2012, http://www.whitehouse.gov/the-press-office/2012/01/24/ remarks-president-state-union-address.

36. "Jobless Benefits Cost So Far: $319 Billion," November 17, 2010, http:// money.cnn.com/2010/11/17/news/economy/unemployment_benefits_cost/index.htm.

37. Hannah Shaw and Chad Stone, "Introduction to Unemployment Insurance," June 25, 2012, http://www.cbpp.org/cms/index.cfm?fa=view&id=1466; Chad Stone, Robert Greenstein, and Martha Coven, "Addressing Long Standing Gaps in Unemployment Insurance Coverage," August 2007, http://www.cbpp.org/ cms/?fa=view&id=517#_ftnref1; Margaret C. Simms and Daniel Kuehn, "Unemployment Insurance during a Recession," December 2008, http://www.urban.org/ UploadedPDF/411808_unemployment_insurance.pdf.

38. Per Kongshoj Madsen, "Flexicurity in Danish—A Model of Labour Market Reform in Europe?," *Intereconomics*, March/April 2008, 75.

39. Van Horn et al., "Out of Work and Losing Hope."

40. Transcript of President Barack Obama's 2012 State of the Union Message to Congress.

41. Martha Coven and Chad Stone, "Unemployment Reforms Should Be Part of Economic Recovery Package," April 2010, http://www.cbpp.org/files/12-19-02ui.pdf.

42. Lori G. Kletzer and Howard F. Rosen, "Reforming Unemployment Insurance for the Twenty-First Century Workforce," 2006, http://www.brookings.edu/ papers/2006/09unemployment_kletzer.aspx.

43. See, for example, Jesse Rothstein, "Unemployment Insurance and Job Search in the Great Recession," National Bureau of Economic Research Working Paper 17534, http://www.nber.org/papers/w17534.

44. For a range of views on this topic, see, for example, Peter Cappelli, *The New Deal at Work: Managing the Market-Driven Workforce* (Cambridge, MA: Harvard Business Press, 1999); Thomas Kochan, *Restoring the American Dream: A Working Family's Agenda for America* (Cambridge, MA: MIT Press, 2005); and Paul Osterman and Beth Shulman, *Good Jobs America: Making Work Better for Everyone* (New York: Russell Sage Foundation, 2011).

45. Donald C. Baumer and Carl E. Van Horn, *The Politics of Unemployment* (Washington, DC: CQ Press, 1995), 208.

46. Jon Cohen and Peyton M. Craighill, "Americans Increasingly View Globalization as a Negative for the U.S.," *Washington Post*, January 28, 2011, http://www.washingtonpost.com/wp-dyn/content/article/2011/01/28/AR2011012801651.html.

47. Baumer and Van Horn, *The Politics of Unemployment*, 208.

Appendix

Work Trends: Americans' Attitudes about Work, Employers, and Government, 1998–2012

Title	Date	Topics	Survey Sample	Number of Respondents/ Sampling Error
Work Trends 1: Americans' Attitudes about Work, Employers, and the Government Report: http://bit.ly/NAM7S0 Media Release: http://bit.ly/MyreJB	Fall 1998	Jobs, the workplace, and economic security	Workers*	1,001 respondents, ±3% sampling error at the 95% confidence level
Work Trends 2: Work and Family: How Employers and Workers Can Strike the Balance Report: http://bit.ly/NpdUbR Media Release: http://bit.ly/QBlxHg	Winter 1999	Jobs, the workplace, and economic security	Workers*	1,000 respondents, ±3% sampling error at the 95% confidence level
Work Trends 3: Working Hard but Staying Poor: A National Survey of the Working Poor and Unemployed Report: http://bit.ly/NlUzUn Media Release: http://bit.ly/QBlPxA	July 1999	Working poor	Workers (with an oversample of low-income workers)*	500 respondents, ±4% sampling error at the 95% confidence level
Work Trends 4: Who Will Let the Good Times Roll? A National Survey on Jobs, the Economy, and the Race for the President Report: http://bit.ly/PYkv7l Media Release: http://bit.ly/R20X7d	September 1999	Jobs, the economy, and the race for president	Workers*	1,000 respondents, ±3% sampling error at the 95% confidence level

Study	Date	Topic	Population	Sample
Work Trends 5: Nothing but Net: American Workers and the Information Economy Report http://bit.ly/OvtDpl Media Release: http://bit.ly/PmKNWk	February 2000	Jobs, the workplace, and information technology	Workers*	1,005 respondents, ±3% sampling error at the 95% confidence level
Work Trends 6: Making the Grade? What American Workers Think Should Be Done to Improve Education Report: http://bit.ly/RUPMOQ Media Release: http://bit.ly/Nph0MY	June 2000	Education	Workers*	1,015 respondents, ±3% sampling error at the 95% confidence level
Work Trends 7: Second Wind: Workers, Retirement, and Social Security Report: http://bit.ly/NEnLoN Media Release: http://bit.ly/NAULzX	September 2000	Retirement and Social Security	Workers*	1,005 respondents, ±3% sampling error at the 95% confidence level
Work Trends 8: Holding On: Americans Assess a Changing Economic Landscape Report: http://bit.ly/NEo1Ey Media Release: http://bit.ly/OikQV3	May 2001	Jobs, the workplace, and economic security	Workers*	1,010 respondents, ±3% sampling error at the 95% confidence level
Work Trends 9: A Workplace Divided: How Americans View Discrimination and Race on the Job Report: http://bit.ly/TEwewC Media Release: http://bit.ly/N37tp2	January 2002	Discrimination in the workplace	Workers*	1,005 respondents, ±3% sampling error at the 95% confidence level

(continued)

Title	Date	Topics	Survey Sample	Number of Respondents/ Sampling Error
Work Trends 10: Standing on Shaky Ground: Employers Sharply Concerned in Aftermath of Recession and Terrorism Report: http://bit.ly/PkbWYq Media Release: http://bit.ly/OimaHI	February 2002	Recession and September 11	Employers	501 respondents, ±4.38% sampling error at the 95% confidence level
Work Trends 11: Taking Stock of Retirement: How Workers and Employers Assess Pensions, Trusts, and the Economy Report: http://bit.ly/PYtBkB Media Release: http://bit.ly/PmLI9e	May 2002	Retirement, pensions, and economic security	Employers and workers*	1,000 respondents, ±4.38% sampling error at the 95% confidence level
Work Trends 12: Restricted Access: A Survey of Employers about People with Disabilities and Lowering Barriers to Work Report: http://bit.ly/N39fGA Media Release: http://bit.ly/RPfClX	March 2003	Employment and people with disabilities	Employers	501 respondents, ±4.38% sampling error at the 95% confidence level
Work Trends 13: The Disposable Worker: Living in a Job-Loss Economy Report: http://bit.ly/MZLlSg Media Release: http://bit.ly/PYw8v7	July 2003	Jobs, the workplace, and economic security	Workers*	1,015 respondents, ±3% sampling error at the 95% confidence level

Title	Date	Topic	Population	Sample
Work Trends 14: Laid Off: American Workers and Employers Assess a Volatile Job Market Report: http://bit.ly/PYwodB Media Release: http://bit.ly/SmuNk3	April 2004	Jobs, the workplace, and economic security	Employers and workers*	1,007 respondents, ±3% sampling error at the 95% confidence level
Work Trends 15: At a Crossroads: American Workers Assess Jobs and Economic Security amid the Race for President Report: http://bit.ly/NCDkkw Media Release: http://bit.ly/NB1kCF	October 2004	Jobs, the workplace, and economic security	Workers*	1,011 respondents, ±3% sampling error at the 95% confidence level
Work Trends 16: A Work-Filled Retirement: Workers' Changing Views on Employment and Leisure Report: http://bit.ly/RUWWmo Media Release: http://bit.ly/PkeWEa	August 2005	Jobs, retirement, and economic security	Workers*	800 respondents, ±3.5% sampling error at the 95% confidence level
Work Trends 17: The Anxious American Worker Report: http://bit.ly/OioDlb Media Release: http://bit.ly/PmRQ1a	August 2008	Jobs, the workplace, and economic security	Workers*	1,000 respondents, ±3.1% sampling error at the 95% confidence level
Work Trends 18: The Distressed American Worker Report: http://bit.ly/OioLBm Media Release: http://bit.ly/NEvDH6	April 2009	Jobs, the workplace, economic security	Workers*	700 respondents, ±4% sampling error at the 95% confidence level

Title	Date	Topics	Survey Sample	Number of Respondents/ Sampling Error
Work Trends 19: Healthy at Work? Unequal Access to Employer Wellness Programs Report: http://bit.ly/NlraD9 Media Release: http://bit.ly/PsfGZz	May 2009	Wellness programs, legal and privacy implications and concerns	Workers*	583 respondents, ±4.1% sampling error at the 95% confidence level
Work Trends 20: The Anguish of Unemployment Media Release/Findings: http://bit.ly/OioVIM Media Release: http://bit.ly/RPkjfq Survey Quotes: http://bit.ly/RUYPiM	September 2009	Economic and social costs of prolonged joblessness	Unemployed workers	1,202 respondents, ±5.1% sampling error at the 95% confidence level
Work Trends 21: The No Confidence Economy Media Release/Findings: http://bit.ly/QByaSE	November 2009	Permanent, fundamental changes seen in U.S. labor market and economy	Workers*	652 respondents, ±4% sampling error at the 95% confidence level
Work Trends 22: What a Difference a Decade Makes: The Declining Job Satisfaction of the American Worker Media Release/Findings: http://bit.ly/NCJ5yx	December 2009	Contrasting levels of worker job security, benefits, outlook 1999 vs. 2009	Workers*	652 respondents, ±4% sampling error at the 95% confidence level
Work Trends 23: No End in Sight: The Agony of Prolonged Unemployment Report: http://bit.ly/OYfgGe Media Release: http://bit.ly/RV3Yrb	May 2010	Reinterviews of unemployed eight months after The Anguish of Unemployment survey	Unemployed workers	908 respondents, ±5.1% sampling error at the 95% confidence level

Work Trends 24: American Workers Assess an Economic Disaster Report: http://bit.ly/NpnP0T Media Release: http://bit.ly/RgjqyX	September 2010	Economic conditions, job security, response of government to high unemployment	Workers*	818 respondents, ±4% sampling error at the 95% confidence level
Work Trends 25: The Shattered American Dream: Unemployed Workers Lose Ground, Hope, and Faith in Their Futures Report: http://bit.ly/QBB0a5 Media Release: http://bit.ly/QBB4qv	December 2010	Reinterviews of unemployed workers sixteen months after The Anguish of Unemployment survey	Unemployed workers	764 respondents, ±5.1% sampling error at the 95% confidence level
Work Trends 26: Unfulfilled Expectations: Recent College Graduates Struggle in a Troubled Economy Report: http://bit.ly/PYTyAB Media Release: http://bit.ly/RPBbmd	May 2011	Employment status, financial shape, and college experience	College graduates from 2006 to 2010	571 respondents, ±4.5% sampling error at the 95% confidence level
Work Trends 27: Out of Work and Losing Hope: The Misery and Bleak Expectations of American Workers Report: http://bit.ly/PYTVuS Media Release: http://bit.ly/R2ijRc	September 2011	Reinterviews of unemployed workers twenty-four months after The Anguish of Unemployment survey	Unemployed workers	1,098 respondents, ±4% sampling error at the 95% confidence level
Work Trends 28: Chasing the American Dream: Recent College Graduates and the Great Recession Report: http://bit.ly/PYUcOz Media Release: http://bit.ly/NCZaUT	May 2012	Employment status, student debt, preparation for the workforce, and expectations for the future	College graduates from 2006 to 2011	571 respondents, ±5% sampling error at the 95% confidence level

(continued)

Title	Date	Topics	Survey Sample	Number of Respondents/ Sampling Error
Work Trends 29: Left Out. Forgotten? Recent High School Graduates and the Great Recession Report: http://bit.ly/NBlzjC Media Release: http://bit.ly/RVtNr4	June 2012	Employment status, economic conditions, preparation for the workforce and college, and expectations for the future	High school graduates from 2006 to 2011	544 respondents, ±4.5% sampling error at the 95% confidence level

Source: John J. Heldrich Center for Workforce Development, Rutgers University.
*Includes adults eighteen years of age or older who are employed full- or part-time or unemployed and seeking full- or part-time work.

Significant Works

AARP Public Policy Institute. *Boomers and the Great Recession: Struggling to Recover*, 2012.

Akabas, Sheila H., and Paul Kurzman. *Work and the Workplace*. New York: Columbia University Press, 2004.

American Society for Training and Development, Society for Human Resource Management. "The Ill-Prepared US Workforce," Conference Board/ASTD/SHRM/Corporate Voices for Working Families, July 2009.

Applebaum, Lauren D., ed. *Reconnecting to Work: Policies to Mitigate Long-Term Unemployment and Its Consequences*. Kalamazoo, MI: Upjohn Institute, 2012.

Arum, Richard, and Josipa Roksa. *Academically Adrift: Limited Learning on College Campuses*. Chicago: University of Chicago Press, 2010.

Atkinson, Robert. *The Past and Future of America's Economy: Long Waves of Innovation That Power Cycles of Growth*. London: Edward Elgar, 2005.

Barnow, Burt S., and Christopher King, eds. *Improving the Odds: Increasing the Effectiveness of Publicly Funded Training*. Washington, DC: Urban Institute Press, 2000.

Bartels, Larry M. *Unequal Democracy*. New York: Russell Sage Foundation and Princeton University Press, 2008.

Bartik, Timothy J., and Susan Houseman, eds. *A Future of Good Jobs?* Kalamazoo, MI: Upjohn Institute, 2008.

Berger, Michael. *Automobile in American History and Culture*. Westport, CT: Greenwood, 2001.

Cappelli, Peter. *The New Deal at Work: Managing the Market-Driven Workforce*. Cambridge, MA: Harvard Business Press, 1999.

———. "Talent Management for the Twenty-First Century." *Harvard Business Review*, March 2008.

Carnevale, Anthony P., Jeff Strohl, and Michelle Melton. "What's It Worth: The Economic Value of College Majors." Georgetown University Center on Education and the Workforce, May 2011, http://cew.georgetown.edu/whatsitworth.

Cohan, William D. *House of Cards*. New York: Doubleday, 2009.

Congressional Budget Office. "CBO Report on TARP." March 11, 2011.

———. "Estimated Impact of the American Recovery and Reinvestment Act on Employment and Economic Output." November 2011.

Cottingham, Phoebe H., and Douglas J. Besharov, eds. *The Workforce Investment Act—Implementation Experiences and Evaluation Findings*. Kalamazoo, MI: Upjohn Institute, 2011.

Council on Adult and Experiential Learning. "Tapping Mature Talent: Policies for a 21st Century Workforce." May 2012. http://www.cael.org/pdfs/TMT_Summary_Policy_Recs_2012.

Council on Competitiveness. "Raising the Competitive Bar for America since 1986." 25th Anniversary Report. May 2011.

Drucker, Peter F. "They're Not Employees, They're People." *Harvard Business Review*. http://hbr.org/2002/02/theyre-not-employees-theyre-people/ar/1.

Eberts, Randall W., and Richard A. Hobbie, eds. *Older and Out of Work*. Kalamazoo, MI: Upjohn Institute, 2008.

Edelman, Peter, Harry Holzer, Eric Seleznow, Andy Van Kleunen, and Elizabeth Watson. "State Workforce Policy: Recent Innovations and an Uncertain Future." Georgetown Center on Poverty, Inequality, and Public Policy and National Skills Coalition. June 2011.

Farber, Henry S. "Job Loss in the Great Recession: Historical Perspective from the Displaced Workers Survey, 1984–2010." National Bureau of Economic Research. Working Paper No. 17040. May 2011.

Farrell, Diana, et al. "Changing the Fortunes of America's Workforce: A Human Capital Challenge." McKinsey Global Institute, June 2009.

Forman, John Barry. *Making America Work*. Washington, DC: Urban Institute Press, 2006.

Friedman, Thomas F. *The World Is Flat*. New York: Farrar, Straus & Giroux, 2005.

Goldin, Claudia, and Lawrence F. Katz. *The Race between Education and Technology*. Cambridge, MA: Belknap Press of Harvard University Press, 2008.

Greenhouse, Steven. *The Big Squeeze: Tough Times for the American Worker*. New York: Random House, 2009.

Greenstone, Michael, and Adam Looney. "Building America's Job Skills with Effective Workforce Programs: A Training Strategy to Raise Wages and Increase Work Opportunities." The Hamilton Project. November 2011.

Grusky, David B., Bruce Western, and Christopher Wimer, eds. *The Great Recession*. New York: Russell Sage Foundation, 2011.

Hammer, Michael, and James Champy. *Reengineering the Corporation*, revised and updated edition New York: HarperCollins, 2003.

Heidkamp, Maria, Nicole Corre, and Carl E.Van Horn, "The New Unemployables: Older Jobseekers Struggle to Find Work during the Great Recession," Sloan Center on Aging & Work and Boston College, Issue Brief 25. October 2010.

Holzer, Harry J., and Marek Hlavac. *A Very Uneven Road: U.S. Labor Markets in the Past 30 Years*. New York: Russell Sage Foundation, March 2012.

Holzer, Harry J., Julia I. Lane, David B. Rosenblum, and Frederik Abdersson. *Where Are All the Good Jobs Going?* New York: Russell Sage Foundation, 2011.

Holzer, Harry J., and Demetra Smith Nightingale, eds. *Reshaping the American Workforce in a Changing Economy.* Washington, DC: Urban Institute, 2007.

Hughes, Kent H. *Building the Next American Century.* Washington, DC: Woodrow Wilson Center Press, 2005.

Johnson, Richard, and Corina Mommaerts. "Age Differences in Job Loss, Job Search, and Reemployment." Washington, DC: Urban Institute, 2011.

Kochan, Thomas. *Restoring the American Dream: A Working Family's Agenda for America.* Cambridge, MA: MIT Press, 2005.

Krueger, Alan B., and Andreas Mueller. "Job Search and Job Finding in a Period of Mass Unemployment: Evidence from High-Frequency Longitudinal Data." Center for Economic Policy Studies, Princeton University. Working Paper No. 215. January 2011.

Krugman, Paul. *End This Depression, Now.* New York: Norton, 2012.

Mann, Thomas, and Norman Ornstein. *It's Even Worse Than It Looks: How the American Constitutional System Collided with the New Politics of Extremism.* New York: Basic Books, 2012.

McLean, Bethany, and Joe Nocera. *All the Devils Are Here.* New York: Viking Penguin Portfolio, 2010.

Mishel, Lawrence, Josh Bivens, Elise Gould, and Heidi Shierholz. *The State of Working America.* 12th edition. Ithaca, NY: Cornell University Press, 2012.

Moss, Phillip, and Chris Tilley. *Stories Employers Tell: Race, Skill, and Hiring in America.* New York: Russell Sage Foundation, 2001.

Munnell, Alicia A., and Steven A. Sass. *Working Longer: The Solution to the Retirement Income Challenge.* Washington: DC: Brookings Institution, 2009.

National Center on Education and the Economy. "Tough Choices or Tough Times." Report of the New Commission on the Skills of the American Workforce, 2007.

Organisation for Economic Co-operation and Development. "Better Skills, Better Jobs, Better Lives: A Strategic Approach to Skills Policies." May 21, 2012. doi: 10.1787/9789264177338-en.

Osterman, Paul, and Beth Shulman. *Good Jobs America: Making Work Better for Everyone.* New York: Russell Sage Foundation, 2011.

Peck, Don. *Pinched: How the Great Recession Has Narrowed Our Futures and What We Can Do about It.* New York: Crown, 2011.

Pew Charitable Trusts Fiscal Analysis Project. "A Year or More: The High Cost of Long-Term Unemployment." April 2010.

Plotnick, Robert D., Marcia K. Meyers, Jennifer Romich, and Steven Rathgeb Smith, eds. *Old Assumptions, New Realities.* New York: Russell Sage Foundation, 2011.

President's Council of Economic Advisors. *Work-Life Balance and the Economics of Workplace Flexibility.* White House, 2010.

Rodgers, William M., III. "Future Work 2.0: Life after the Great Recession." Working Paper. Heldrich Center for Workforce Development, Rutgers University. January 2012.

Rothstein, Jesse. "Unemployment Insurance and Job Search in the Great Recession." Brookings Papers on Economic Activity. Economic Studies Program, Brookings Institution. March 2012.

Smith, Hedrick. *Who Stole the American Dream?* New York: Random House, 2012.

Soares, Louis. "Working Learners: Educating Our Entire Workforce for Success in the 21st Century." Washington, DC: Center for American Progress, 2009.

Uchitelle, Louis. *The Disposable American: Layoffs and Their Consequences.* New York: Knopf, 2006.

U.S. Department of Commerce, National Economic Council. "The Competitiveness and Innovative Capacity of the United States." January 2012.

U.S. Department of Education, Office of Vocational and Adult Education. "Investing in America's Future: A Blueprint for Transforming Career and Technical Education." April 2012.

U.S. Department of Labor, Employment and Training Administration. *Report of the Task Force on Aging of the American Workforce.* February 2008.

U.S. Government Accountability Office. "Unemployed Older Workers." GAO-Pub No. 12-445. April 2012.

Van Horn, Carl E., and Maria Heidkamp. "Older and Out of Work: Employer, Government, and Non-Profit Assistance." Sloan Center for Aging and Work, Boston College. October 2008.

Wandner, Stephen A. *Solving the Reemployment Puzzle: From Research to Policy.* Kalamazoo, MI: Upjohn Institute, 2010.

Index

Page references to figures are in *italics*.